Moonstruck

VOL 1: MAGIC TO BREW

Writer
GRACE ELLIS

Artist
SHAE BEAGLE

Pleasant Mountain Sisters Artist
KATE LETH

Colorist
CAITLIN QUIRK

Letterer
CLAYTON COWLES

Editor/Designer
LAURENN MCCUBBIN

LAURENN · SHAE · GRACE · CAITLIN · CLAYTON · KATE

teammoonstruck@gmail.com • @teammoonstruck • #moonstruckcomic

IMAGE COMICS, INC.
Robert Kirkman—Chief Operating Officer
Erik Larsen—Chief Financial Officer
Todd McFarlane—President
Marc Silvestri—Chief Executive Officer
Jim Valentino—Vice President

Eric Stephenson—Publisher
Corey Hart—Director of Sales
Jeff Boison—Director of Publishing Planning
& Book Trade Sales
Chris Ross—Director of Digital Sales
Jeff Stang—Director of Specialty Sales
Kat Salazar—Director of PR & Marketing
Drew Gill—Art Director
Heather Doornink—Production Director
Nicole Lapalme—Controller

IMAGECOMICS.COM

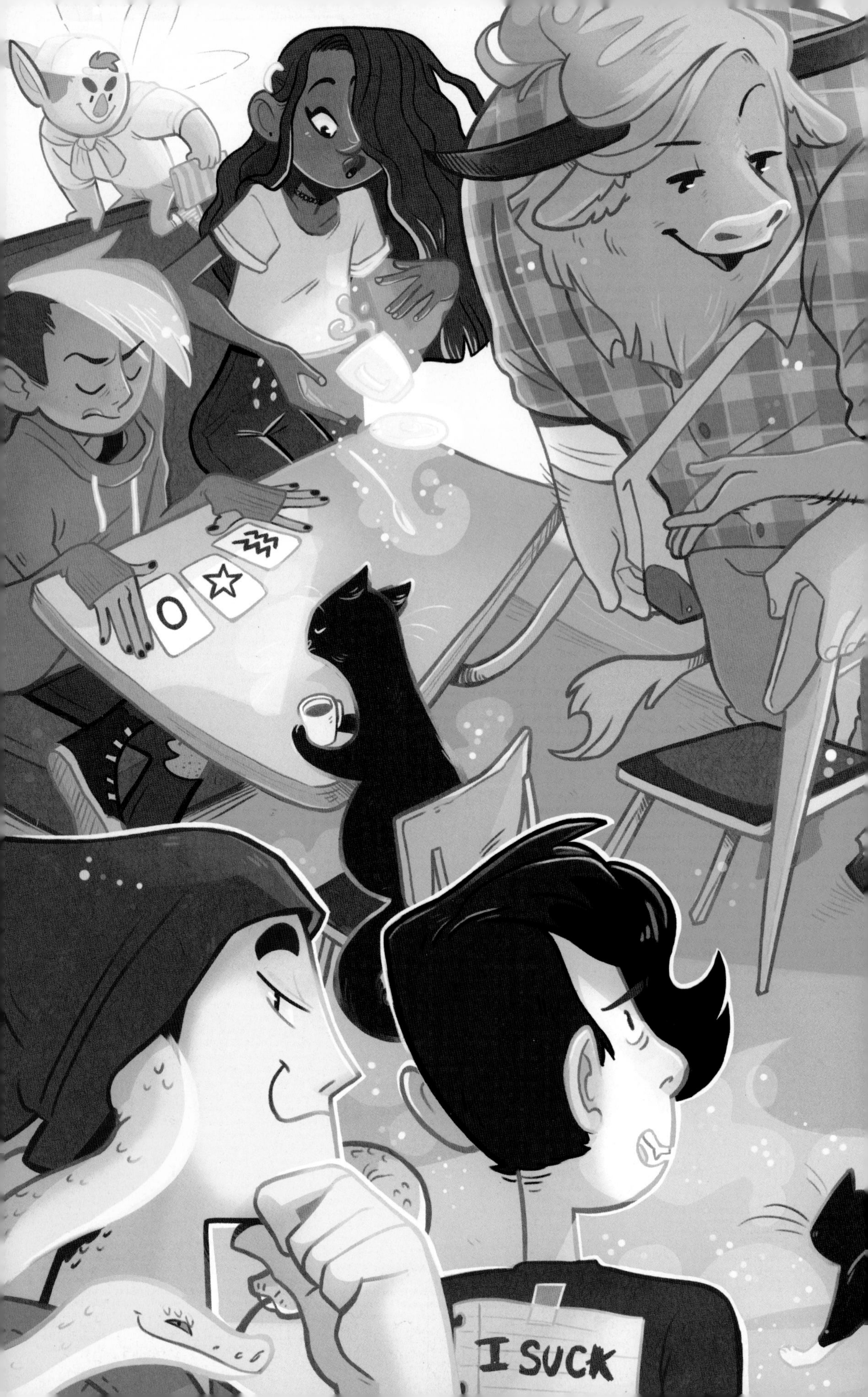
I SUCK

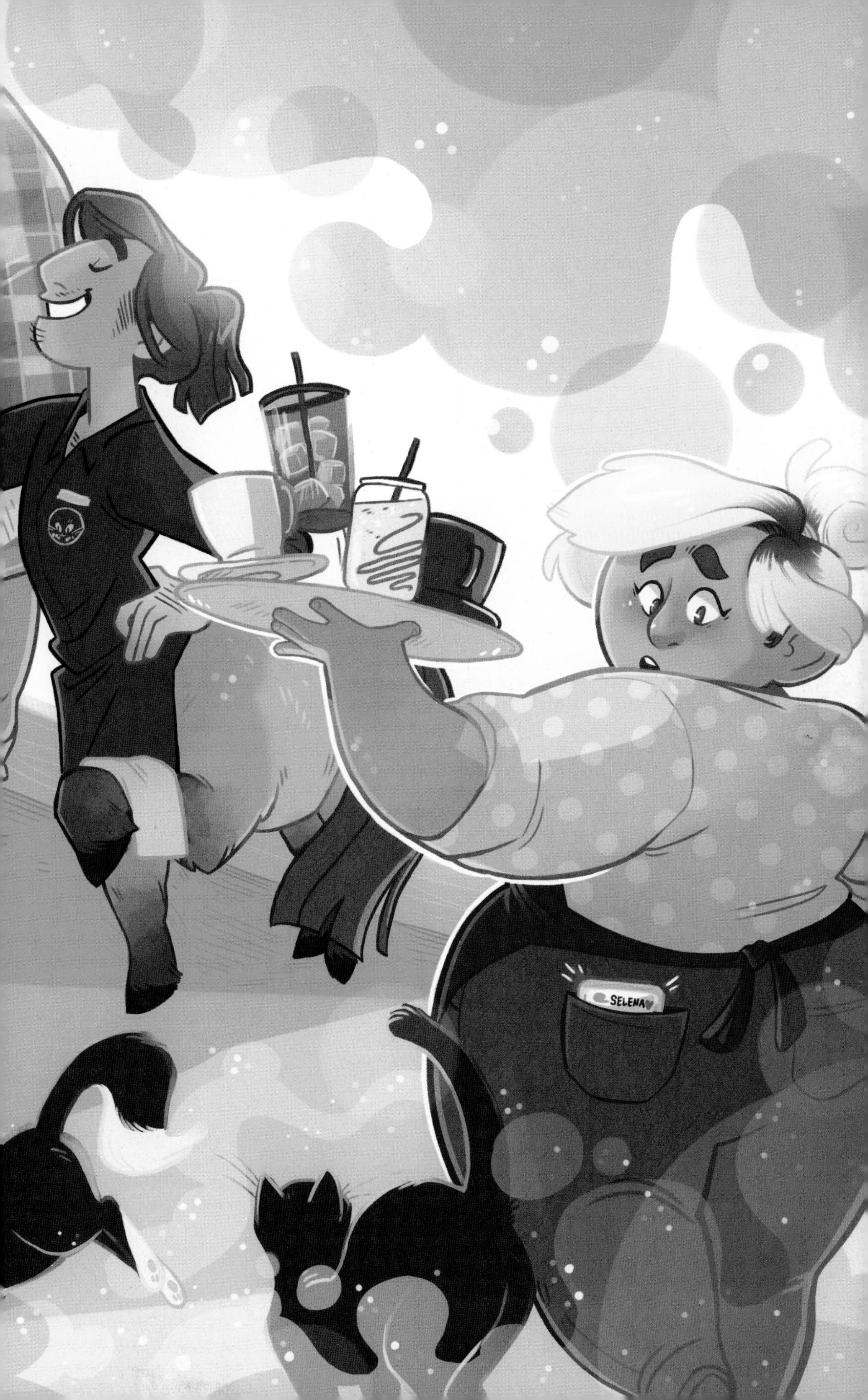
SELENA

CHAPTER ONE

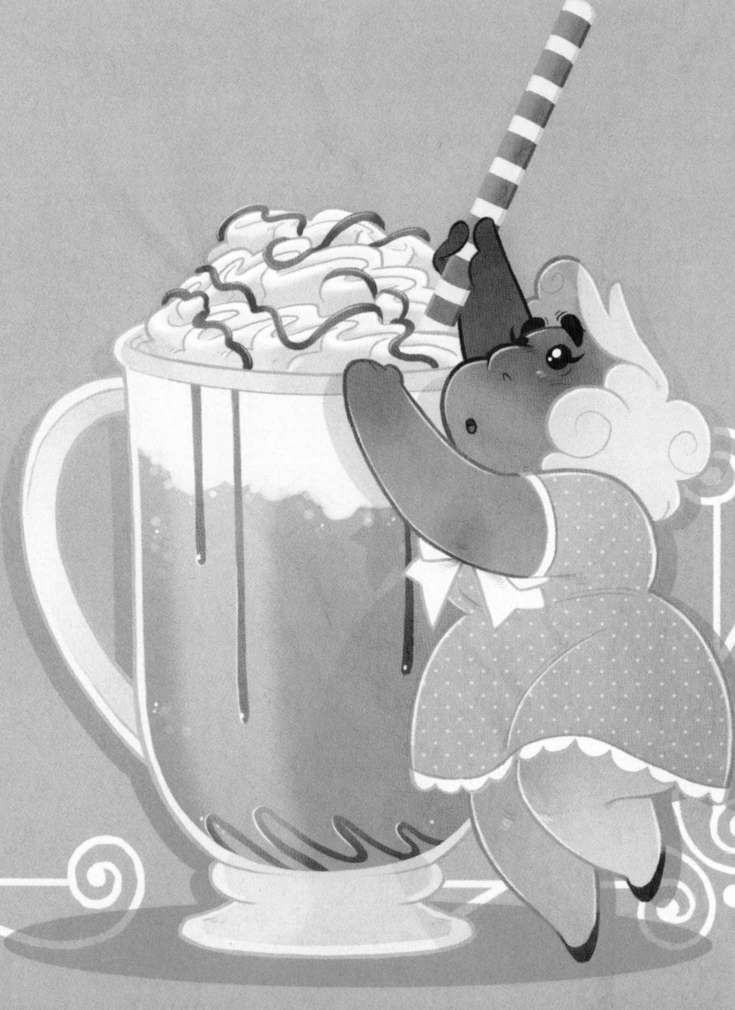

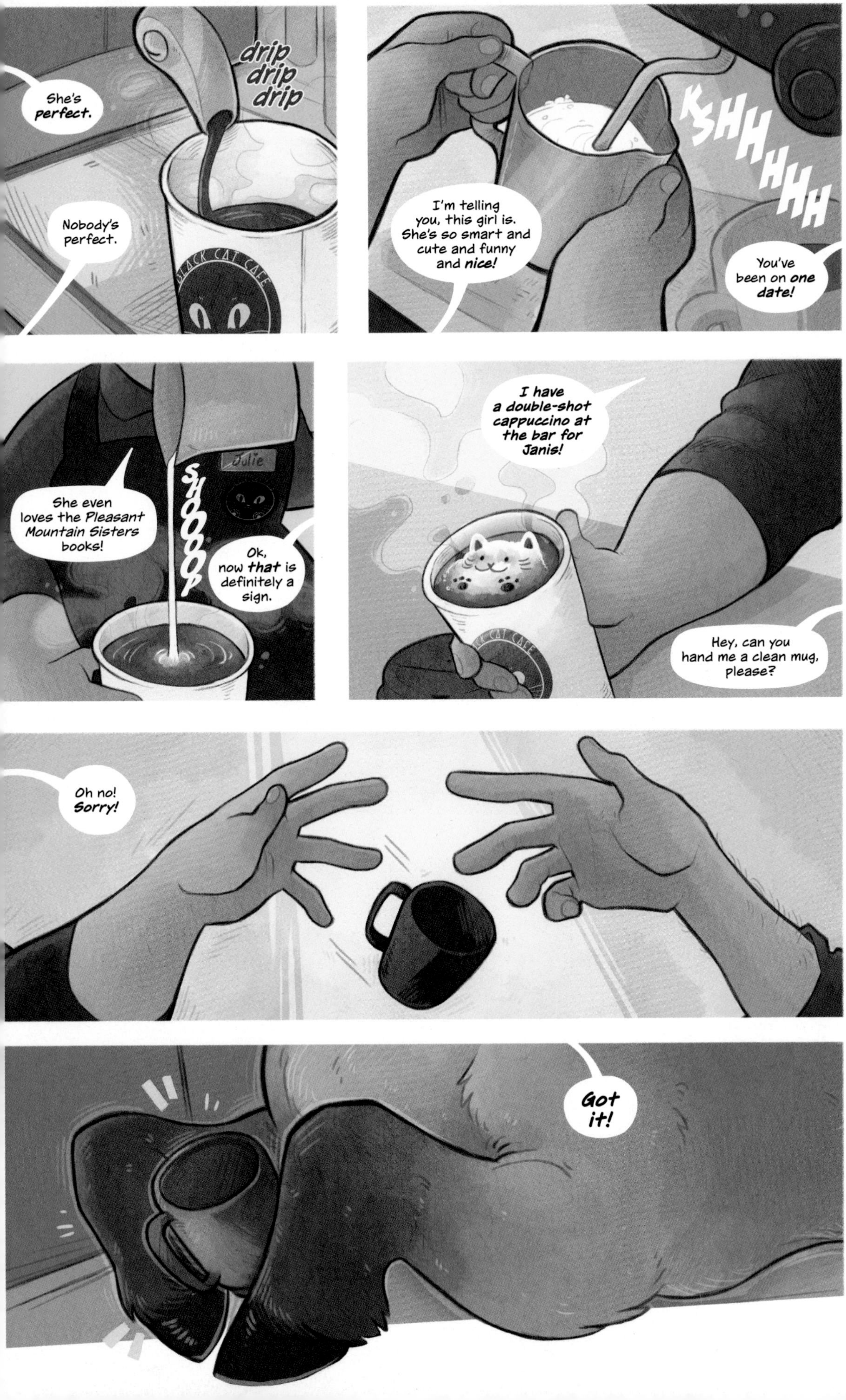
drip drip drip
She's *perfect.*
Nobody's perfect.
I'm telling you, this girl is. She's so smart and cute and funny and *nice!*
KSHHHHHH
You've been on *one date!*
Julie
She even loves the *Pleasant Mountain Sisters* books!
SHOOOOP
Ok, now *that* is definitely a sign.
I have a double-shot cappuccino at the bar for Janis!
Hey, can you hand me a clean mug, please?
Oh no! *Sorry!*
Got it!

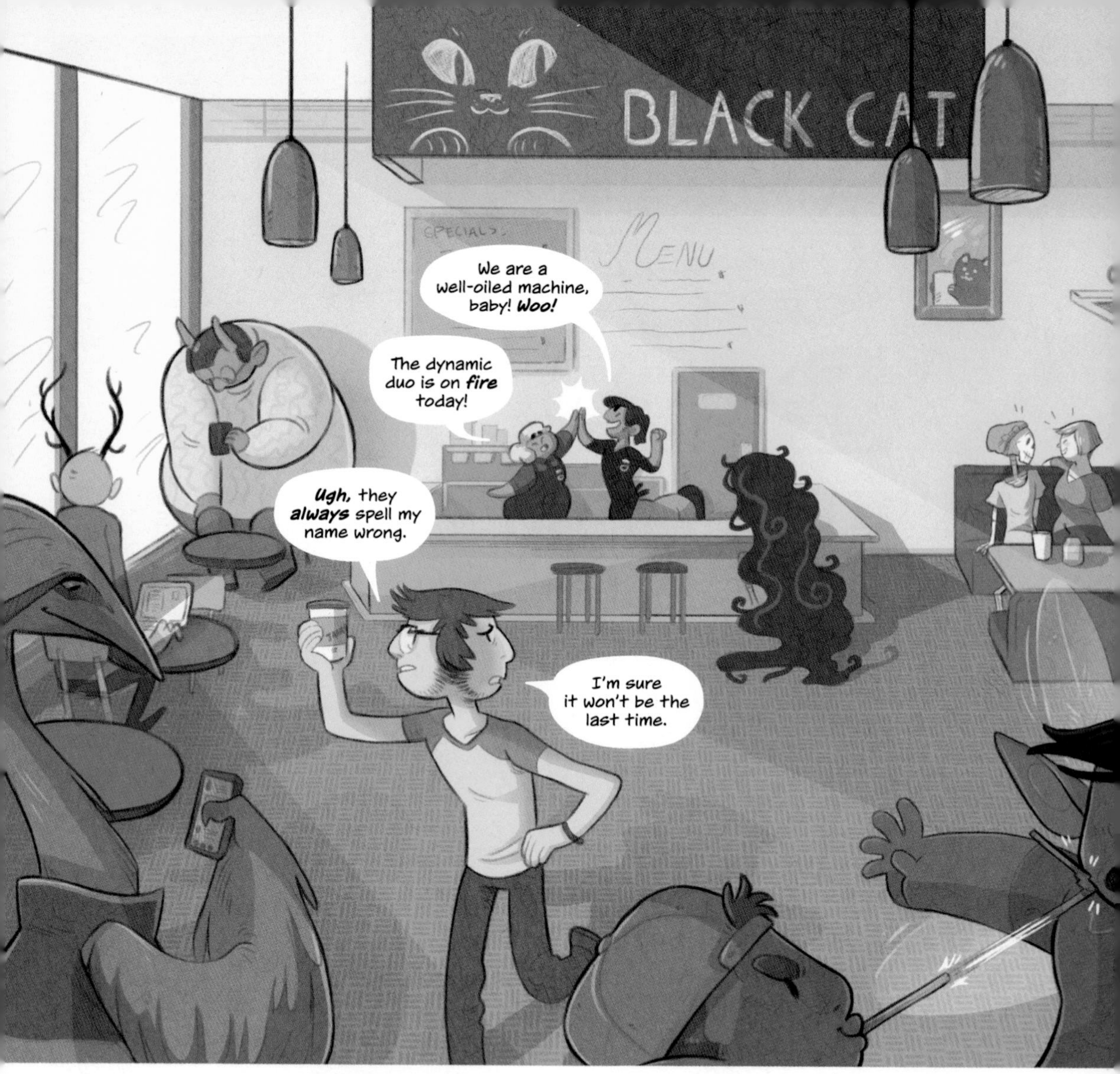
BLACK CAT
SPECIALS
MENU
We are a well-oiled machine, baby! Woo!
The dynamic duo is on fire today!
Ugh, they always spell my name wrong.
I'm sure it won't be the last time.

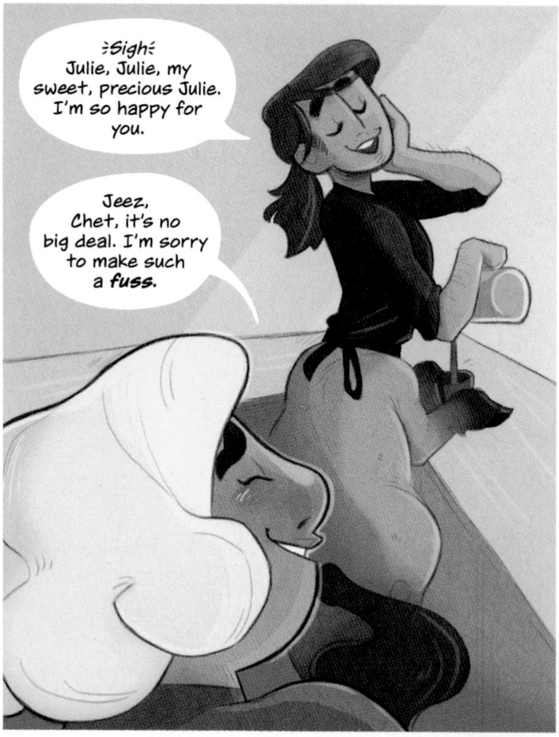
Sigh
Julie, Julie, my sweet, precious Julie. I'm so happy for you.
Jeez, Chet, it's no big deal. I'm sorry to make such a fuss.

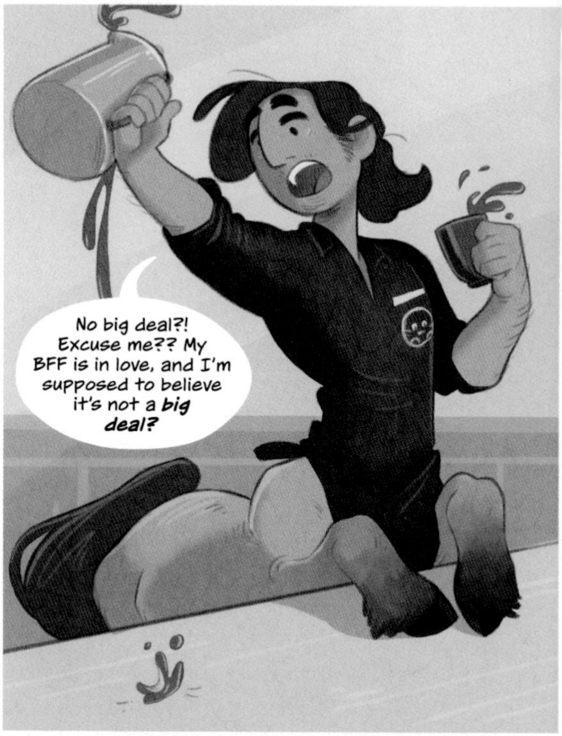
No big deal?! Excuse me?? My BFF is in love, and I'm supposed to believe it's not a big deal?

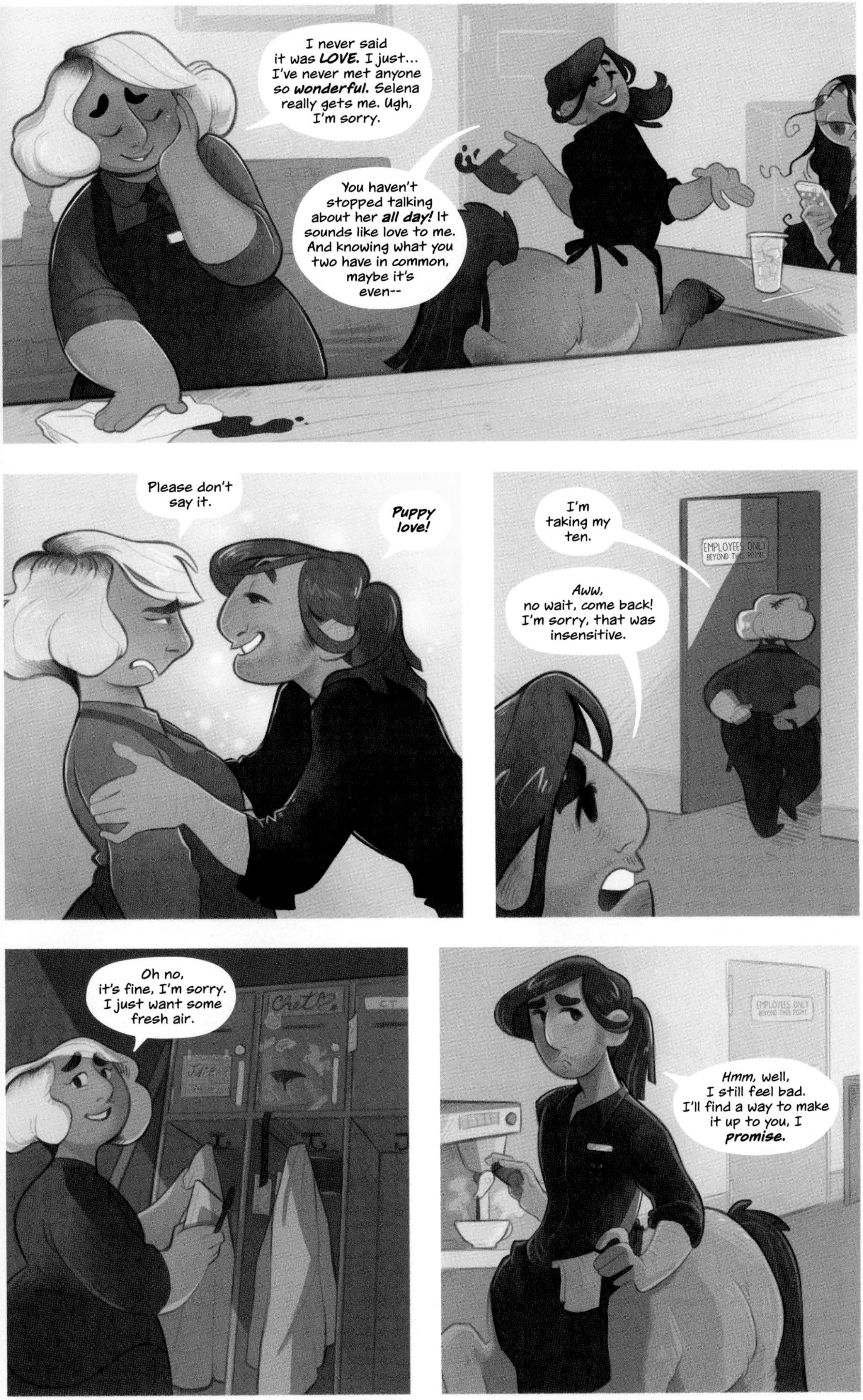

I never said it was **LOVE.** I just... I've never met anyone so **wonderful.** Selena really gets me. Ugh, I'm sorry.
You haven't stopped talking about her ***all day!*** It sounds like love to me. And knowing what you two have in common, maybe it's even--
Please don't say it.
Puppy love!
I'm taking my ten.
EMPLOYEES ONLY BEYOND THIS POINT
Aww, no wait, come back! I'm sorry, that was insensitive.
Oh no, it's fine, I'm sorry. I just want some fresh air.
Hmm, well, I still feel bad. I'll find a way to make it up to you, I ***promise.***

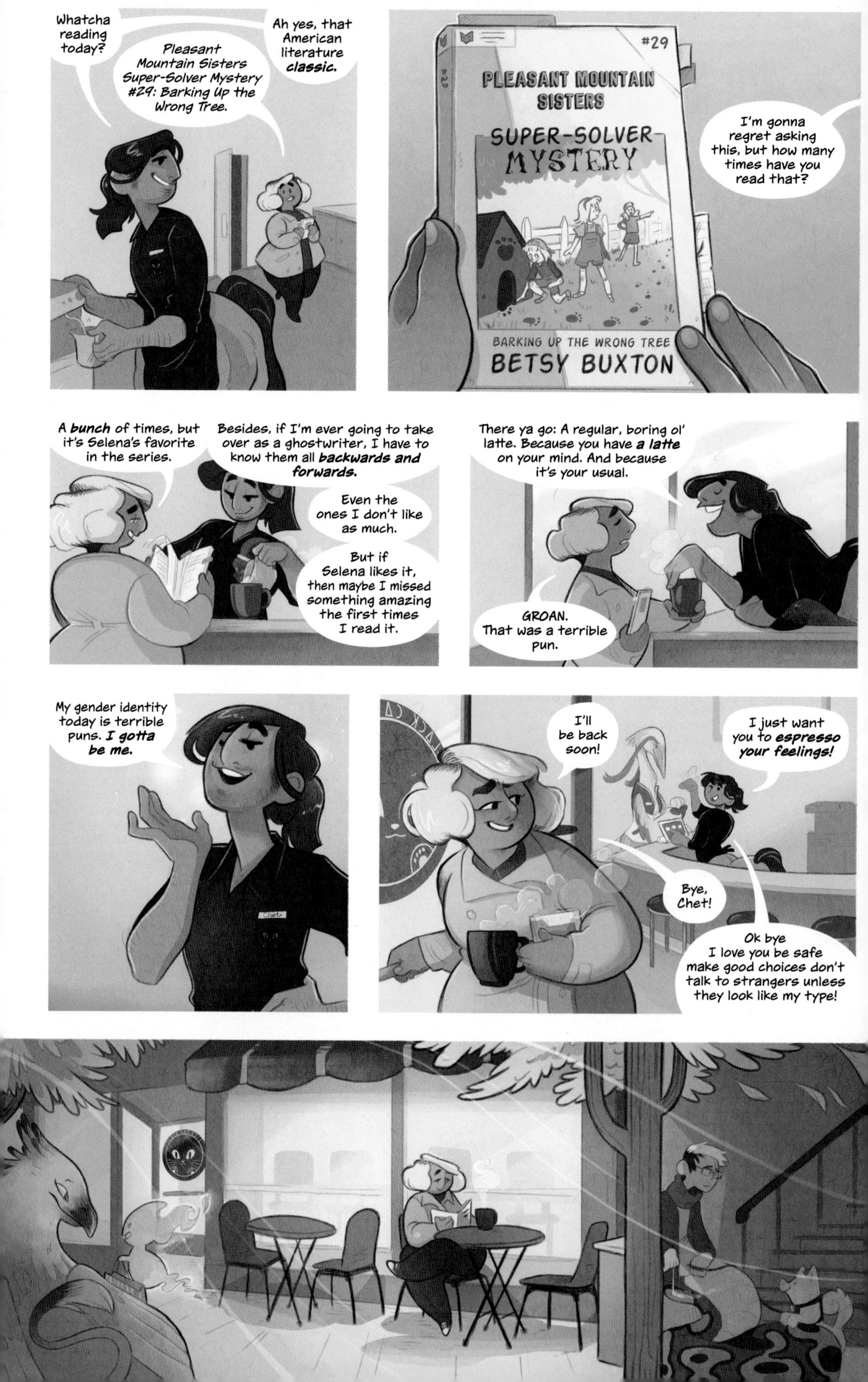
Whatcha reading today?
Pleasant Mountain Sisters Super-Solver Mystery #29: Barking Up the Wrong Tree.
Ah yes, that American literature **classic.**
#29
PLEASANT MOUNTAIN SISTERS
SUPER-SOLVER MYSTERY
BARKING UP THE WRONG TREE
BETSY BUXTON
I'm gonna regret asking this, but how many times have you read that?
A **bunch** of times, but it's Selena's favorite in the series.
Besides, if I'm ever going to take over as a ghostwriter, I have to know them all **backwards and forwards.**
Even the ones I don't like as much.
But if Selena likes it, then maybe I missed something amazing the first times I read it.
There ya go: A regular, boring ol' latte. Because you have **a latte** on your mind. And because it's your usual.
GROAN. That was a terrible pun.
My gender identity today is terrible puns. **I gotta be me.**
I'll be back soon!
I just want you to **espresso your feelings!**
Bye, Chet!
Ok bye I love you be safe make good choices don't talk to strangers unless they look like my type!

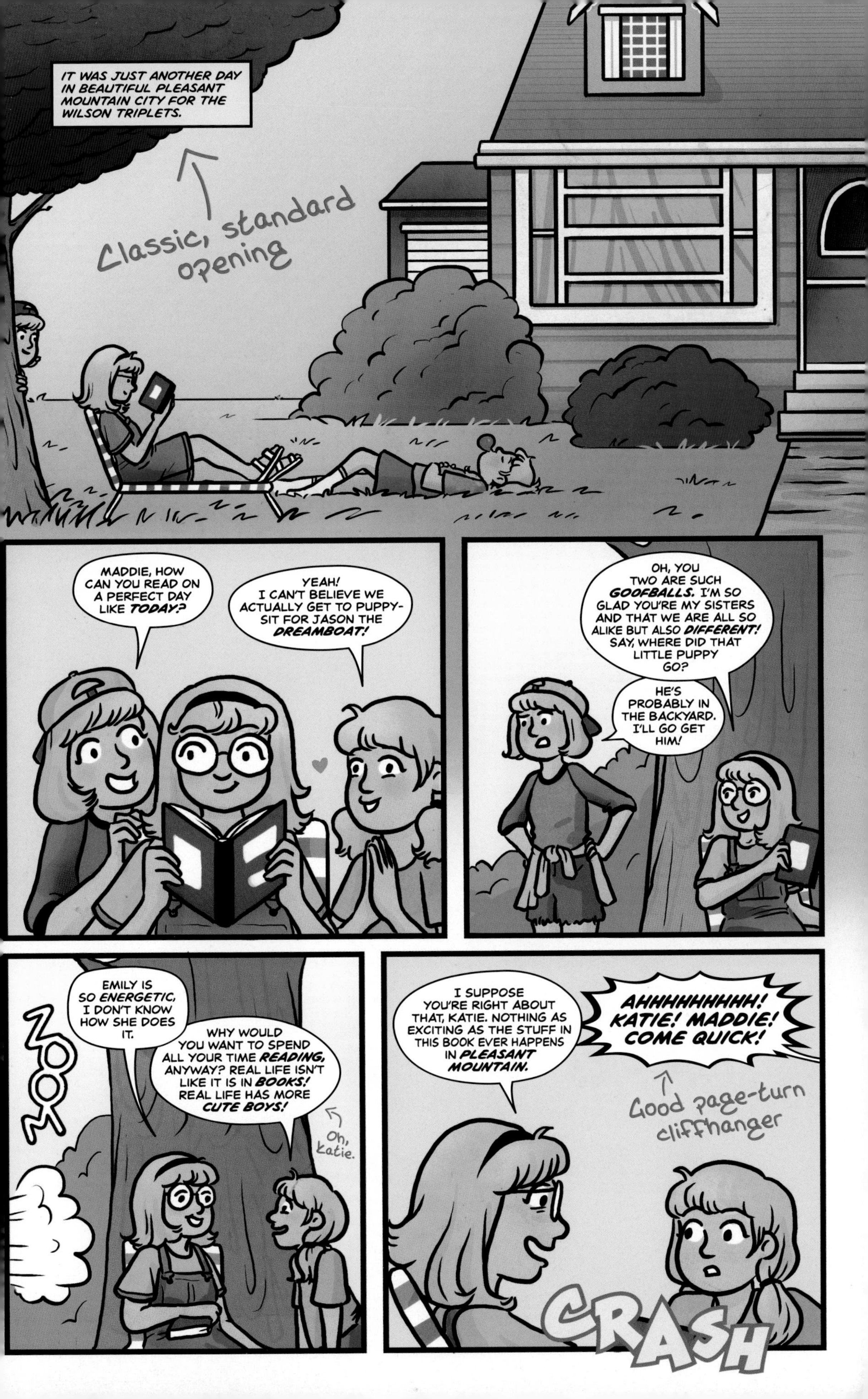
IT WAS JUST ANOTHER DAY IN BEAUTIFUL PLEASANT MOUNTAIN CITY FOR THE WILSON TRIPLETS.
Classic, standard opening
MADDIE, HOW CAN YOU READ ON A PERFECT DAY LIKE TODAY?
YEAH! I CAN'T BELIEVE WE ACTUALLY GET TO PUPPY-SIT FOR JASON THE DREAMBOAT!
OH, YOU TWO ARE SUCH GOOFBALLS. I'M SO GLAD YOU'RE MY SISTERS AND THAT WE ARE ALL SO ALIKE BUT ALSO DIFFERENT! SAY, WHERE DID THAT LITTLE PUPPY GO?
HE'S PROBABLY IN THE BACKYARD. I'LL GO GET HIM!
ZOOM
EMILY IS SO ENERGETIC, I DON'T KNOW HOW SHE DOES IT.
WHY WOULD YOU WANT TO SPEND ALL YOUR TIME READING, ANYWAY? REAL LIFE ISN'T LIKE IT IS IN BOOKS! REAL LIFE HAS MORE CUTE BOYS!
Oh, Katie.
I SUPPOSE YOU'RE RIGHT ABOUT THAT, KATIE. NOTHING AS EXCITING AS THE STUFF IN THIS BOOK EVER HAPPENS IN PLEASANT MOUNTAIN.
AHHHHHHHHHH! KATIE! MADDIE! COME QUICK!
Good page-turn cliffhanger
CRASH

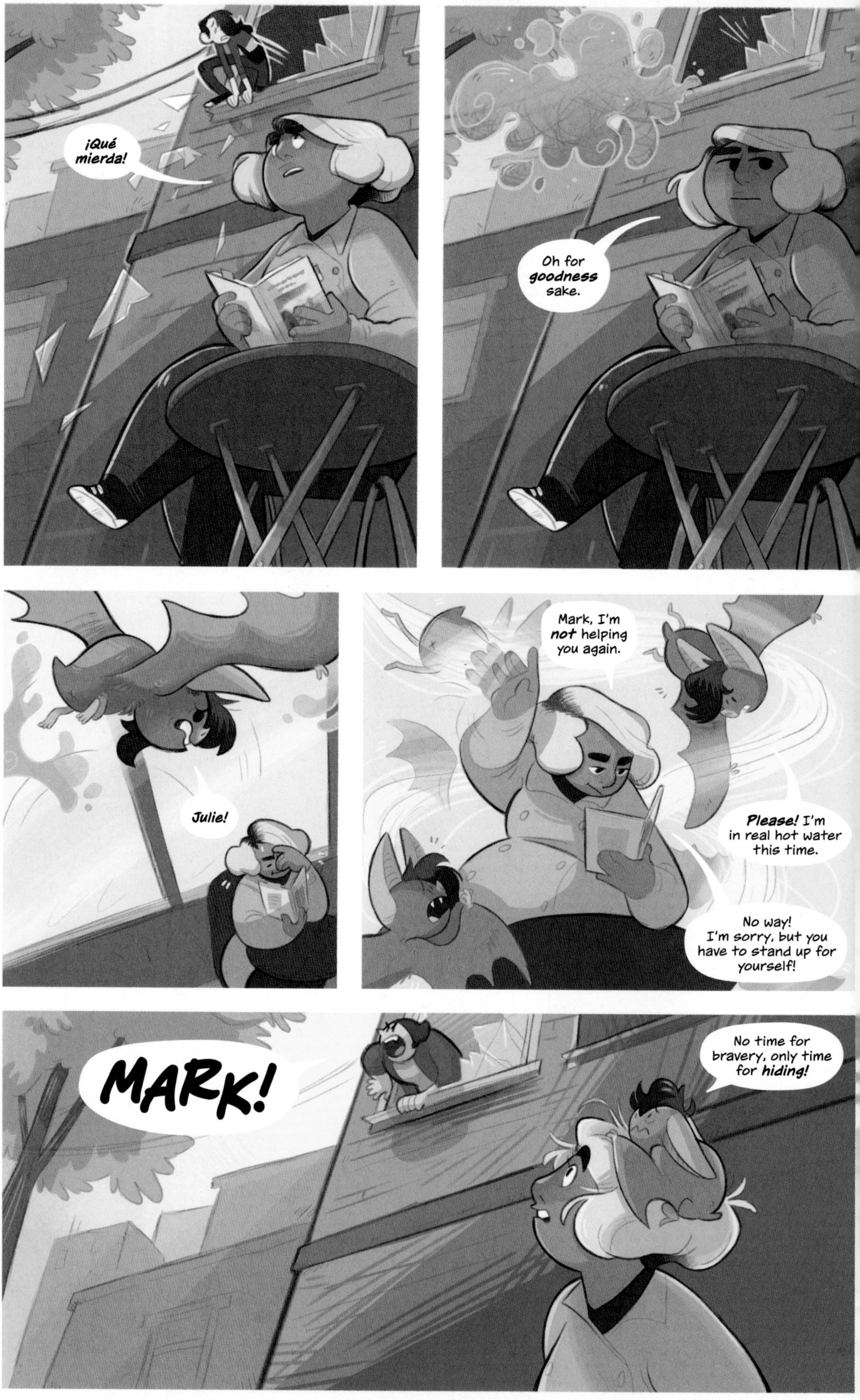
¡Qué mierda!
Oh for goodness sake.
Julie!
Mark, I'm not helping you again.
Please! I'm in real hot water this time.
No way! I'm sorry, but you have to stand up for yourself!
MARK!
No time for bravery, only time for hiding!

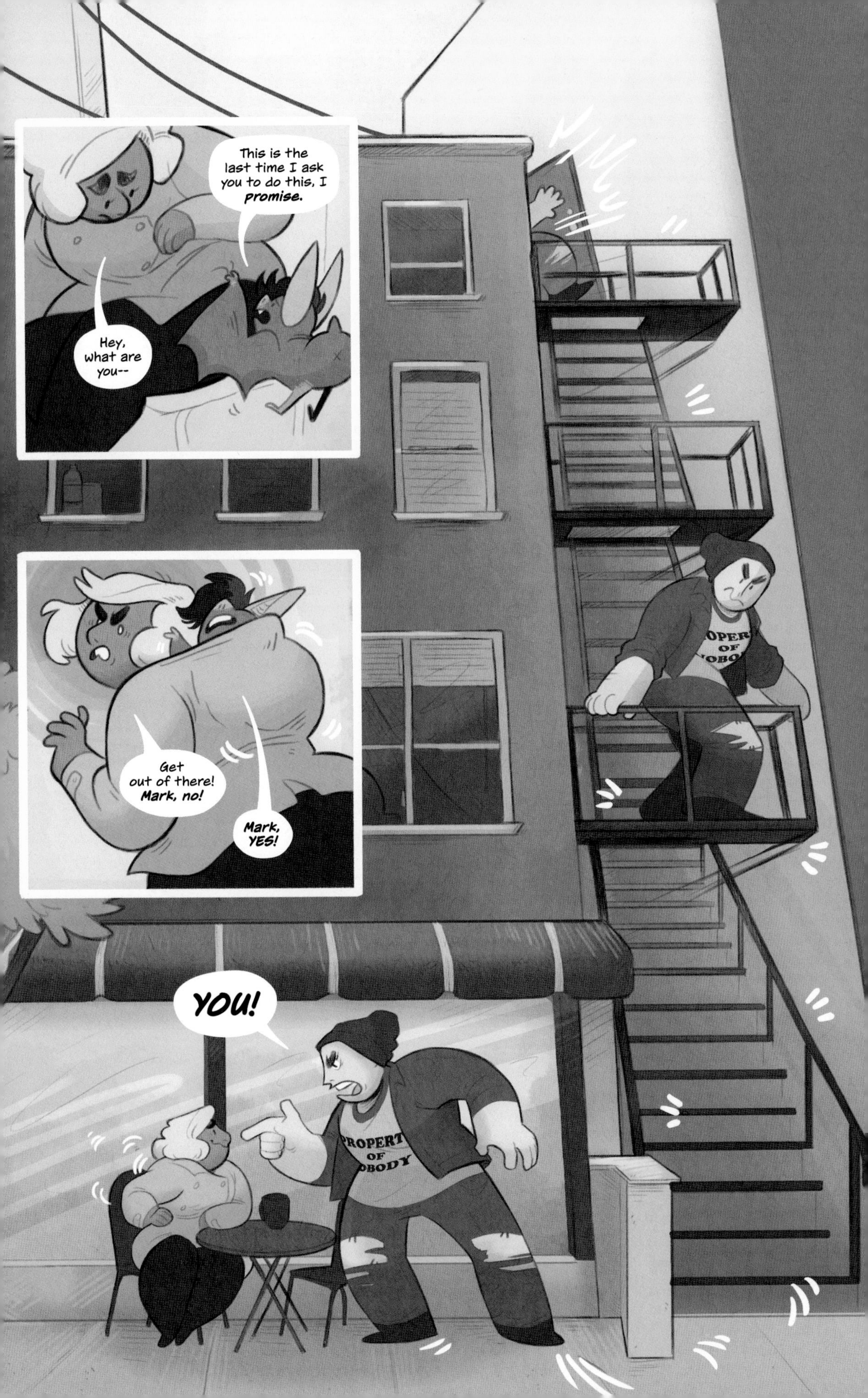
This is the last time I ask you to do this, I *promise.*
Hey, what are you--
Get out of there! *Mark, no!*
Mark, YES!
YOU!
PROPERTY OF NOBODY

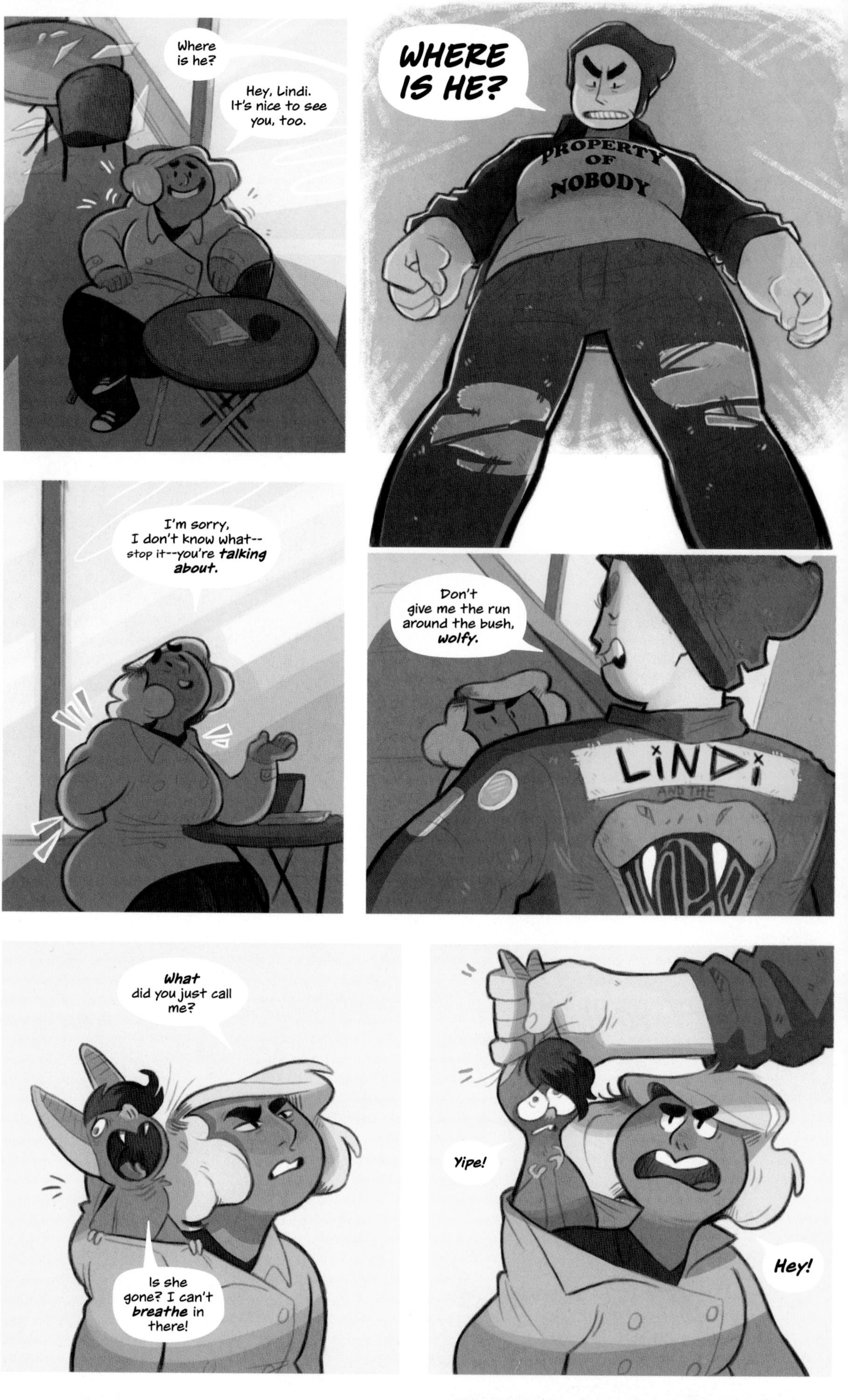
Where is he?
Hey, Lindi. It's nice to see you, too.
WHERE IS HE?
PROPERTY OF NOBODY
I'm sorry, I don't know what-- stop it--you're *talking about.*
Don't give me the run around the bush, *wolfy.*
LiNDi
What did you just call me?
Is she gone? I can't *breathe* in there!
Yipe!
Hey!

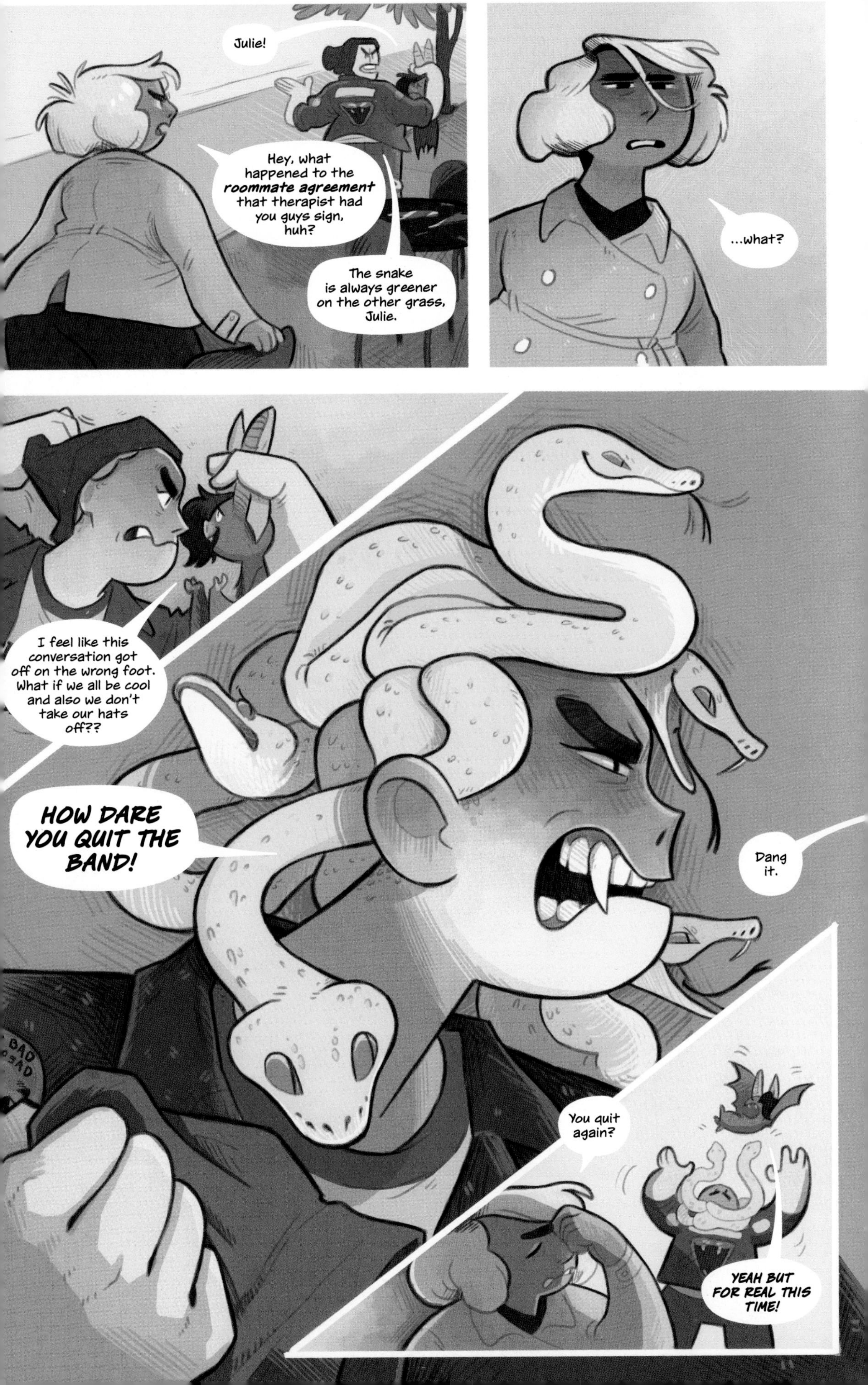
Julie!
Hey, what happened to the **roommate agreement** that therapist had you guys sign, huh?
The snake is always greener on the other grass, Julie.
...what?
I feel like this conversation got off on the wrong foot. What if we all be cool and also we don't take our hats off??
HOW DARE YOU QUIT THE BAND!
Dang it.
You quit again?
YEAH BUT FOR REAL THIS TIME!

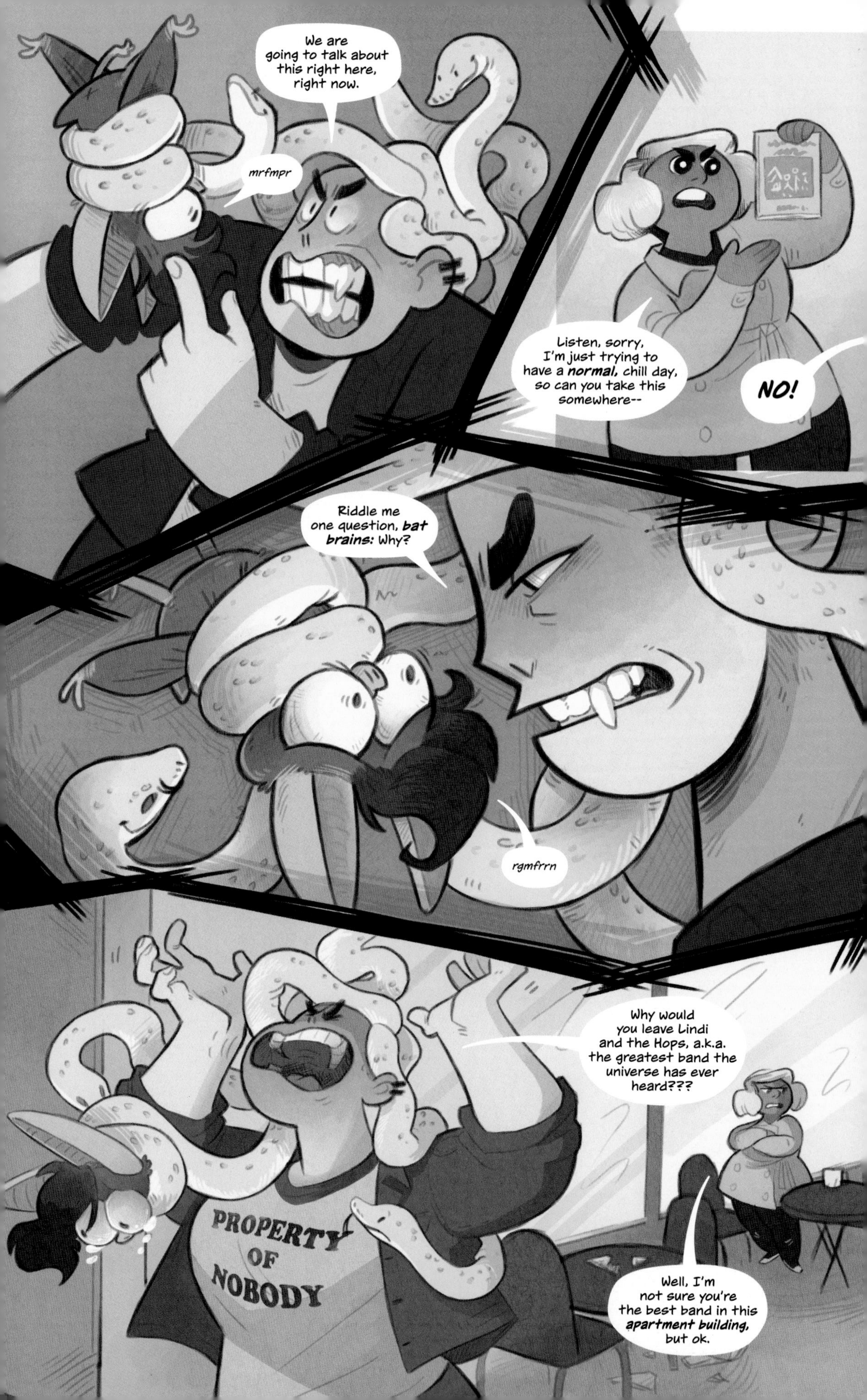
We are going to talk about this right here, right now.
mrfmpr
Listen, sorry, I'm just trying to have a **normal,** chill day, so can you take this somewhere--
NO!
Riddle me one question, **bat brains:** Why?
rgmfrrn
Why would you leave Lindi and the Hops, a.k.a. the greatest band the universe has ever heard???
PROPERTY OF NOBODY
Well, I'm not sure you're the best band in this **apartment building,** but ok.

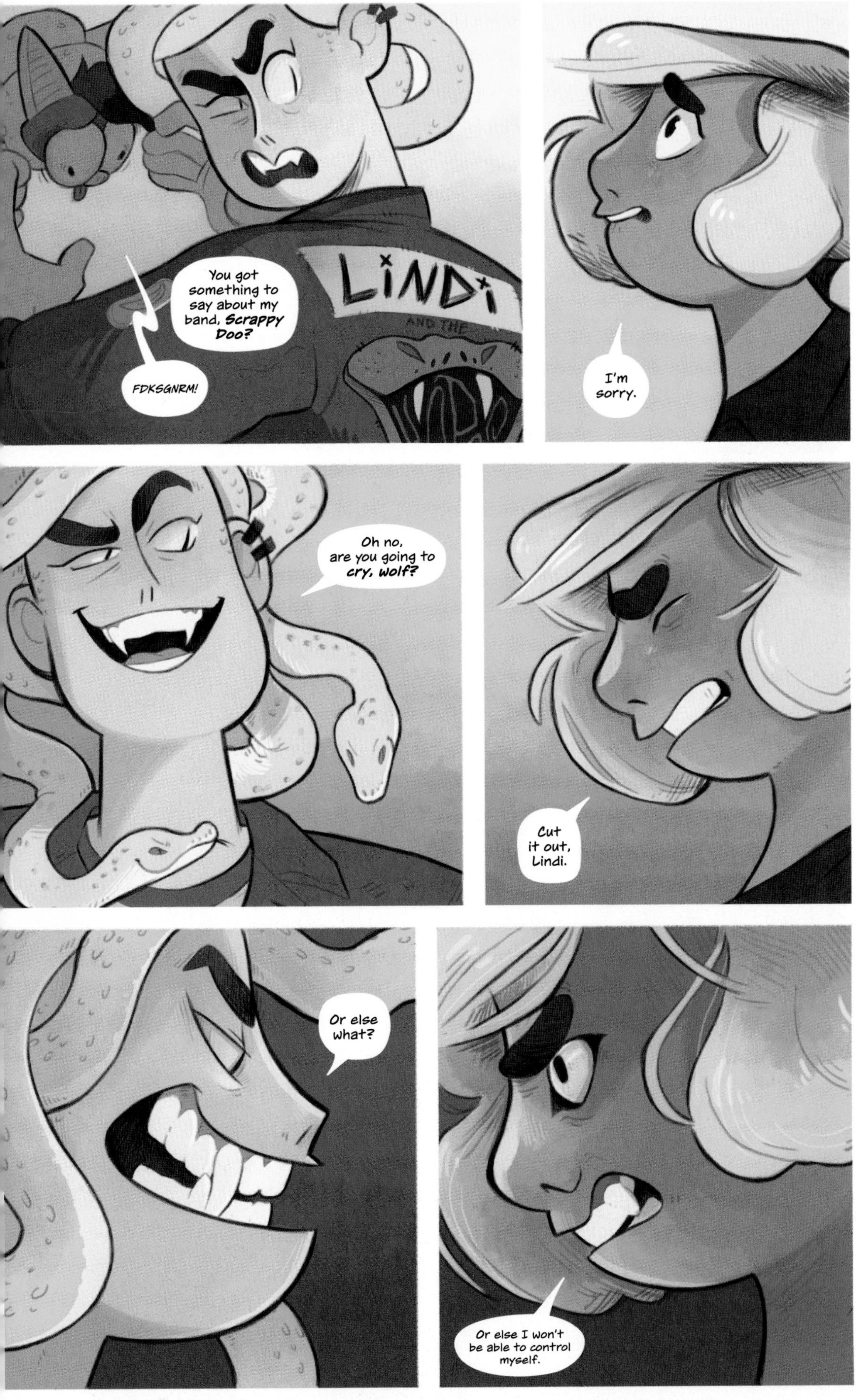
You got something to say about my band, Scrappy Doo?
FDKSGNRM!
I'm sorry.
Oh no, are you going to cry, wolf?
Cut it out, Lindi.
Or else what?
Or else I won't be able to control myself.

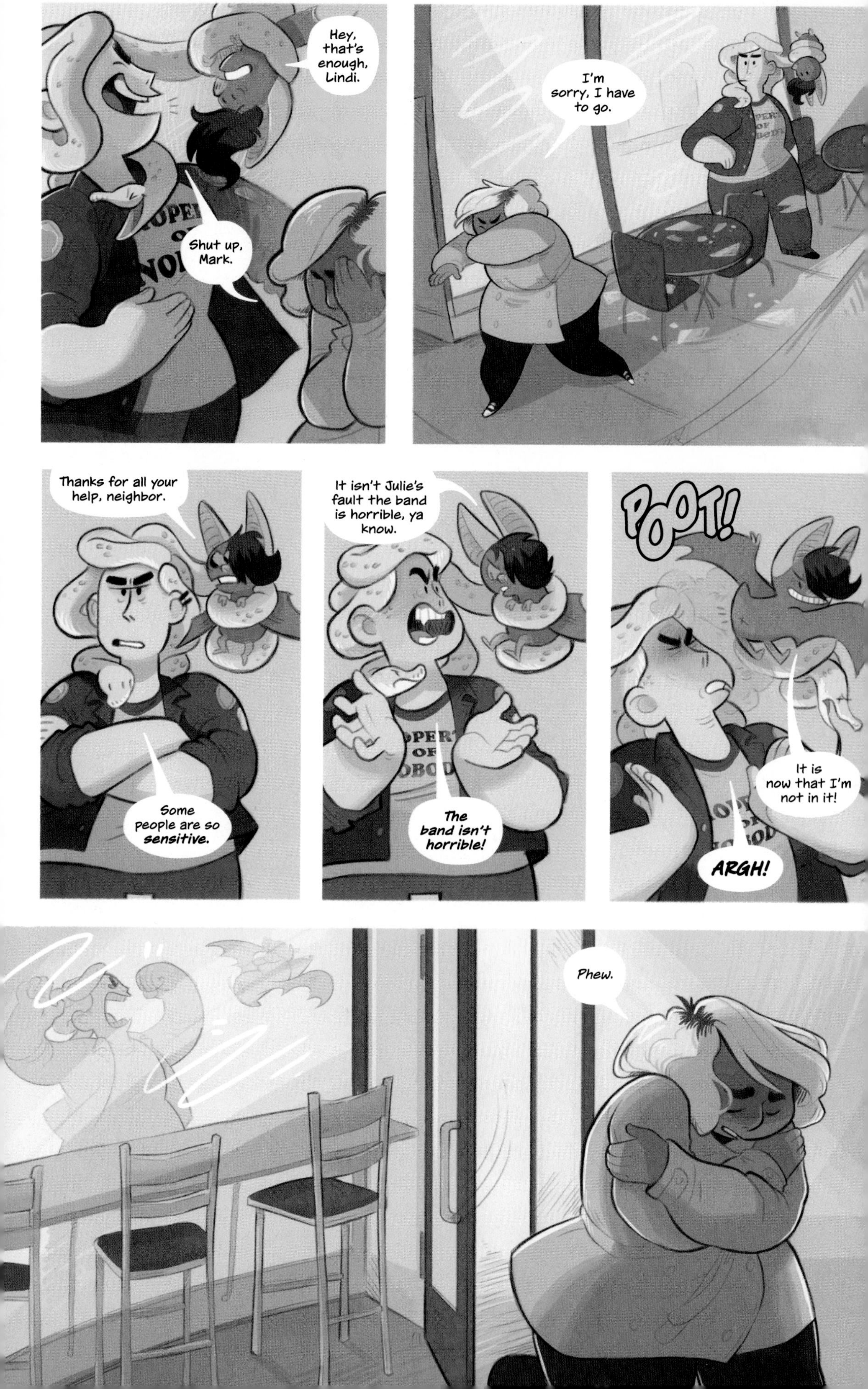

Hey, that's enough, Lindi.
Shut up, Mark.
I'm sorry, I have to go.
Thanks for all your help, neighbor.
Some people are so *sensitive.*
It isn't Julie's fault the band is horrible, ya know.
The band isn't horrible!
POOT!
It is now that I'm not in it!
ARGH!
Phew.

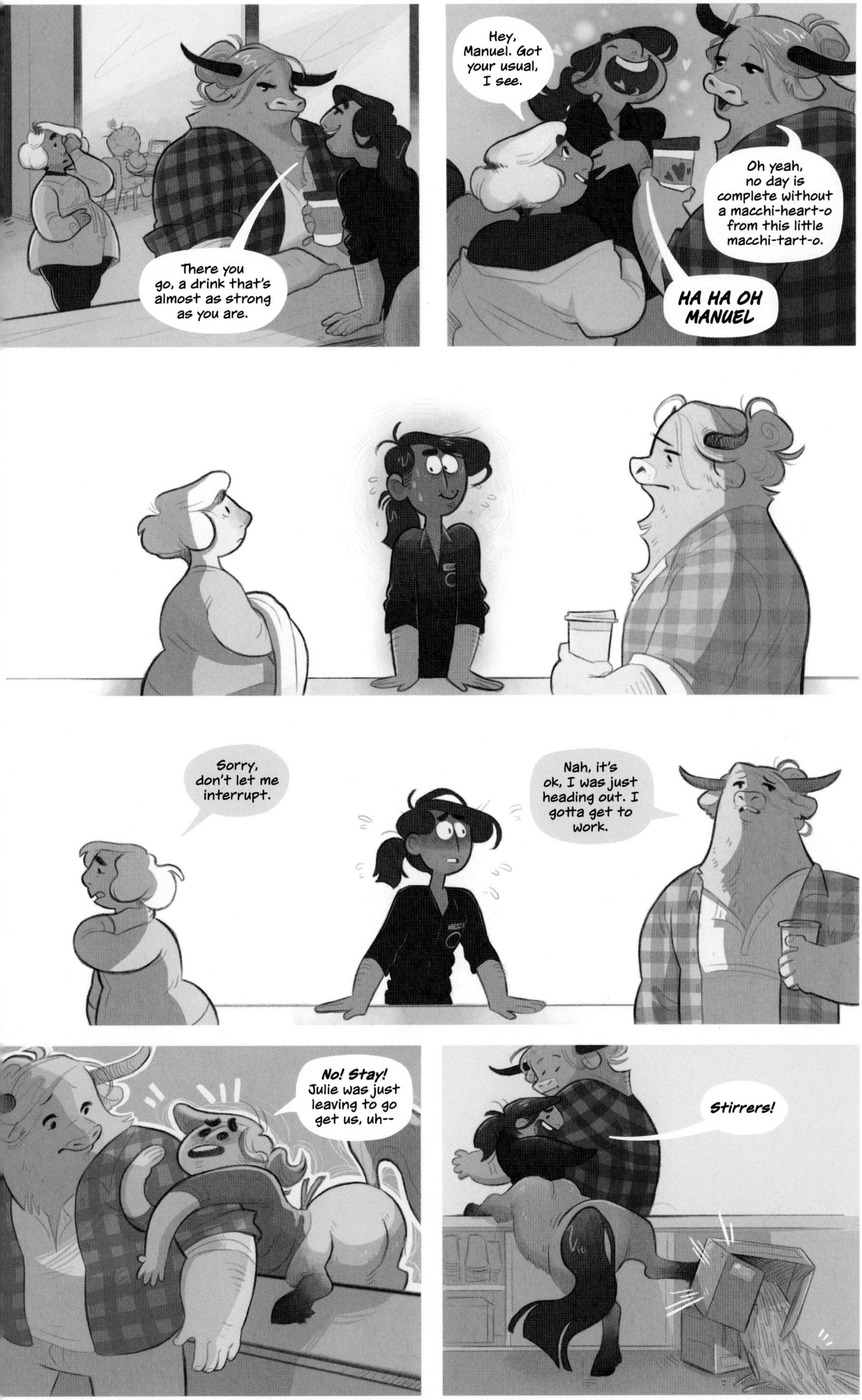
There you go, a drink that's almost as strong as you are.
Hey, Manuel. Got your usual, I see.
Oh yeah, no day is complete without a macchi-heart-o from this little macchi-tart-o.
HA HA OH MANUEL
Sorry, don't let me interrupt.
Nah, it's ok, I was just heading out. I gotta get to work.
No! Stay! Julie was just leaving to go get us, uh--
Stirrers!

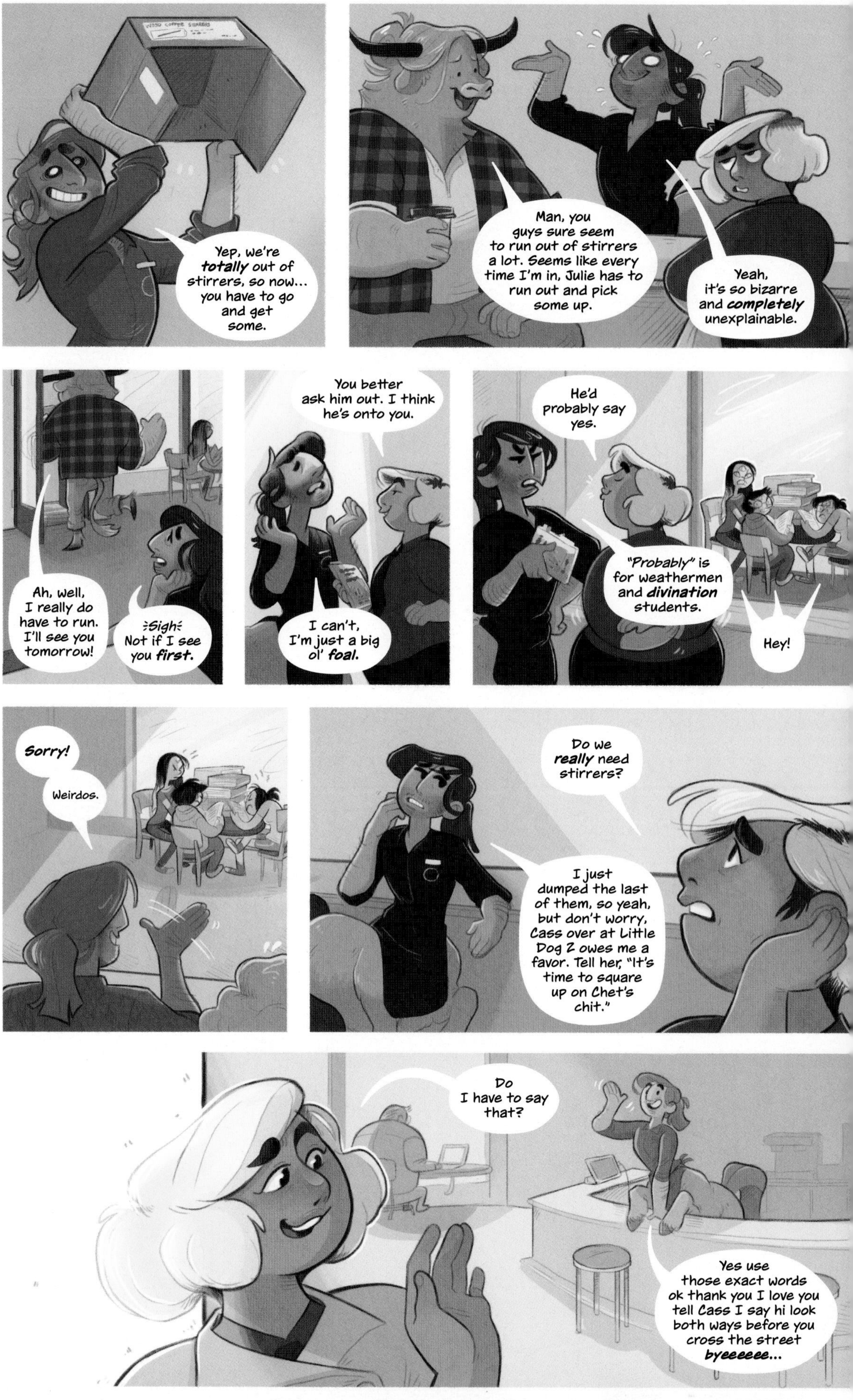

Yep, we're *totally* out of stirrers, so now... you have to go and get some.
Man, you guys sure seem to run out of stirrers a lot. Seems like every time I'm in, Julie has to run out and pick some up.
Yeah, it's so bizarre and *completely* unexplainable.
Ah, well, I really do have to run. I'll see you tomorrow!
Sigh Not if I see you *first.*
You better ask him out. I think he's onto you.
I can't, I'm just a big ol' *foal.*
He'd probably say yes.
"*Probably*" is for weathermen and *divination* students.
Hey!
Sorry!
Weirdos.
Do we *really* need stirrers?
I just dumped the last of them, so yeah, but don't worry, Cass over at Little Dog 2 owes me a favor. Tell her, "It's time to square up on Chet's chit."
Do I have to say that?
Yes use those exact words ok thank you I love you tell Cass I say hi look both ways before you cross the street *byeeeeee...*

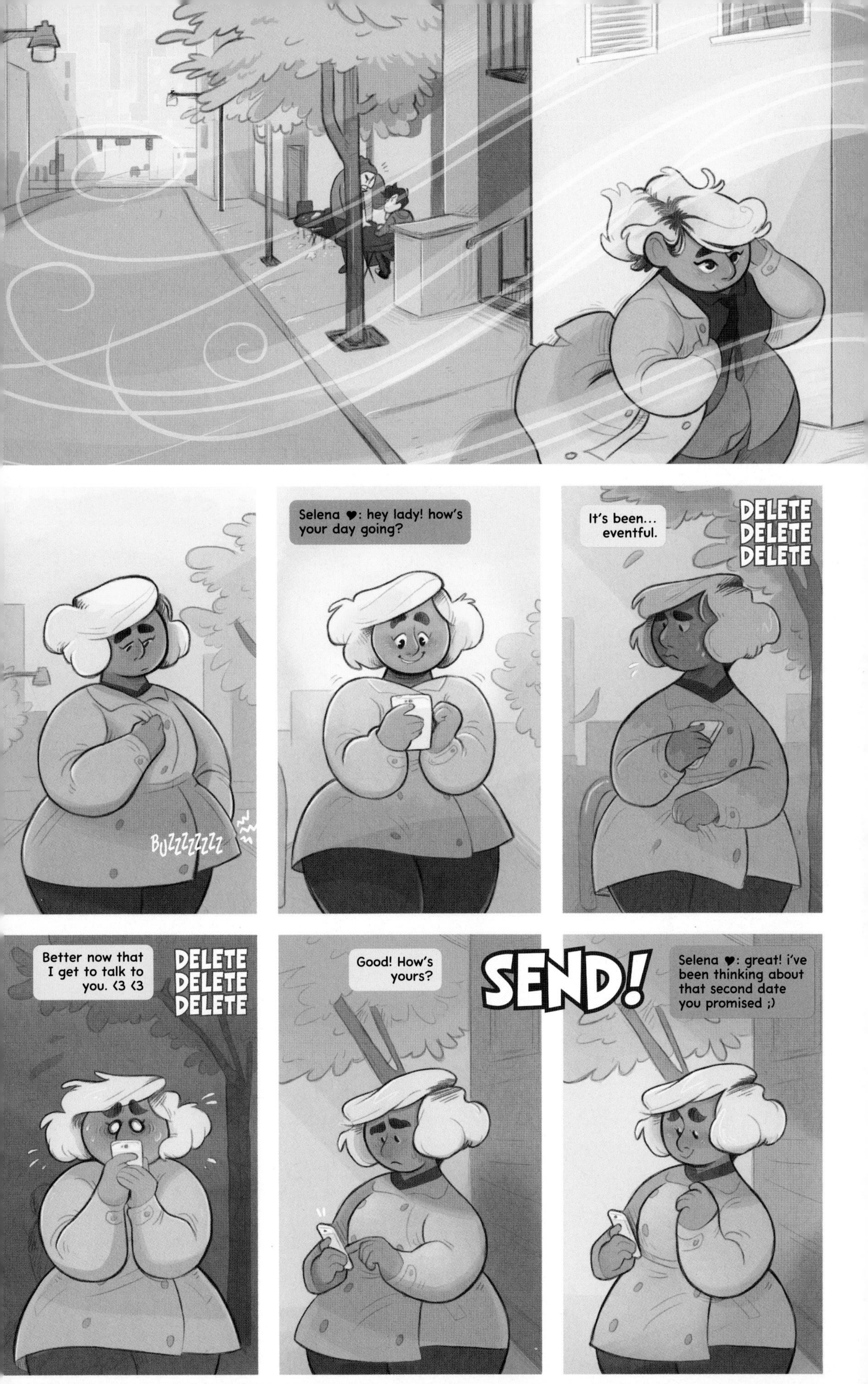
BUZZZZZZZZ
Selena ♥: hey lady! how's your day going?
It's been... eventful.
DELETE DELETE DELETE
Better now that I get to talk to you. <3 <3
DELETE DELETE DELETE
Good! How's yours?
SEND!
Selena ♥: great! i've been thinking about that second date you promised ;)

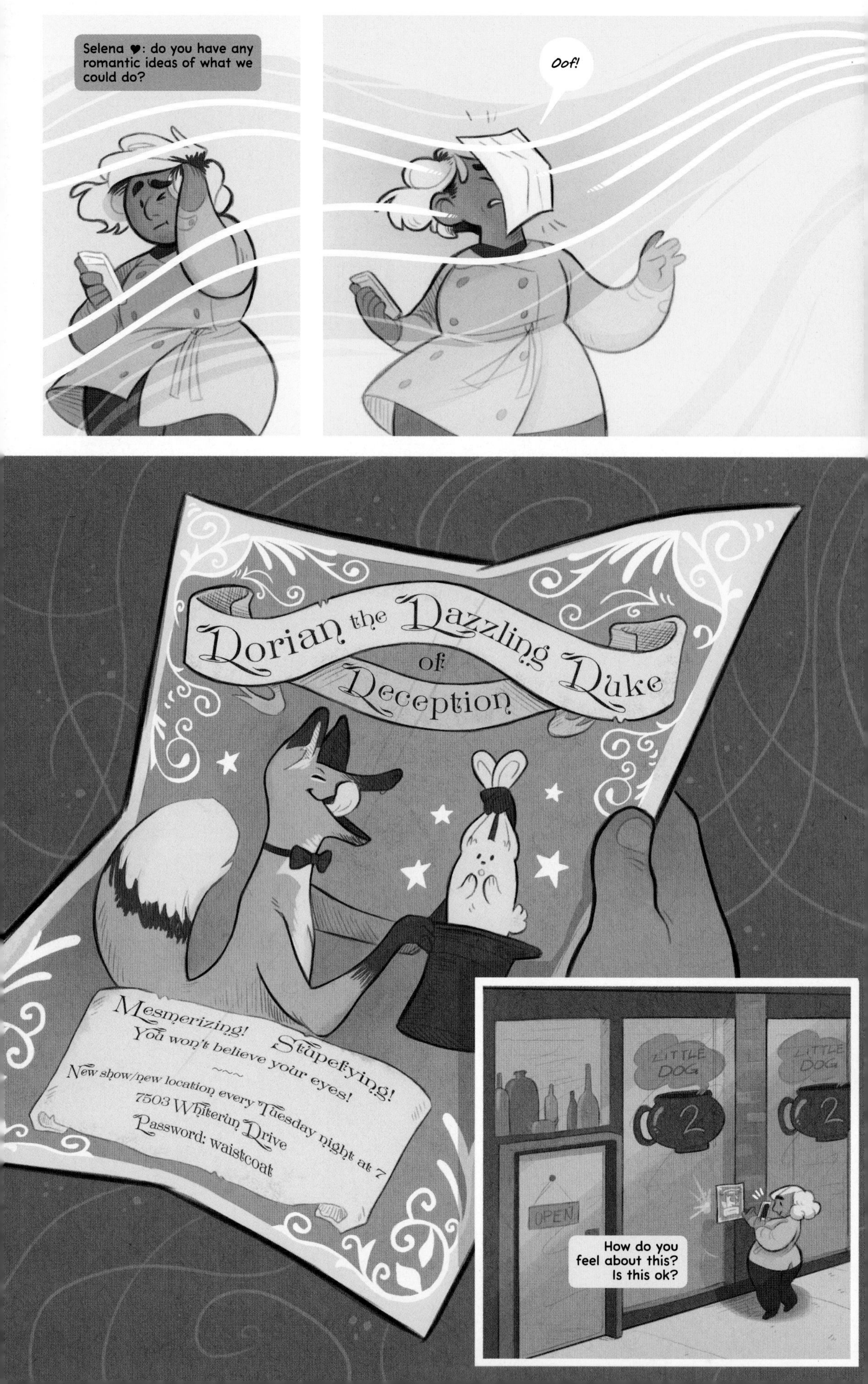
Selena ♥: do you have any romantic ideas of what we could do?
Oof!
Dorian the Dazzling Duke of Deception
Mesmerizing! Stupefying!
You won't believe your eyes!
~~~
New show/new location every Tuesday night at 7
7503 Whiterun Drive
Password: waistcoat
LITTLE DOG
2
LITTLE DOG
2
OPEN
How do you feel about this? Is this ok?
~~~

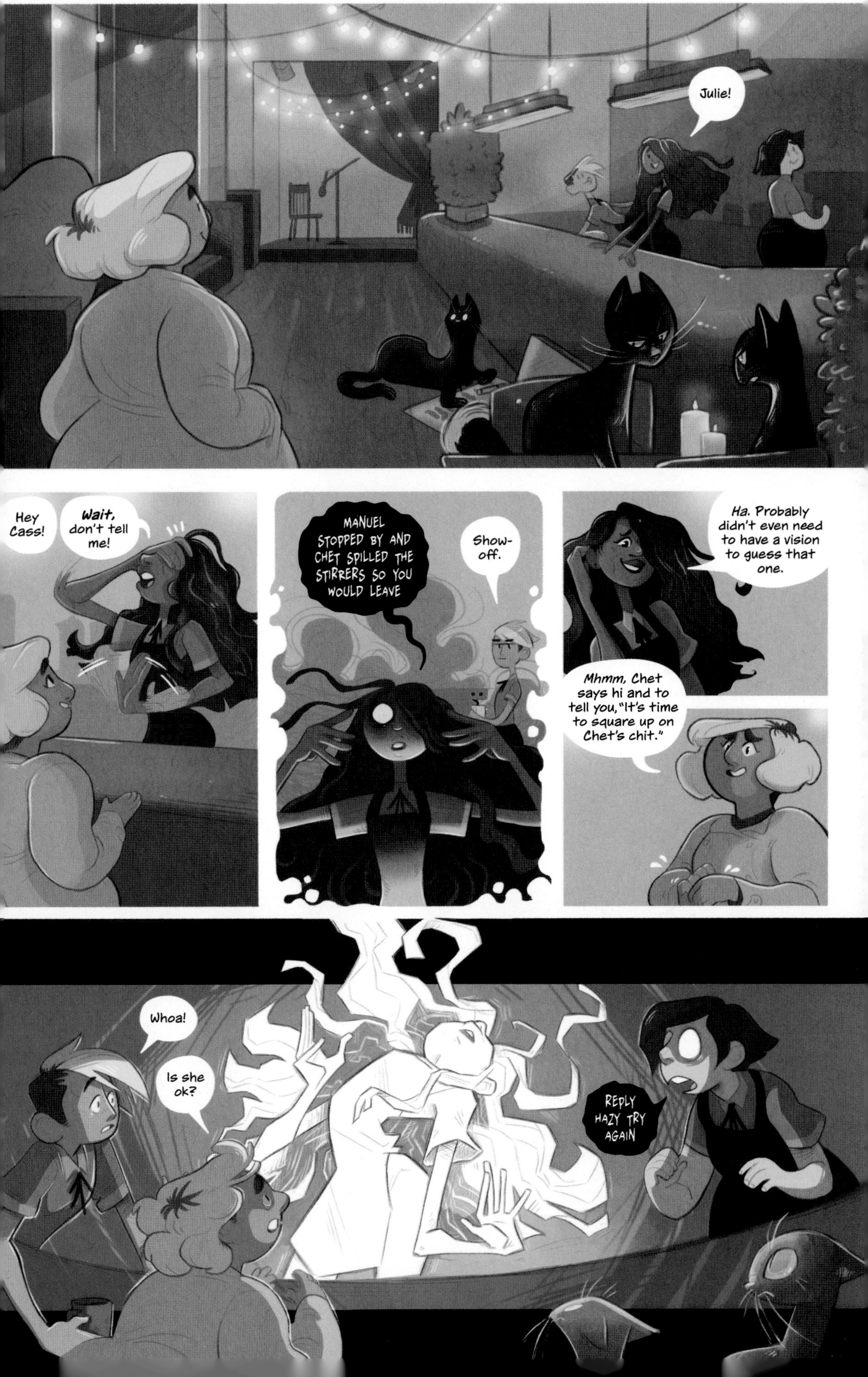
Julie!
Hey Cass!
Wait, don't tell me!
MANUEL STOPPED BY AND CHET SPILLED THE STIRRERS SO YOU WOULD LEAVE
Show-off.
Ha. Probably didn't even need to have a vision to guess that one.
Mhmm, Chet says hi and to tell you, "It's time to square up on Chet's chit."
Whoa!
Is she ok?
REPLY HAZY TRY AGAIN

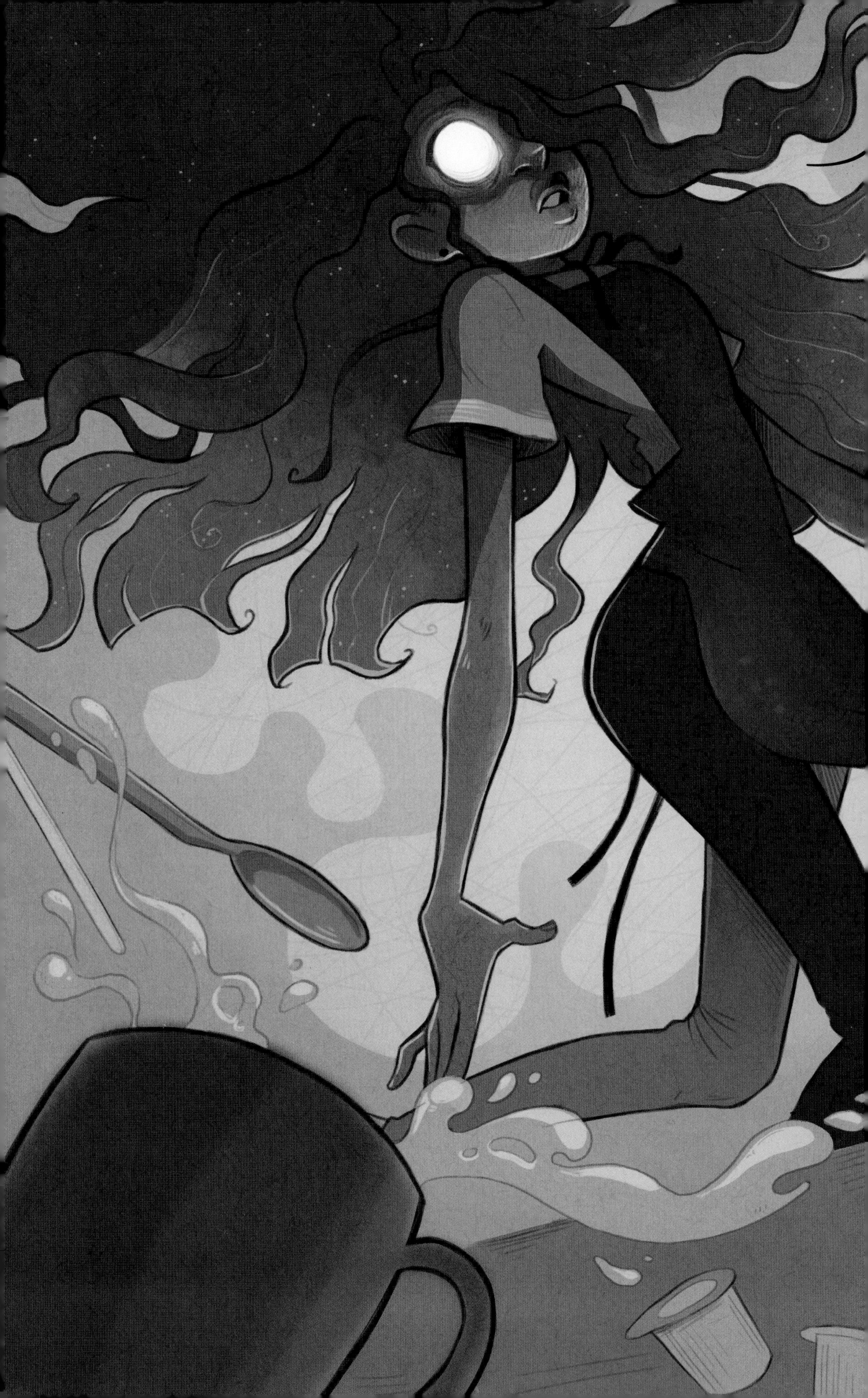

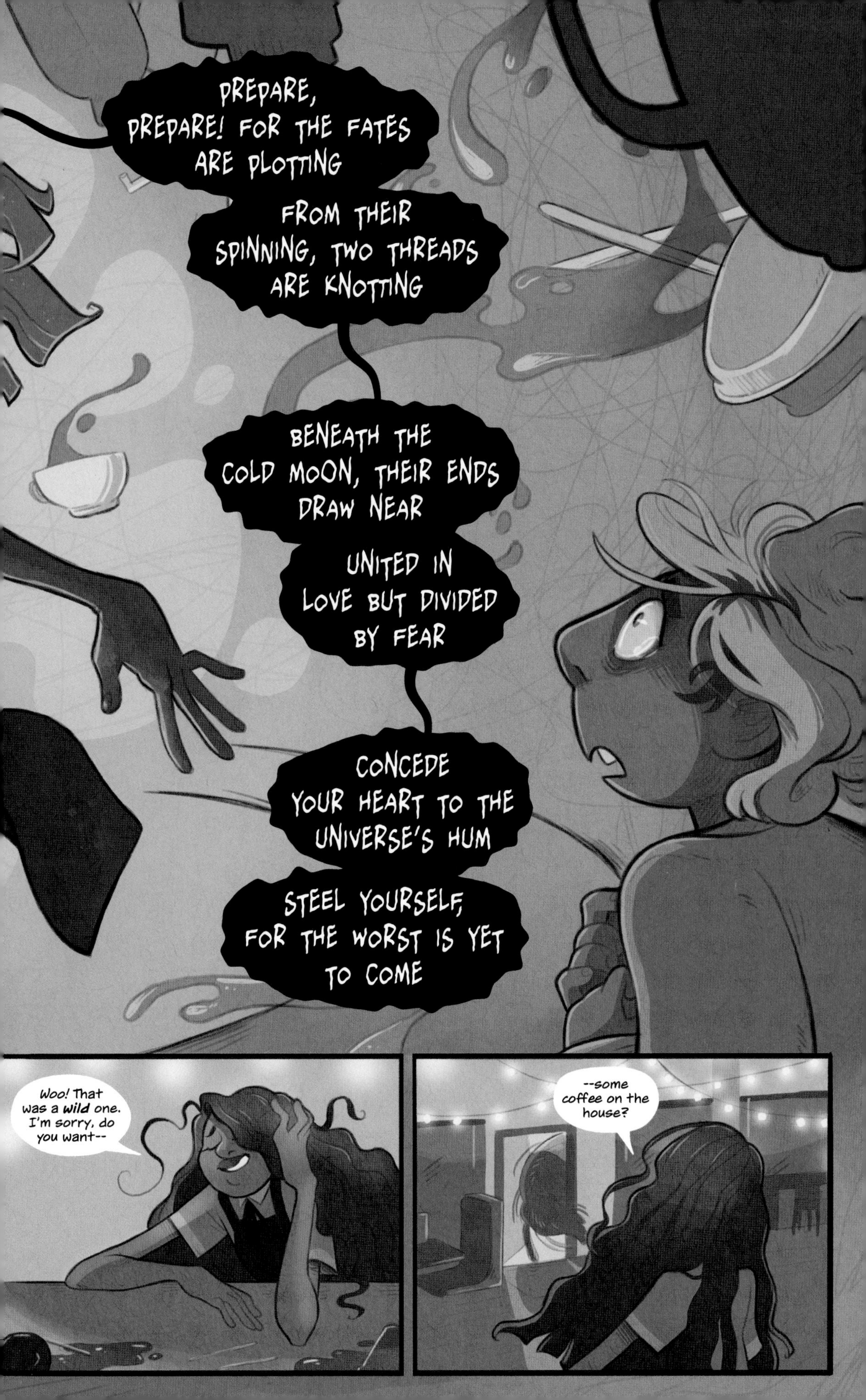
PREPARE, PREPARE! FOR THE FATES ARE PLOTTING
FROM THEIR SPINNING, TWO THREADS ARE KNOTTING
BENEATH THE COLD MOON, THEIR ENDS DRAW NEAR
UNITED IN LOVE BUT DIVIDED BY FEAR
CONCEDE YOUR HEART TO THE UNIVERSE'S HUM
STEEL YOURSELF, FOR THE WORST IS YET TO COME
Woo! That was a wild one. I'm sorry, do you want--
--some coffee on the house?

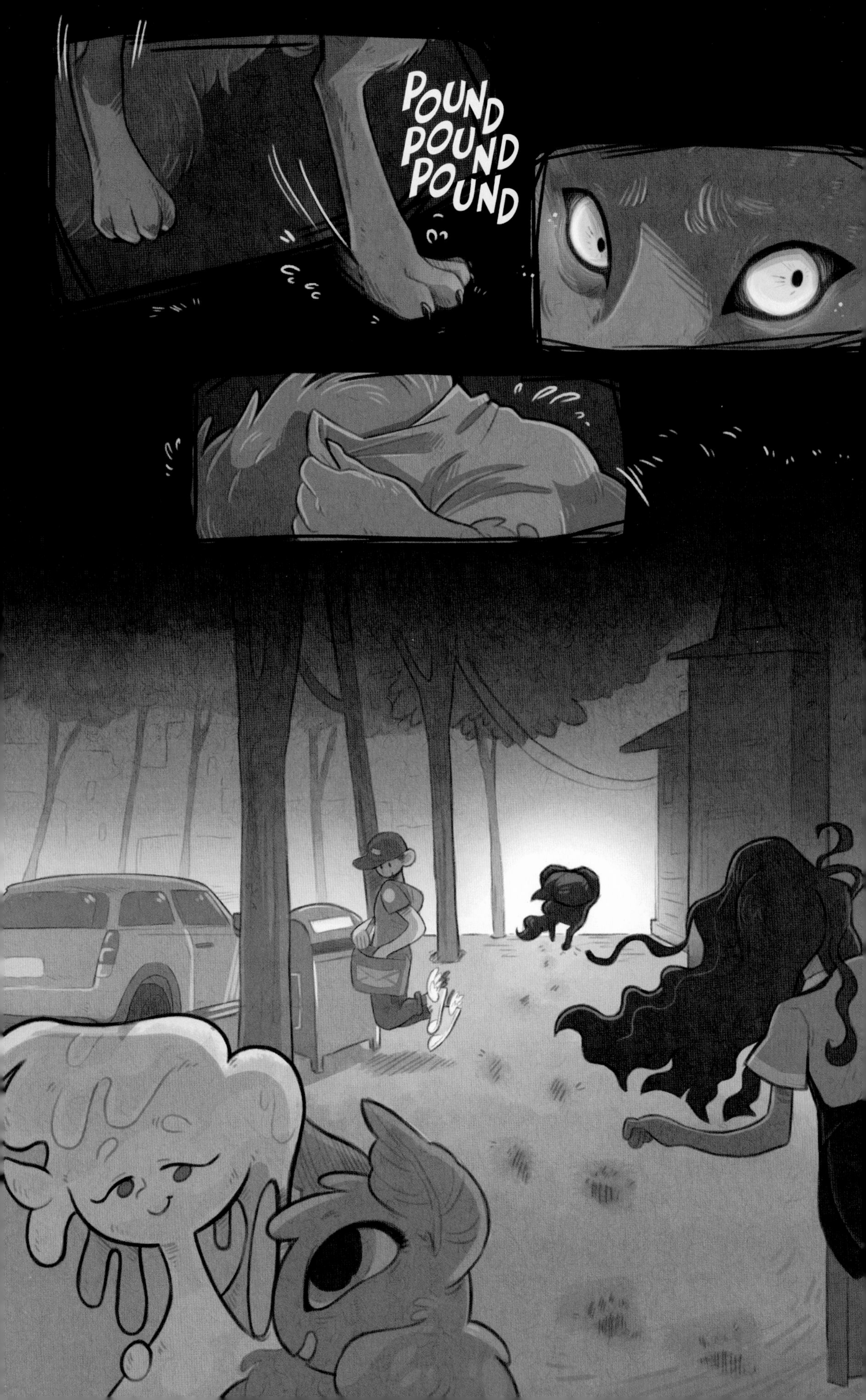
POUND
POUND
POUND

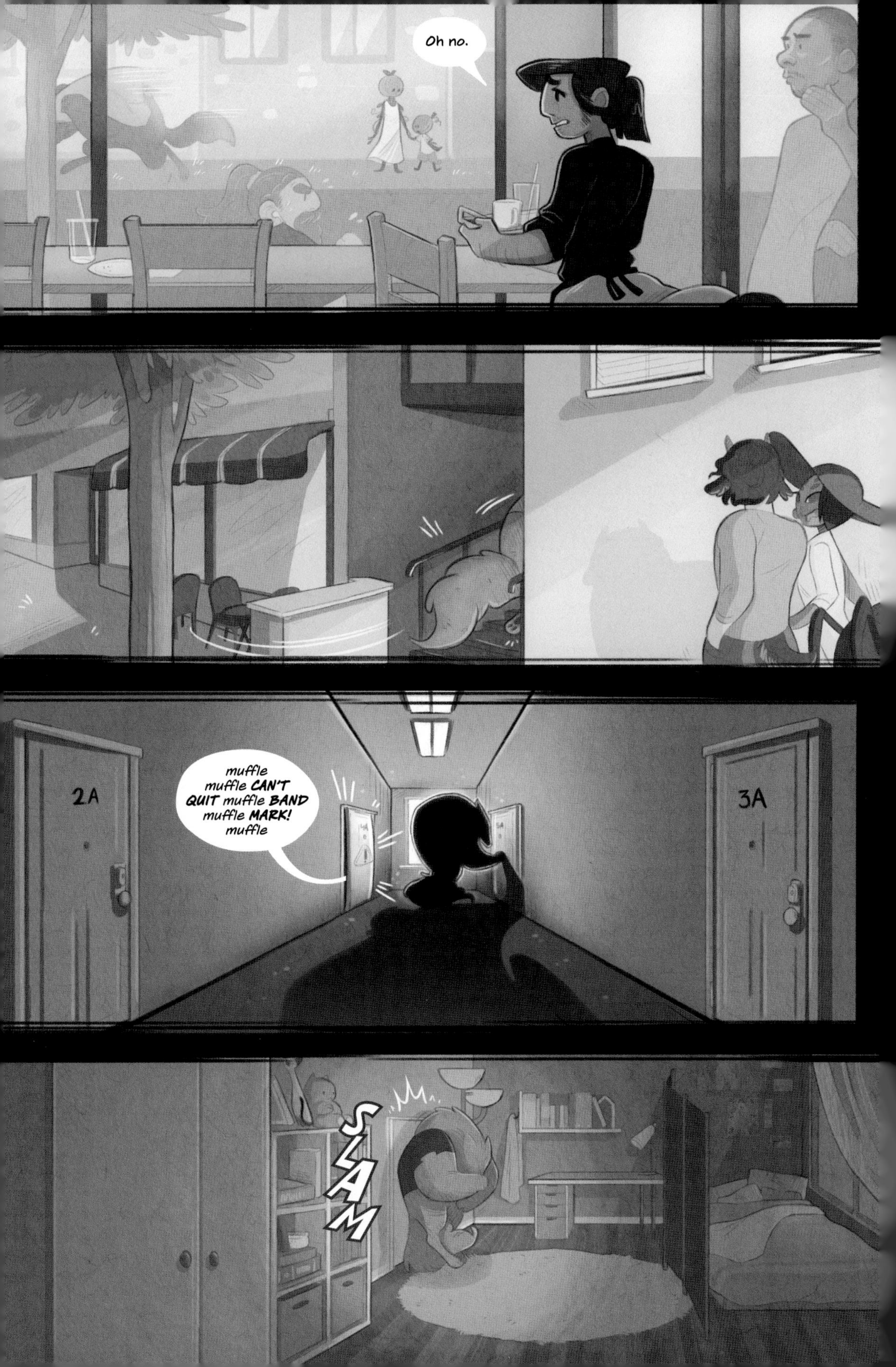
Oh no.
muffle muffle CAN'T QUIT muffle BAND muffle MARK! muffle
2A
3A
SLAM

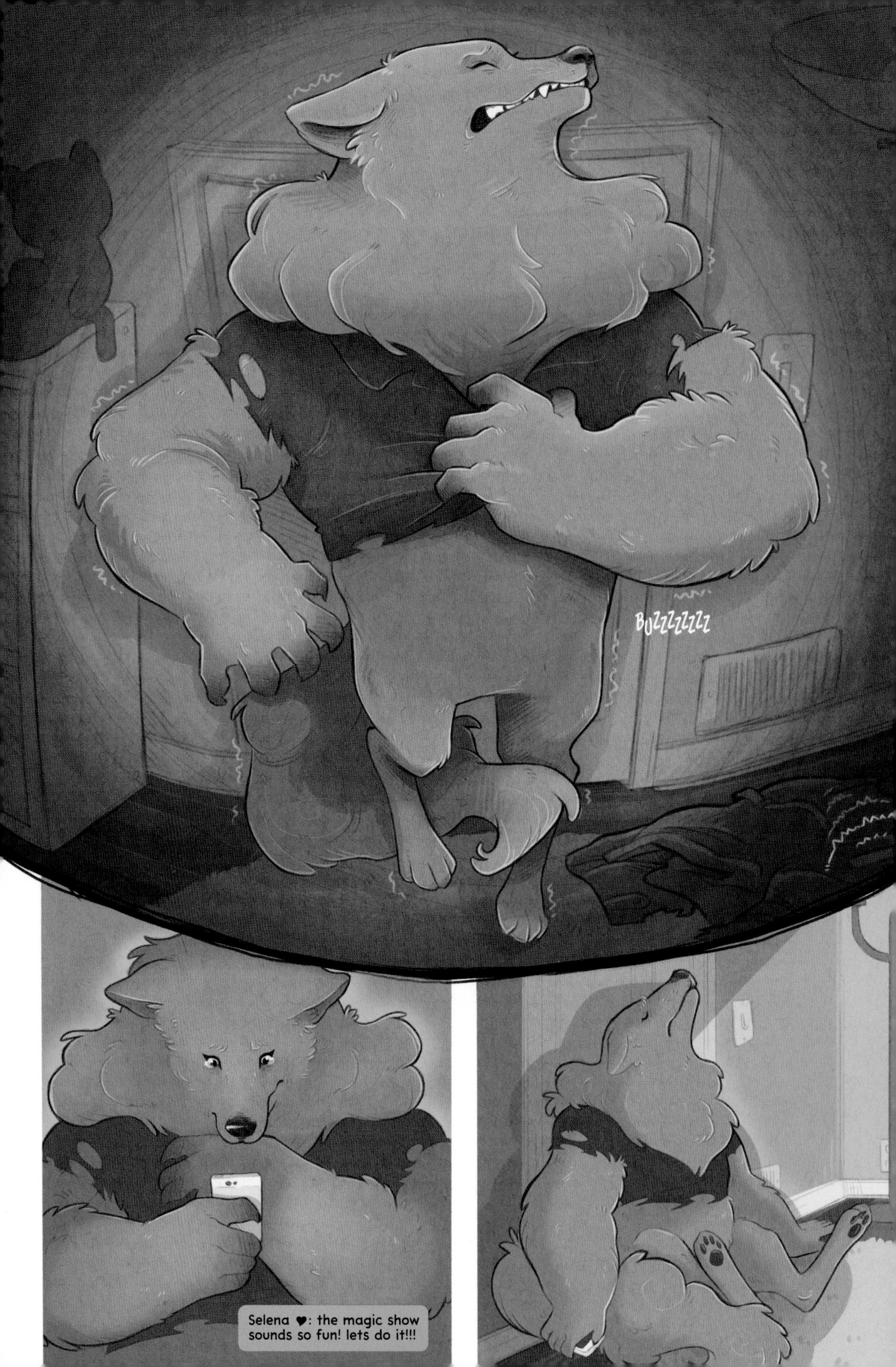
BUZZZZZZZ
Selena ♥: the magic show sounds so fun! lets do it!!!

ASK A KNOW-IT-ALL

Each month, we feature advice from a different local celebrity with a unique perspective.

This month's Know-It-All is Tallulah Atoll, who you may recognize from her work as the Arts and Entertainment Editor for the Blitheton Beacon Press. Tally is a BSU alumna who enjoys music and long swims by the beach.

Dear Know-It-All,
I love my husband, but I also am in love with his secretary. How do I best introduce the idea of a polyamorous relationship?
-Polly Wolly Canoodle

Dear Polly,
It sounds like you've got yourself into a real pickle! Have you considered seducing them both with your siren song and then drowning them? I've found that works wonders!

Dear Know-It-All,
My boss can be a real piece of work. He always finds a way to put himself in the spotlight, while I'm stuck doing all the behind-the-scenes work. It's like I'm invisible to him. What should I do?
-Andy in Agony

Dear Andy,
Bosses can sure be a pain! I recommend this tried and true technique: Drown him! You'll thank me later.

Dear Know-It-All,
I feel like no one takes me seriously as an artist. I mean, I don't actually make any art, but I think that it's unfair for people to use that as a way to measure my talent. How can I get them to take me seriously?
-Angsty Arteest

Dear 'Teest,
Be provocative! If you really want to get the attention of the art community, a surefire way to do it is to drown them all. You'd be doing them a favor, trust me. What creates more great art than than pain and suffering

(besides hard work, perseverance, money, access to resources, and the ability to take criticism)!

Dear Know-It-All,
I've run out of Netflix binge shows. What should I watch now?
-Procrastinating in Phoenix

Dear P.P.,
You can't go wrong with "Grace and Frankie."

Dear Know-It-All,
The coastal watermaster insists on shining our lighthouse lens every nine seconds when it's listed on ships' manifests as blinking every six! Someone is going to get hurt! How do I convince him to change it back?
-Six Seconds To Sandbars

Dear Six,
Wow, what a complicated problem! First of all, you should consider drowning the coastal watermaster. But don't rule out leaving the light at nine seconds! You don't know who's on those ships! Maybe they heard, I don't know, someone singing from the rocks and they're just trying to investigate without some life-saving light flashing in their eyes all the time. Actually, you know what? Why don't you come on down and check out those super cool rocks yourself, Six. Yes, that's right, follow the singing, a little closer, don't stop now... that's it...

PAGE OF WAND
THE HERM

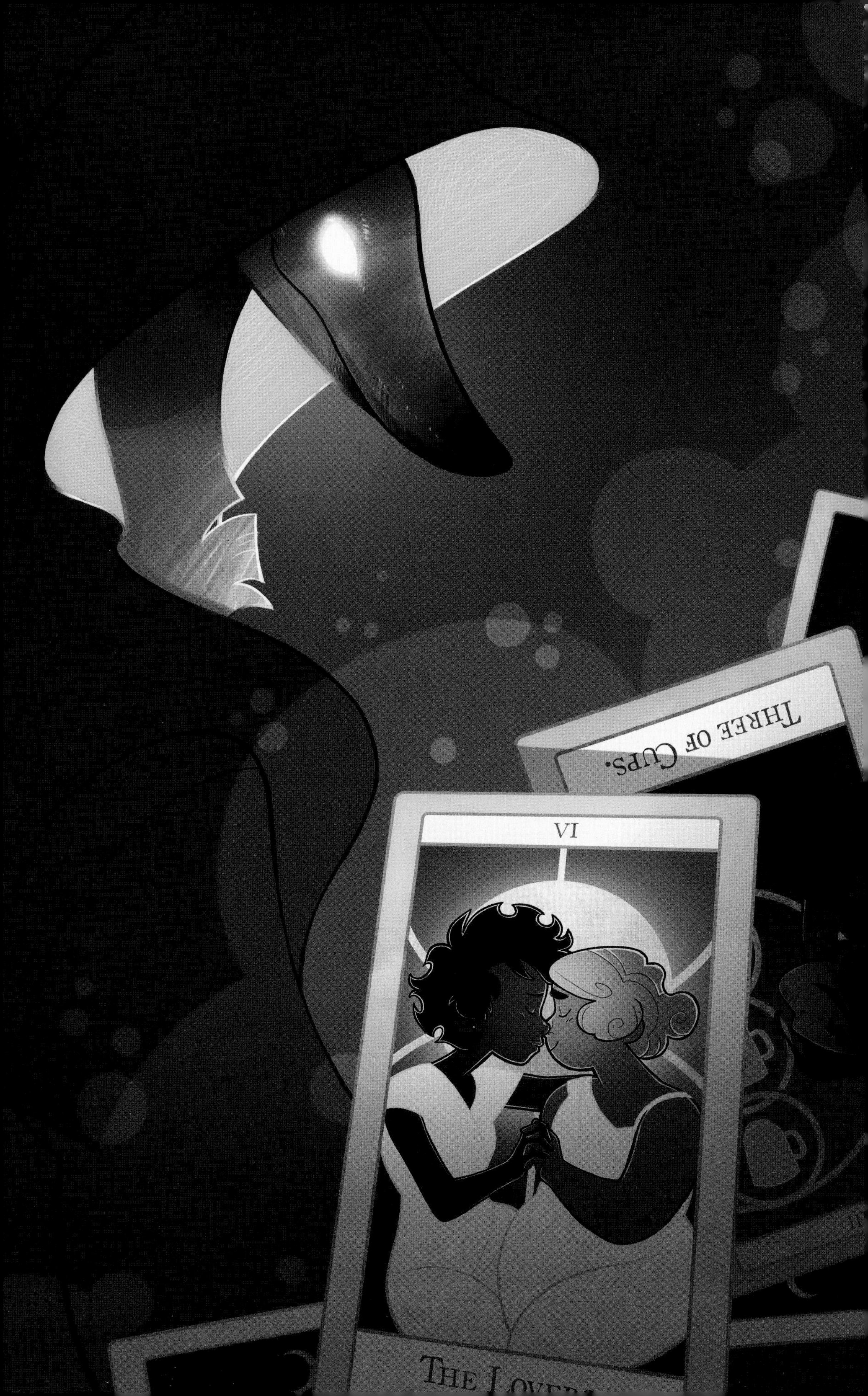
THREE OF CUPS.
VI
THE LOVE

CHAPTER TWO

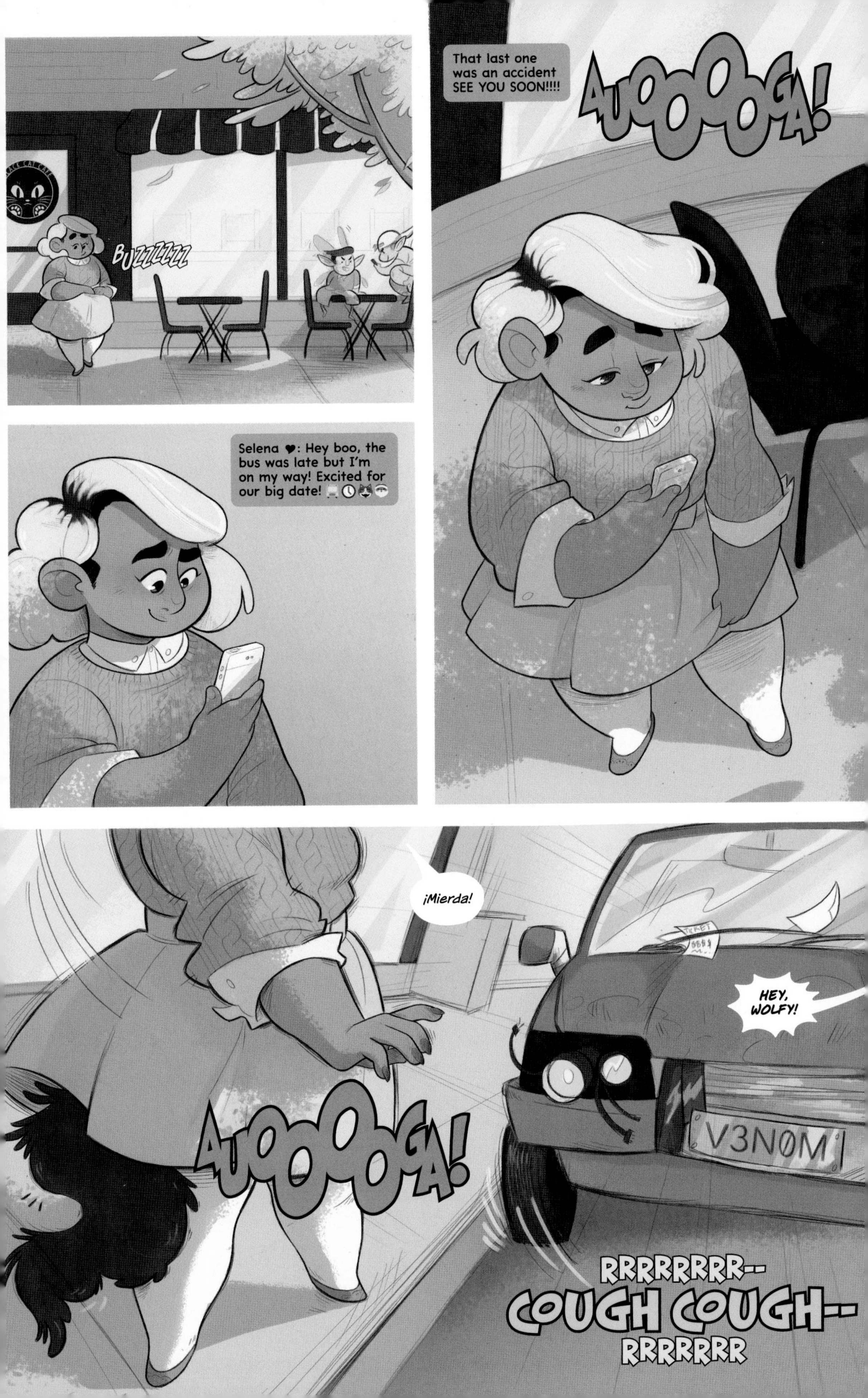
BUZZZZZZZ
Selena ♥: Hey boo, the bus was late but I'm on my way! Excited for our big date!
That last one was an accident SEE YOU SOON!!!!
AUOOOOGA!
¡Mierda!
AUOOOOGA!
HEY, WOLFY!
V3NØM
RRRRRRRR--
COUGH COUGH--
RRRRRRR

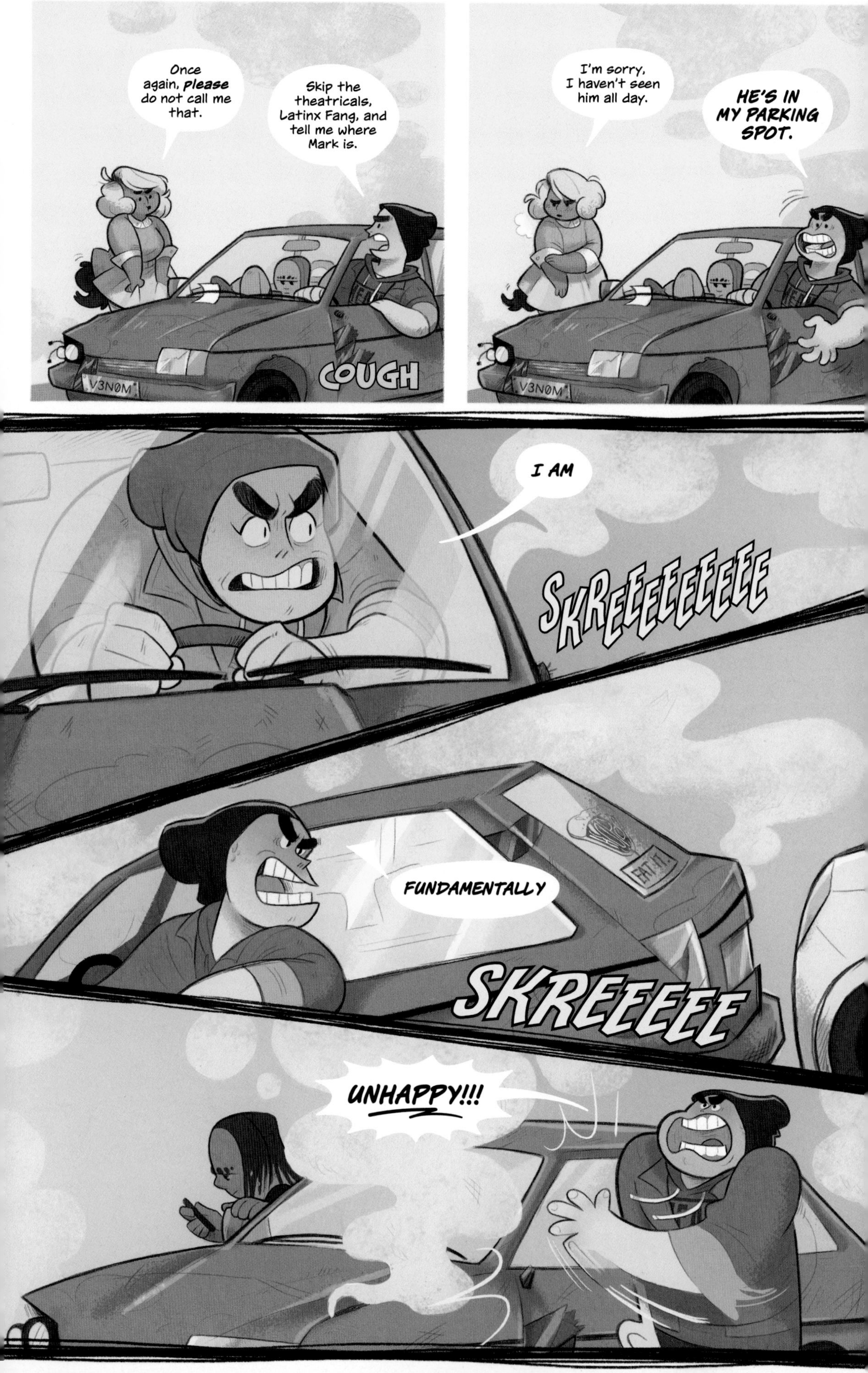
Once again, *please* do not call me that.
Skip the theatricals, Latinx Fang, and tell me where Mark is.
COUGH
V3N0M
I'm sorry, I haven't seen him all day.
HE'S IN MY PARKING SPOT.
V3N0M
I AM
SKREEEEEEEEE
FUNDAMENTALLY
EAT IT.
SKREEEEEE
UNHAPPY!!!

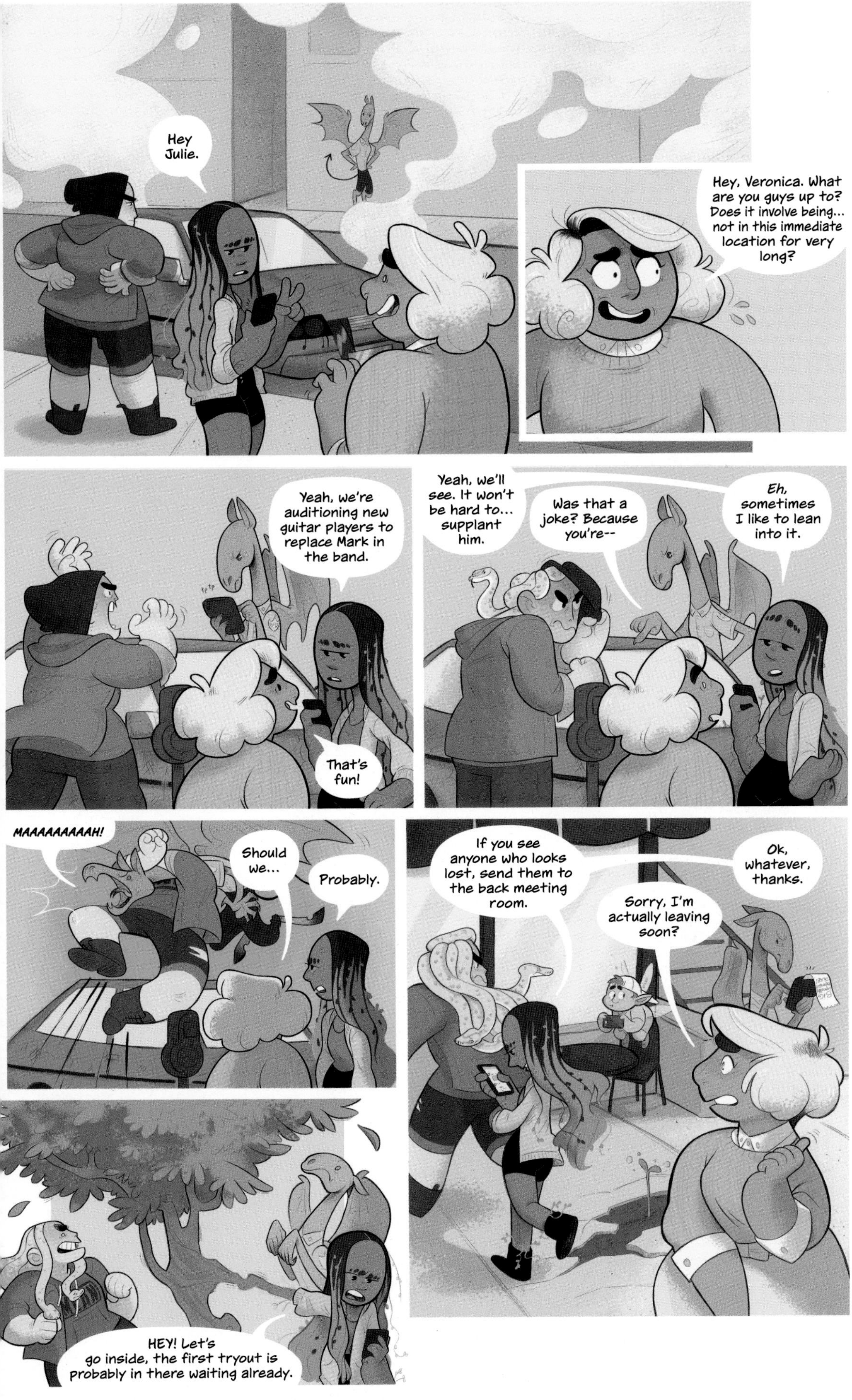
Hey Julie.
Hey, Veronica. What are you guys up to? Does it involve being... not in this immediate location for very long?
Yeah, we're auditioning new guitar players to replace Mark in the band.
That's fun!
Yeah, we'll see. It won't be hard to... supplant him.
Was that a joke? Because you're--
Eh, sometimes I like to lean into it.
MAAAAAAAAAH!
Should we...
Probably.
HEY! Let's go inside, the first tryout is probably in there waiting already.
If you see anyone who looks lost, send them to the back meeting room.
Ok, whatever, thanks.
Sorry, I'm actually leaving soon?

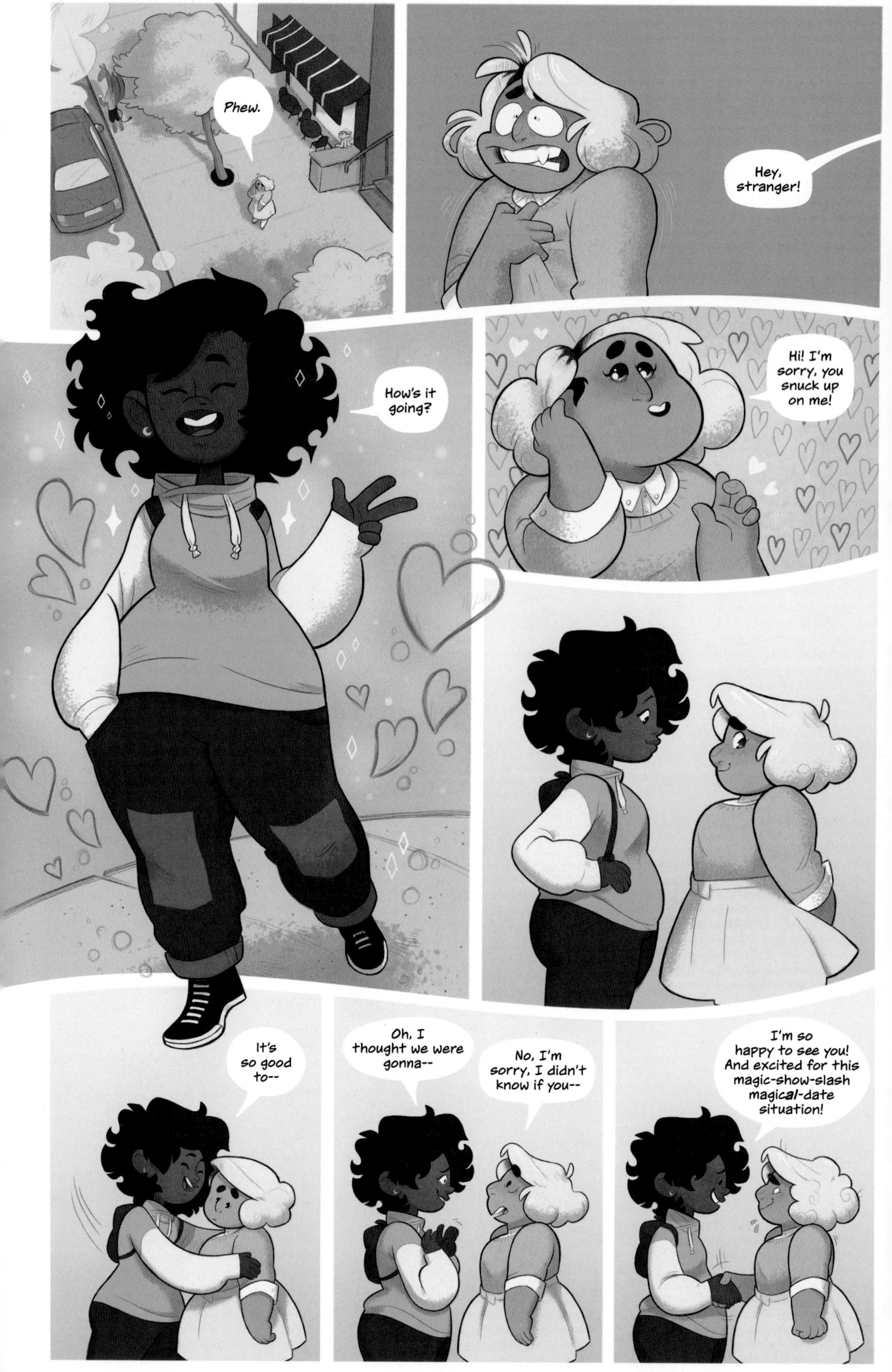
Phew.
Hey, stranger!
How's it going?
Hi! I'm sorry, you snuck up on me!
It's so good to--
Oh, I thought we were gonna--
No, I'm sorry, I didn't know if you--
I'm so happy to see you! And excited for this magic-show-slash magical-date situation!

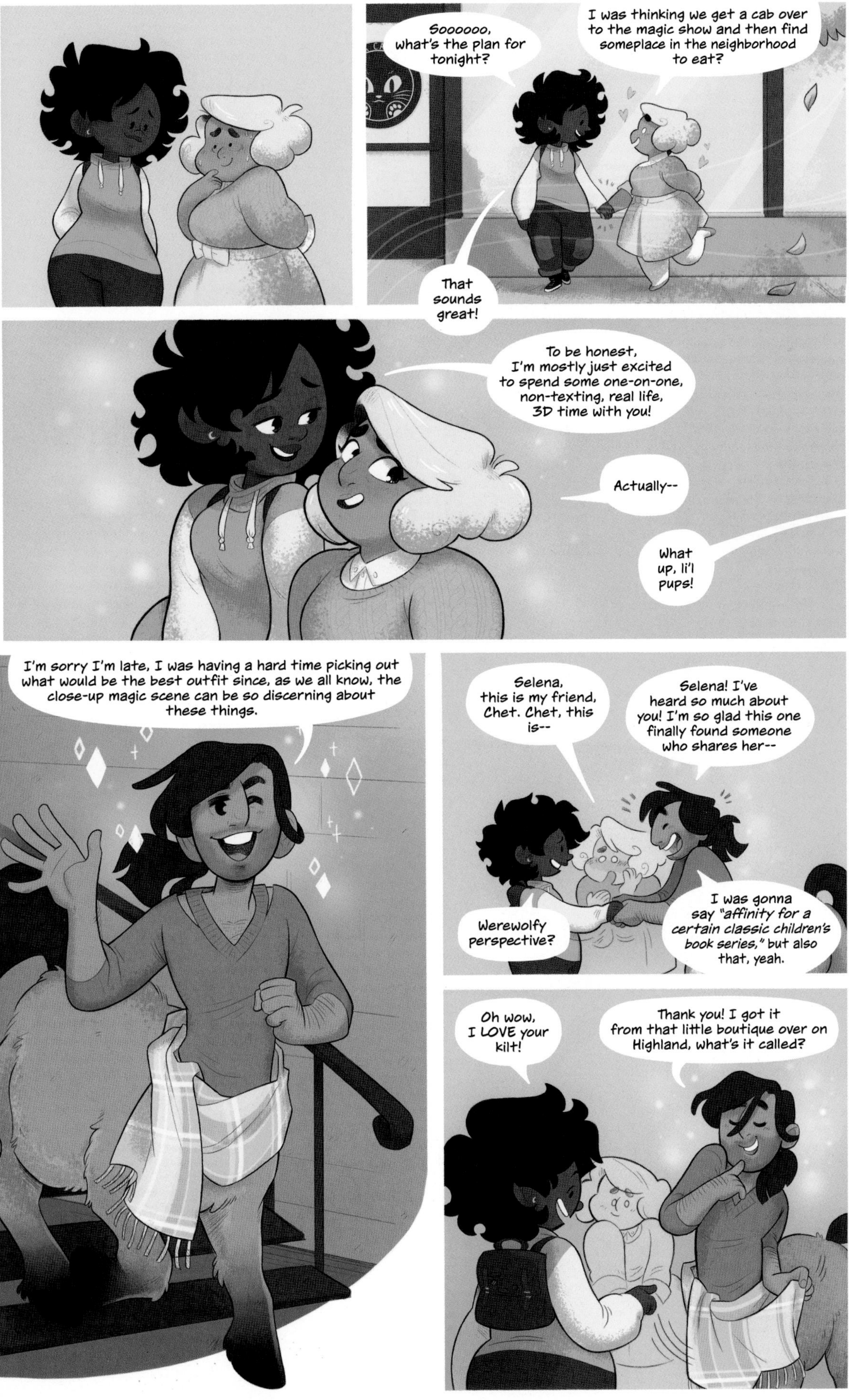
Sooooooo, what's the plan for tonight?
I was thinking we get a cab over to the magic show and then find someplace in the neighborhood to eat?
That sounds great!
To be honest, I'm mostly just excited to spend some one-on-one, non-texting, real life, 3D time with you!
Actually--
What up, li'l pups!
I'm sorry I'm late, I was having a hard time picking out what would be the best outfit since, as we all know, the close-up magic scene can be so discerning about these things.
Selena, this is my friend, Chet. Chet, this is--
Selena! I've heard so much about you! I'm so glad this one finally found someone who shares her--
Werewolfy perspective?
I was gonna say "affinity for a certain classic children's book series," but also that, yeah.
Oh wow, I LOVE your kilt!
Thank you! I got it from that little boutique over on Highland, what's it called?

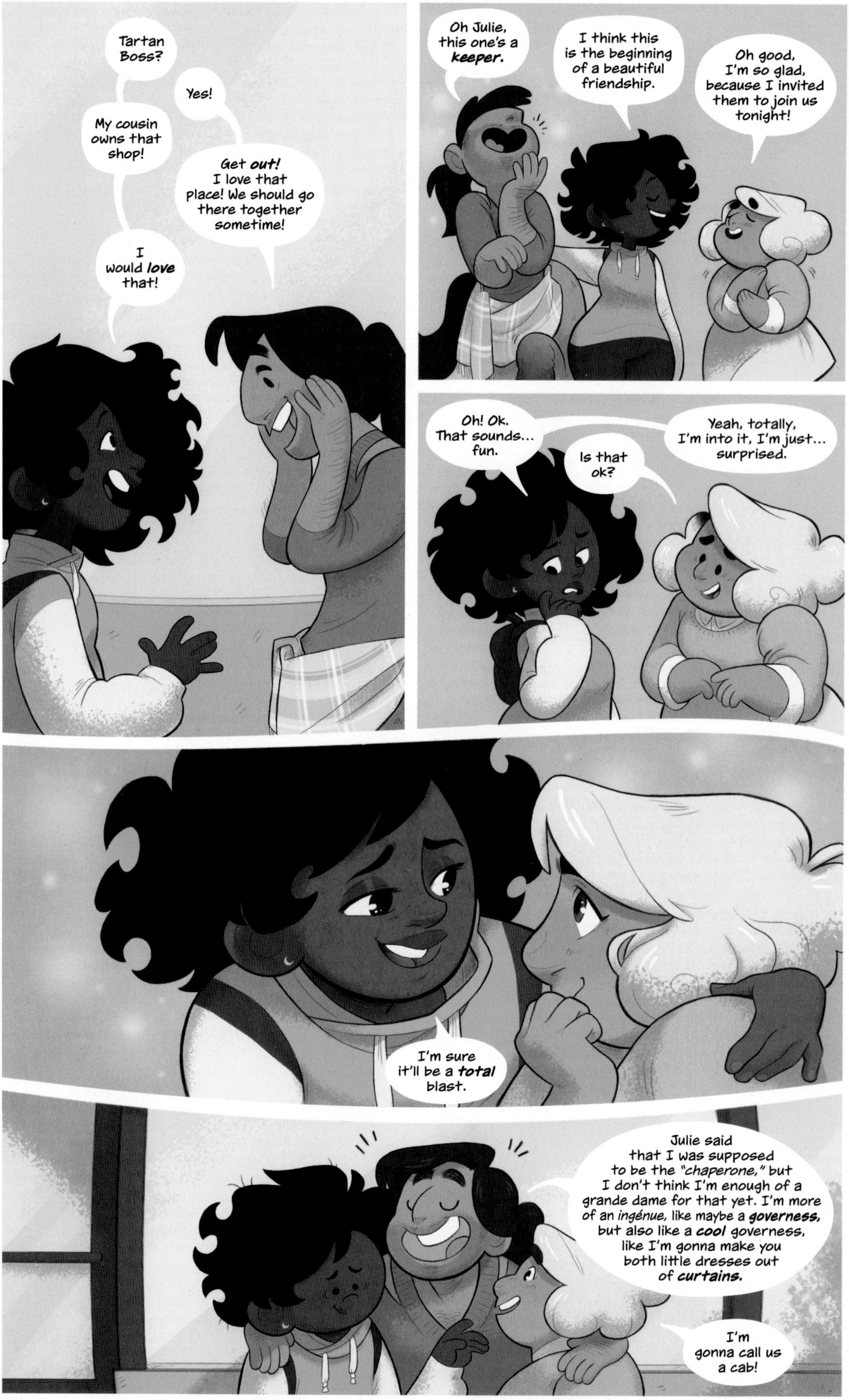
Tartan Boss?
Yes!
My cousin owns that shop!
Get *out!* I love that place! We should go there together sometime!
I would *love* that!
Oh Julie, this one's a ***keeper.***
I think this is the beginning of a beautiful friendship.
Oh good, I'm so glad, because I invited them to join us tonight!
Oh! Ok. That sounds... fun.
Is that ok?
Yeah, totally, I'm into it, I'm just... surprised.
I'm sure it'll be a ***total*** blast.
Julie said that I was supposed to be the *"chaperone,"* but I don't think I'm enough of a grande dame for that yet. I'm more of an *ingénue*, like maybe a ***governess,*** but also like a ***cool*** governess, like I'm gonna make you both little dresses out of ***curtains.***
I'm gonna call us a cab!

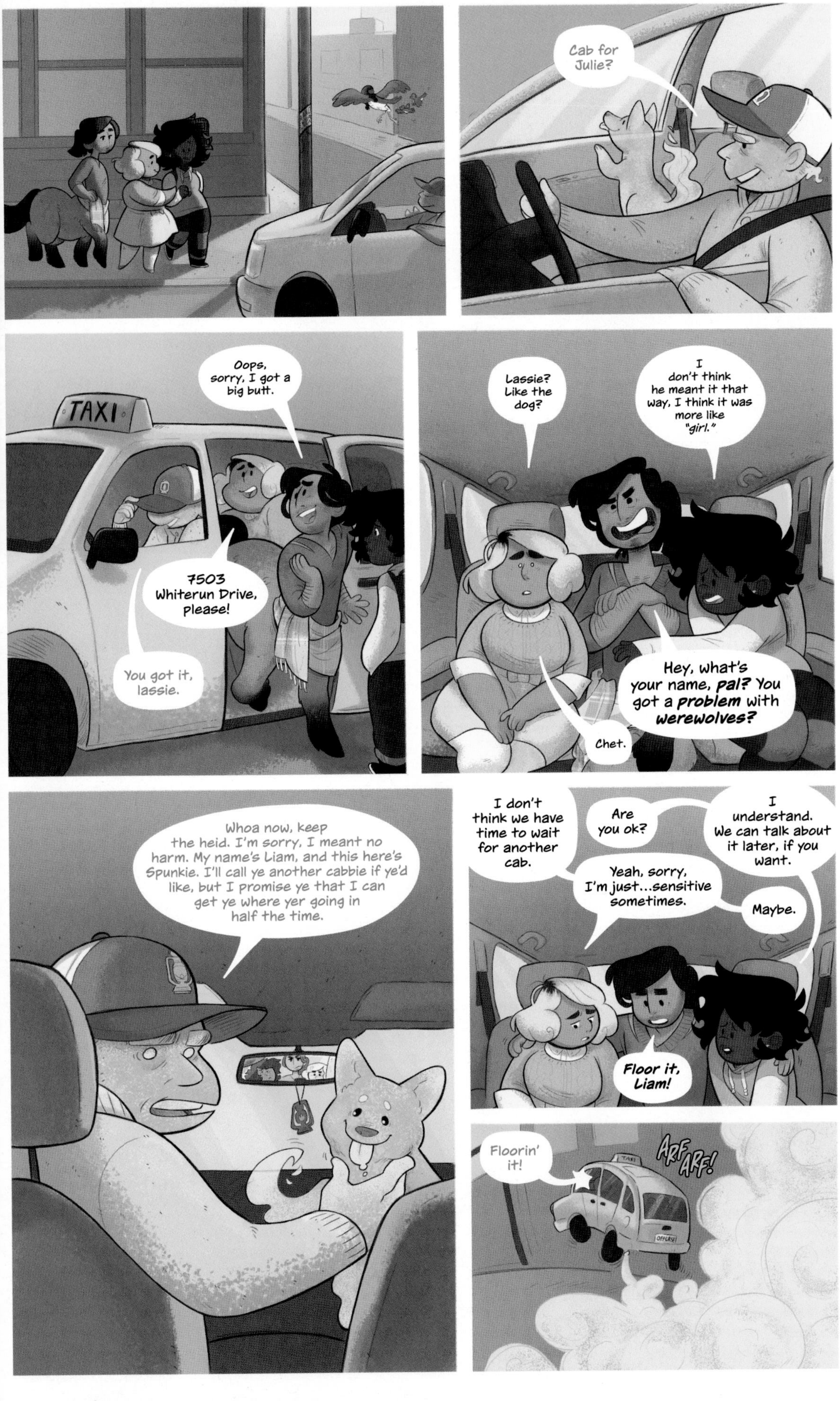
Cab for Julie?
TAXI
Oops, sorry, I got a big butt.
7503 Whiterun Drive, please!
You got it, lassie.
Lassie? Like the dog?
I don't think he meant it that way, I think it was more like "girl."
Hey, what's your name, pal? You got a problem with werewolves?
Chet.
Whoa now, keep the heid. I'm sorry, I meant no harm. My name's Liam, and this here's Spunkie. I'll call ye another cabbie if ye'd like, but I promise ye that I can get ye where yer going in half the time.
I don't think we have time to wait for another cab.
Are you ok?
I understand. We can talk about it later, if you want.
Yeah, sorry, I'm just...sensitive sometimes.
Maybe.
Floor it, Liam!
Floorin' it!
ARF ARF!

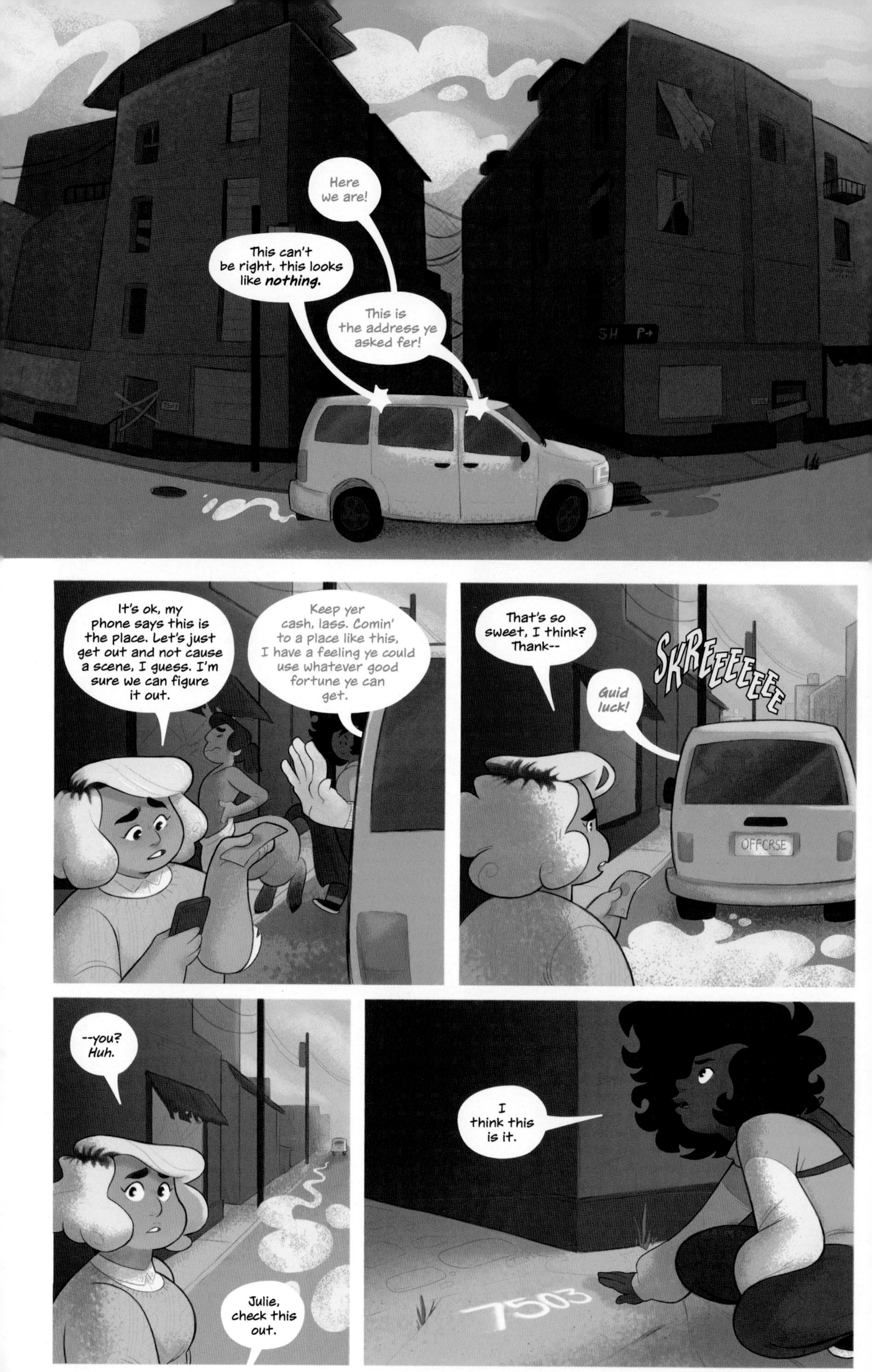

Here we are!
This can't be right, this looks like ***nothing.***
This is the address ye asked fer!
SH
P
It's ok, my phone says this is the place. Let's just get out and not cause a scene, I guess. I'm sure we can figure it out.
Keep yer cash, lass. Comin' to a place like this, I have a feeling ye could use whatever good fortune ye can get.
That's so sweet, I think? Thank--
SKREEEEEEEE
Guid luck!
OFFCRSE
--you? Huh.
Julie, check this out.
I think this is it.
7503

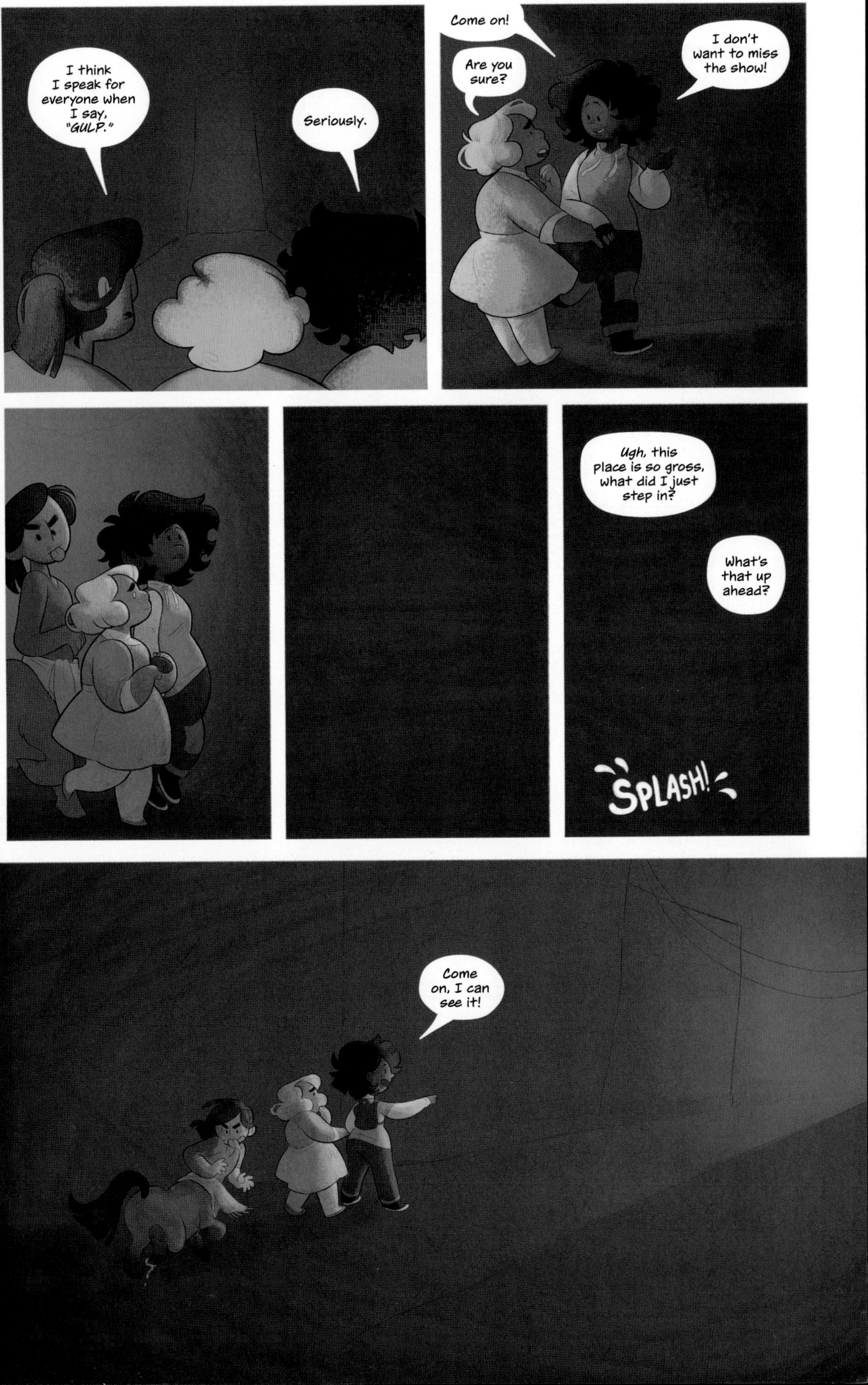
I think I speak for everyone when I say, "GULP."
Seriously.
Come on!
Are you sure?
I don't want to miss the show!
Ugh, this place is so gross, what did I just step in?
What's that up ahead?
SPLASH!
Come on, I can see it!

Pleasant Mountain Sisters

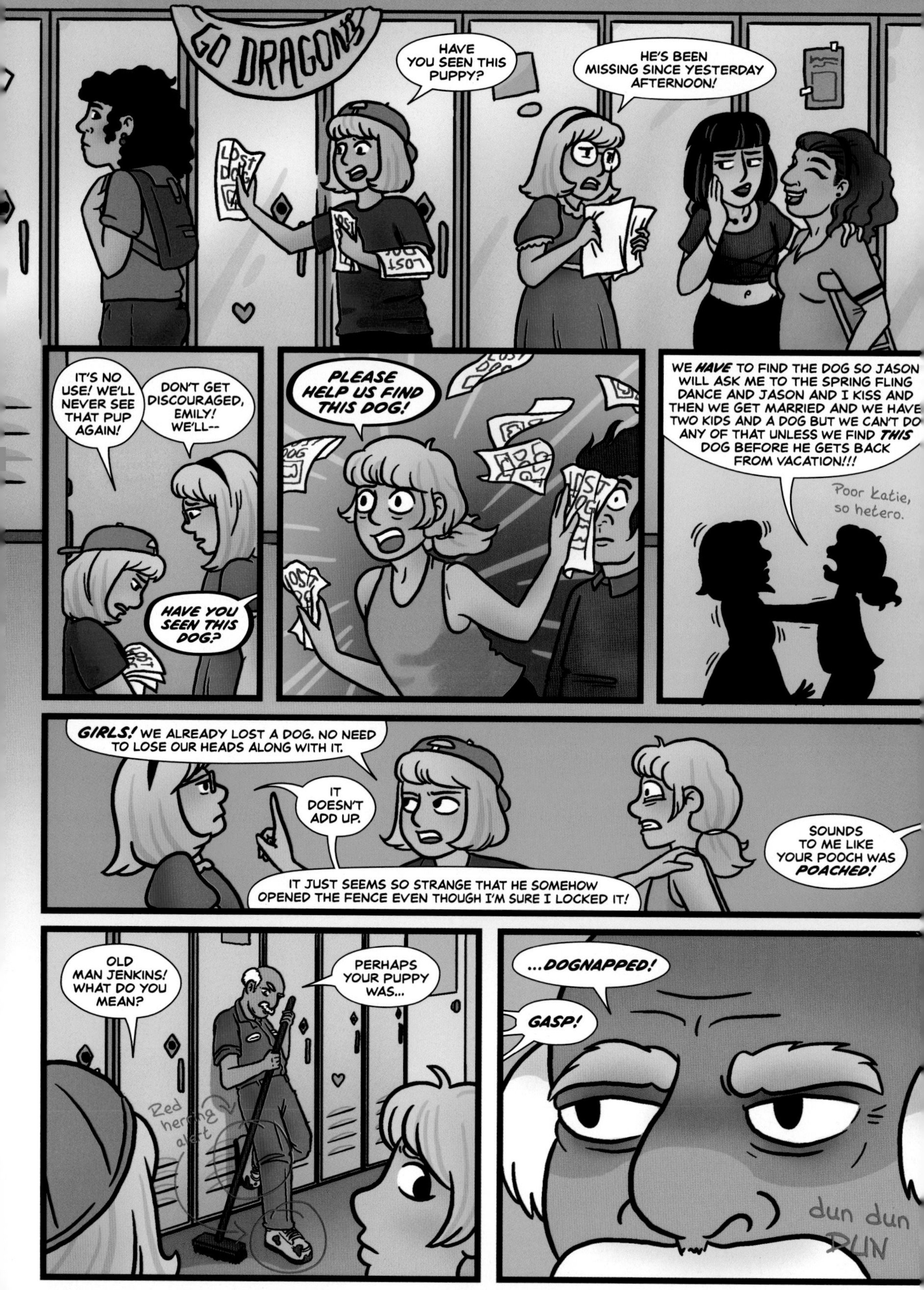

GO DRAGONS
LOST DOG
HAVE YOU SEEN THIS PUPPY?
HE'S BEEN MISSING SINCE YESTERDAY AFTERNOON!
IT'S NO USE! WE'LL NEVER SEE THAT PUP AGAIN!
DON'T GET DISCOURAGED, EMILY! WE'LL--
HAVE YOU SEEN THIS DOG?
PLEASE HELP US FIND THIS DOG!
LOST DOG
WE HAVE TO FIND THE DOG SO JASON WILL ASK ME TO THE SPRING FLING DANCE AND JASON AND I KISS AND THEN WE GET MARRIED AND WE HAVE TWO KIDS AND A DOG BUT WE CAN'T DO ANY OF THAT UNLESS WE FIND THIS DOG BEFORE HE GETS BACK FROM VACATION!!!
Poor Katie, so hetero.
GIRLS! WE ALREADY LOST A DOG. NO NEED TO LOSE OUR HEADS ALONG WITH IT.
IT DOESN'T ADD UP.
IT JUST SEEMS SO STRANGE THAT HE SOMEHOW OPENED THE FENCE EVEN THOUGH I'M SURE I LOCKED IT!
SOUNDS TO ME LIKE YOUR POOCH WAS POACHED!
OLD MAN JENKINS! WHAT DO YOU MEAN?
PERHAPS YOUR PUPPY WAS...
Red herring alert
...DOGNAPPED!
GASP!
dun dun DUN

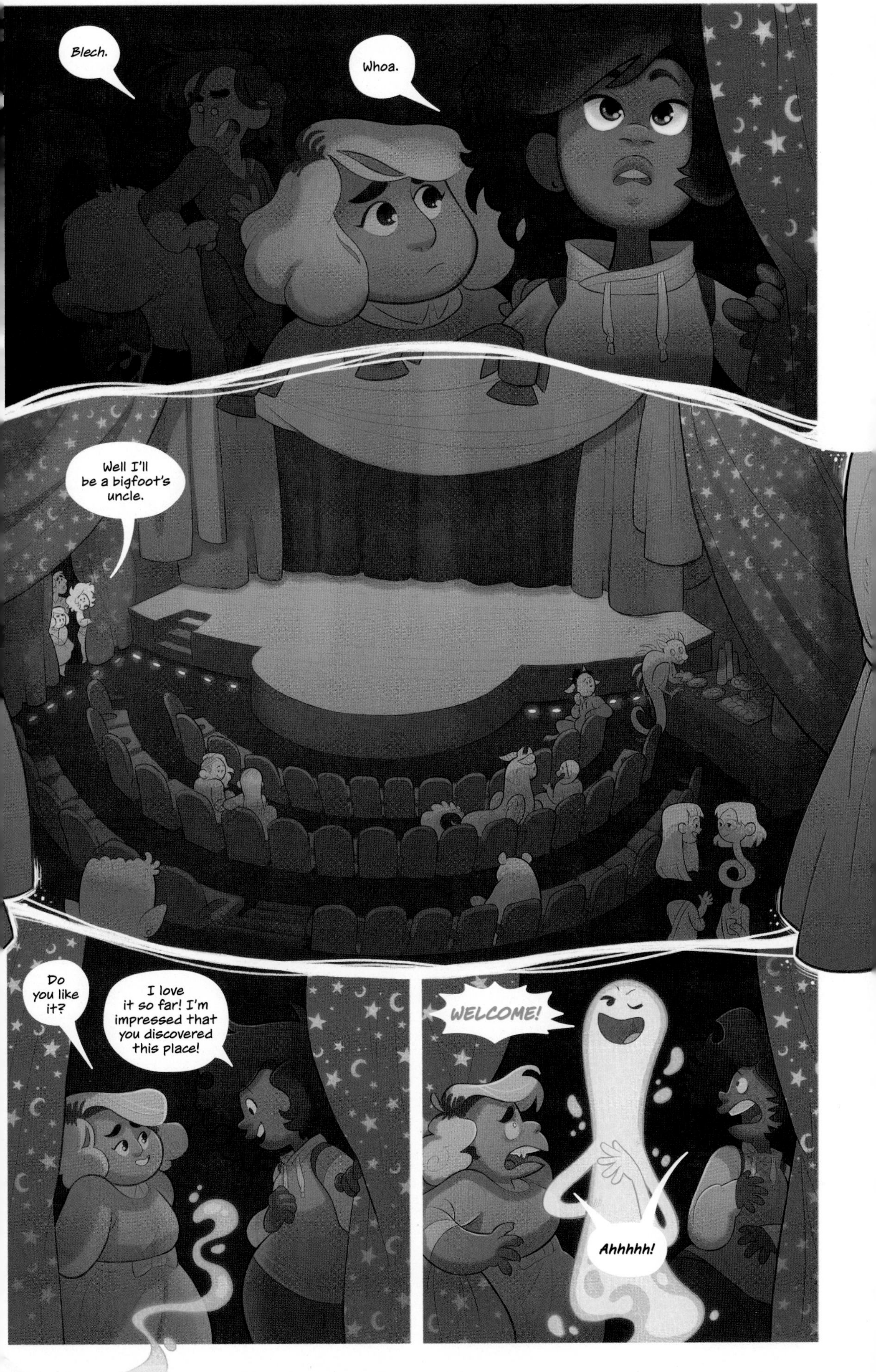
Blech.
Whoa.
Well I'll be a bigfoot's uncle.
Do you like it?
I love it so far! I'm impressed that you discovered this place!
WELCOME!
Ahhhhh!

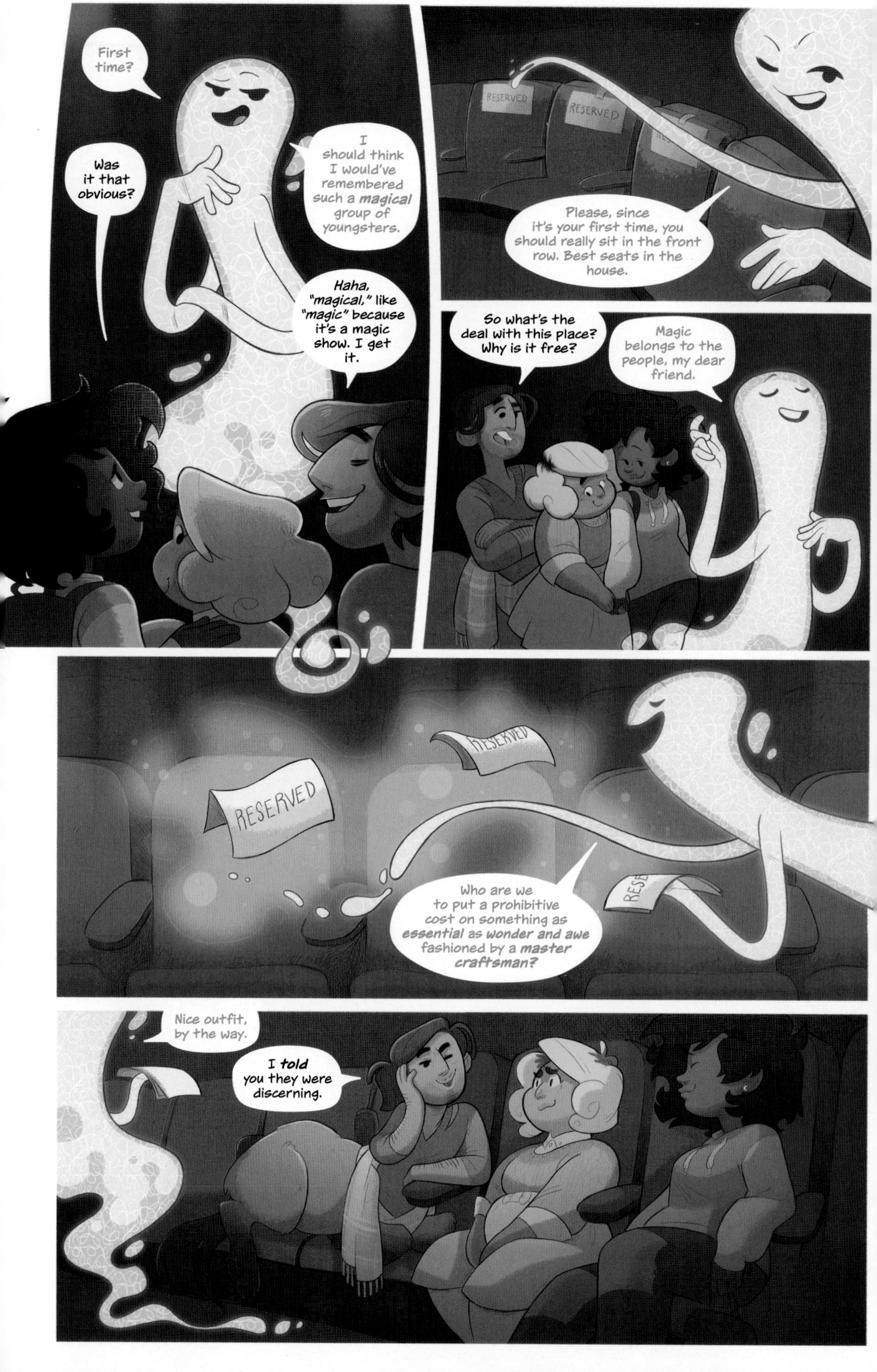
First time?
Was it that obvious?
I should think I would've remembered such a *magical* group of youngsters.
Haha, "magical," like "magic" because it's a magic show. I get it.
RESERVED
RESERVED
Please, since it's your first time, you should really sit in the front row. Best seats in the house.
So what's the deal with this place? Why is it free?
Magic belongs to the people, my dear friend.
RESERVED
RESERVED
Who are we to put a prohibitive cost on something as *essential* as *wonder and awe* fashioned by a *master craftsman?*
Nice outfit, by the way.
I *told* you they were discerning.

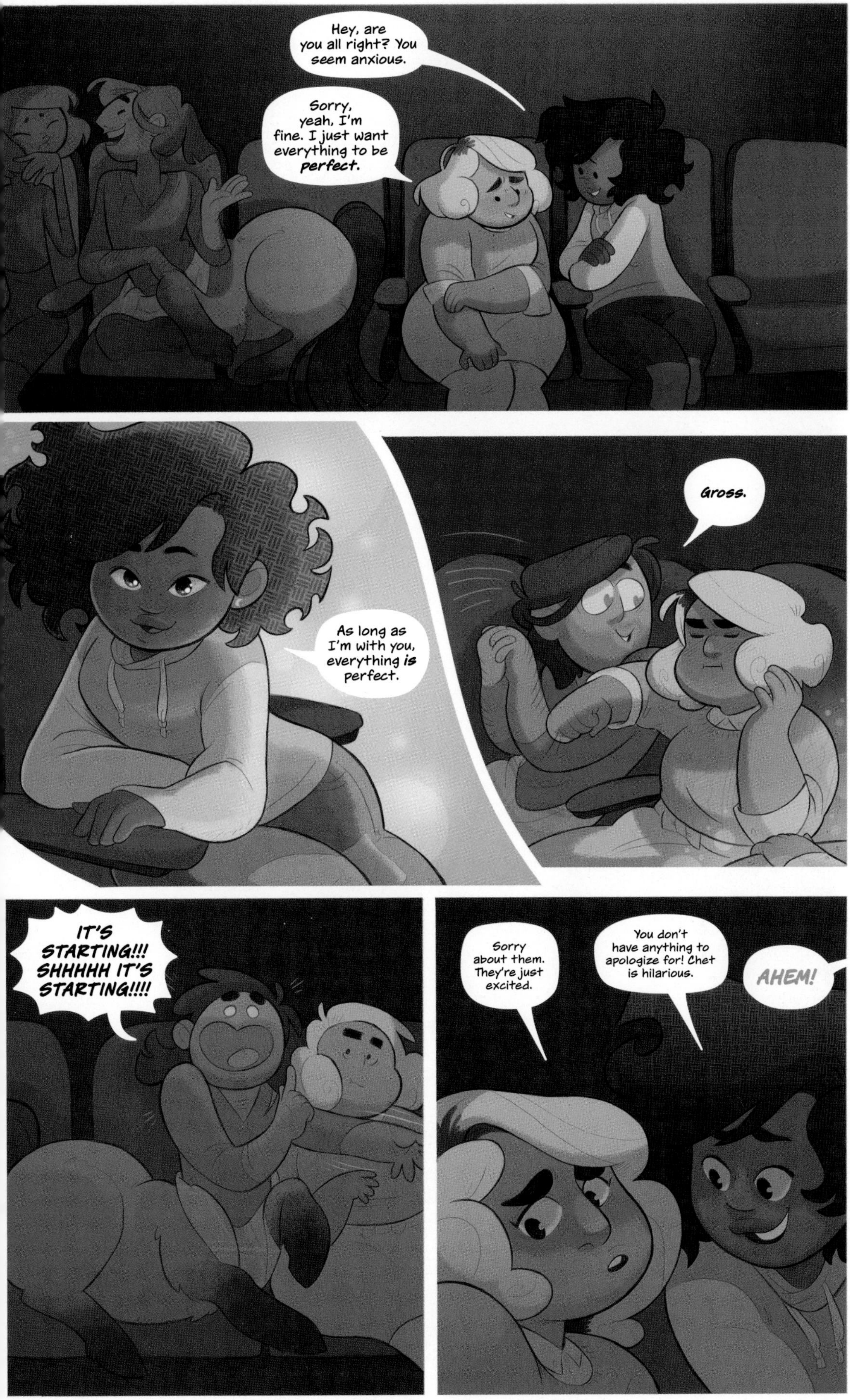
Hey, are you all right? You seem anxious.
Sorry, yeah, I'm fine. I just want everything to be *perfect.*
As long as I'm with you, everything *is* perfect.
Gross.
IT'S STARTING!!! SHHHHH IT'S STARTING!!!!
Sorry about them. They're just excited.
You don't have anything to apologize for! Chet is hilarious.
AHEM!

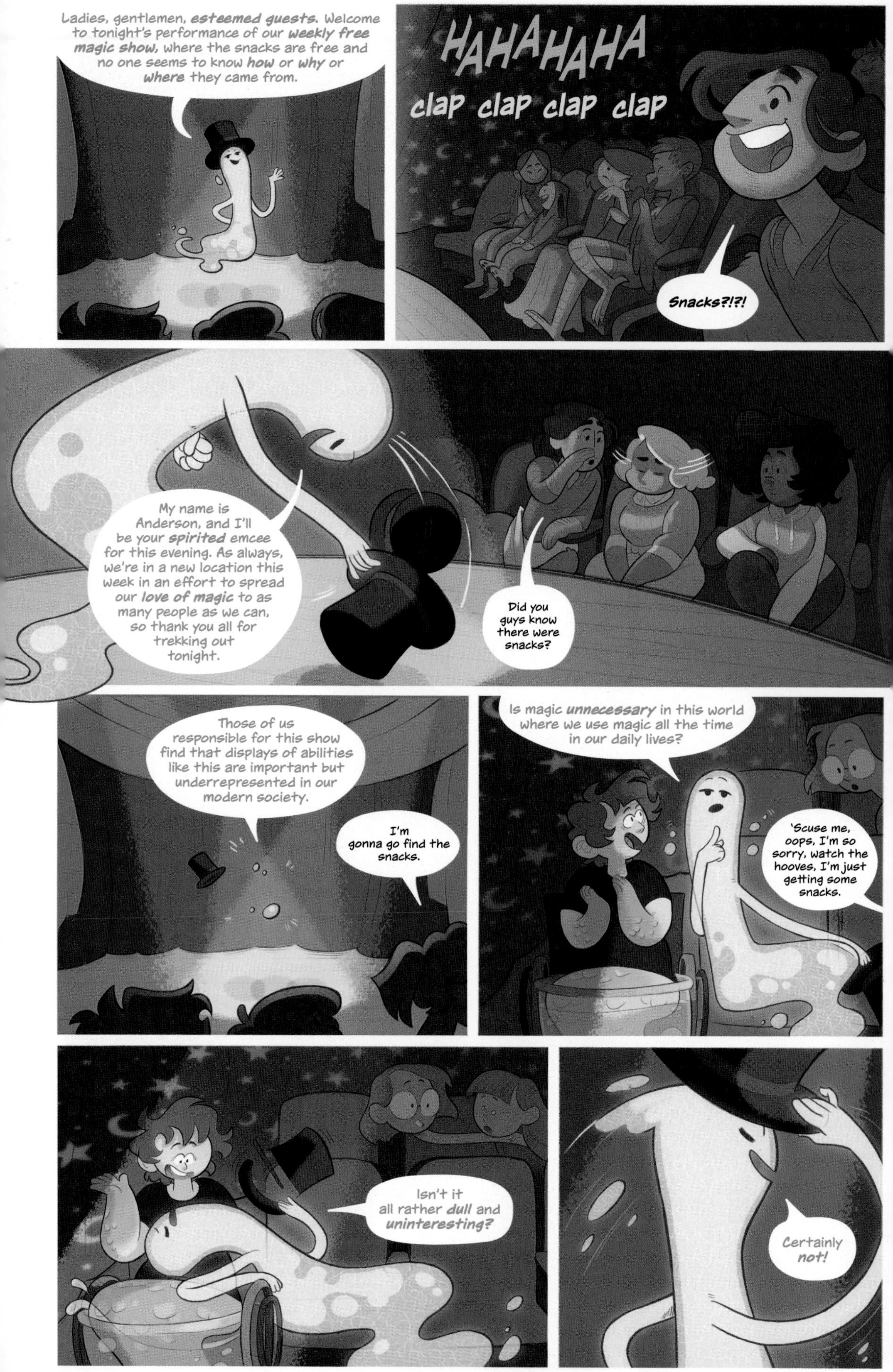
Ladies, gentlemen, esteemed guests. Welcome to tonight's performance of our weekly free magic show, where the snacks are free and no one seems to know how or why or where they came from.
HAHAHAHA
clap clap clap clap
Snacks?!?!
My name is Anderson, and I'll be your spirited emcee for this evening. As always, we're in a new location this week in an effort to spread our love of magic to as many people as we can, so thank you all for trekking out tonight.
Did you guys know there were snacks?
Those of us responsible for this show find that displays of abilities like this are important but underrepresented in our modern society.
I'm gonna go find the snacks.
Is magic unnecessary in this world where we use magic all the time in our daily lives?
'Scuse me, oops, I'm so sorry, watch the hooves, I'm just getting some snacks.
Isn't it all rather dull and uninteresting?
Certainly not!

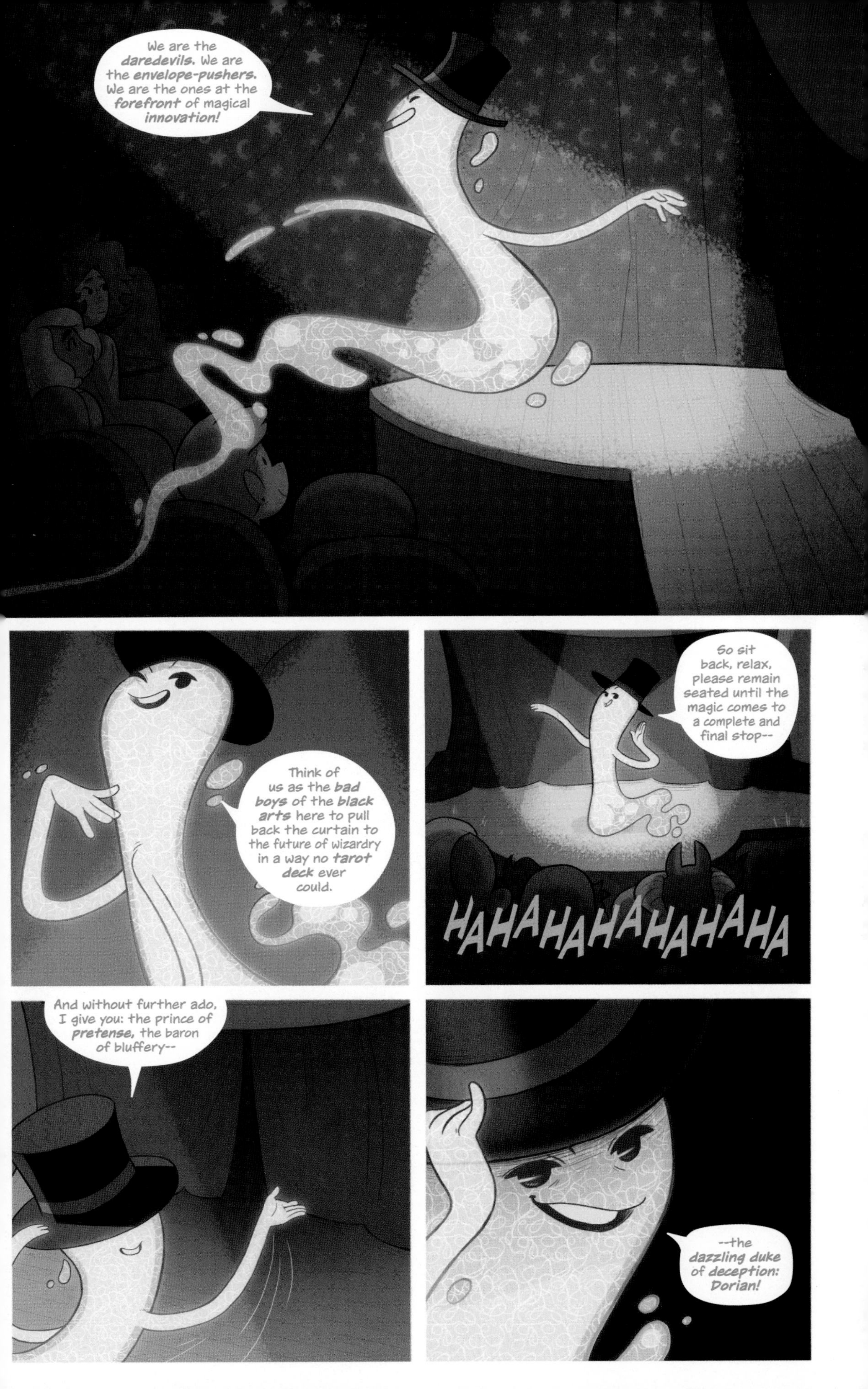
We are the daredevils. We are the envelope-pushers. We are the ones at the forefront of magical innovation!
Think of us as the bad boys of the black arts here to pull back the curtain to the future of wizardry in a way no tarot deck ever could.
So sit back, relax, please remain seated until the magic comes to a complete and final stop--
HAHAHAHAHAHAHAHA
And without further ado, I give you: the prince of pretense, the baron of bluffery--
--the dazzling duke of deception: Dorian!

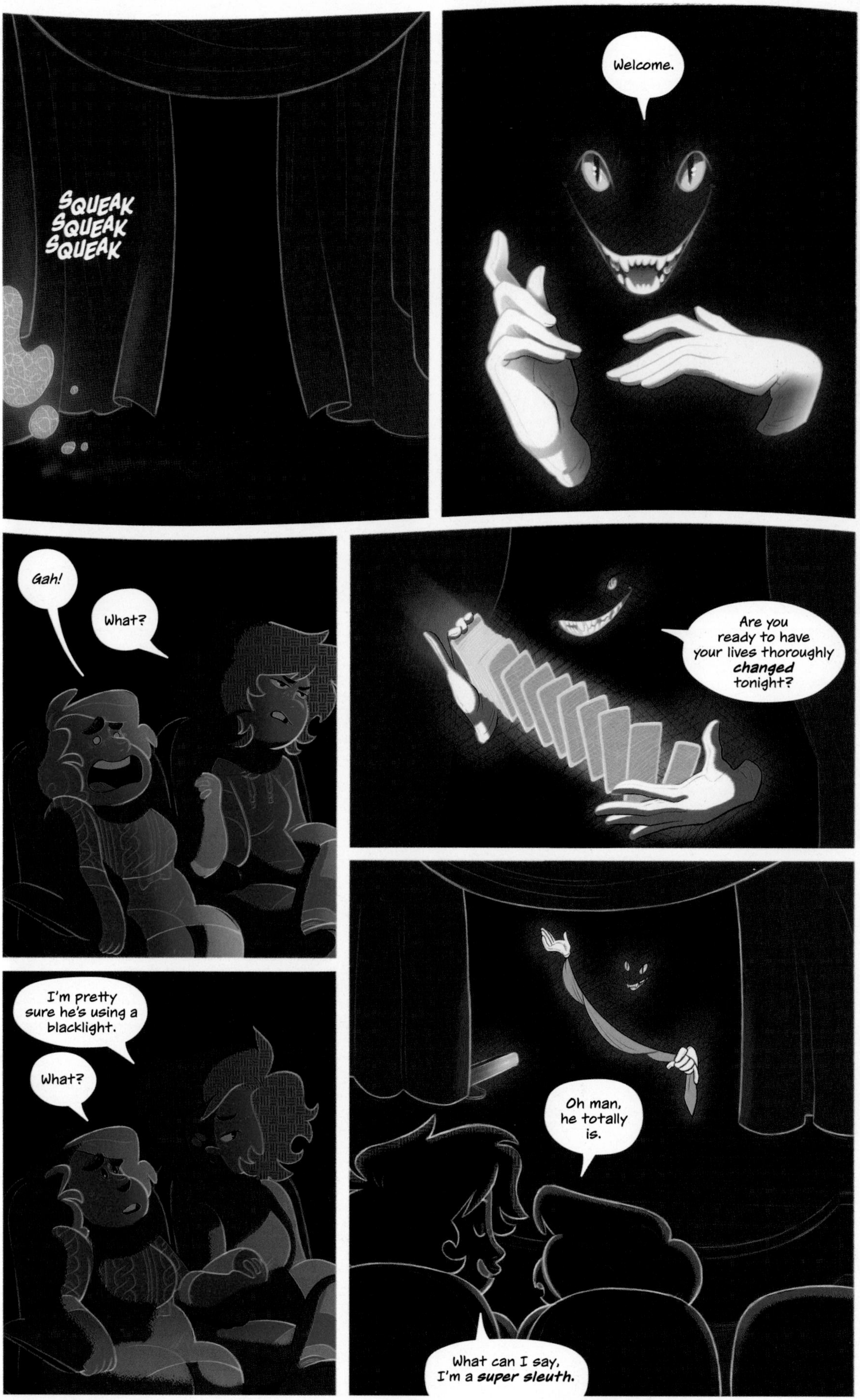
SQUEAK SQUEAK SQUEAK
Welcome.
Gah!
What?
Are you ready to have your lives thoroughly changed tonight?
I'm pretty sure he's using a blacklight.
What?
Oh man, he totally is.
What can I say, I'm a super sleuth.

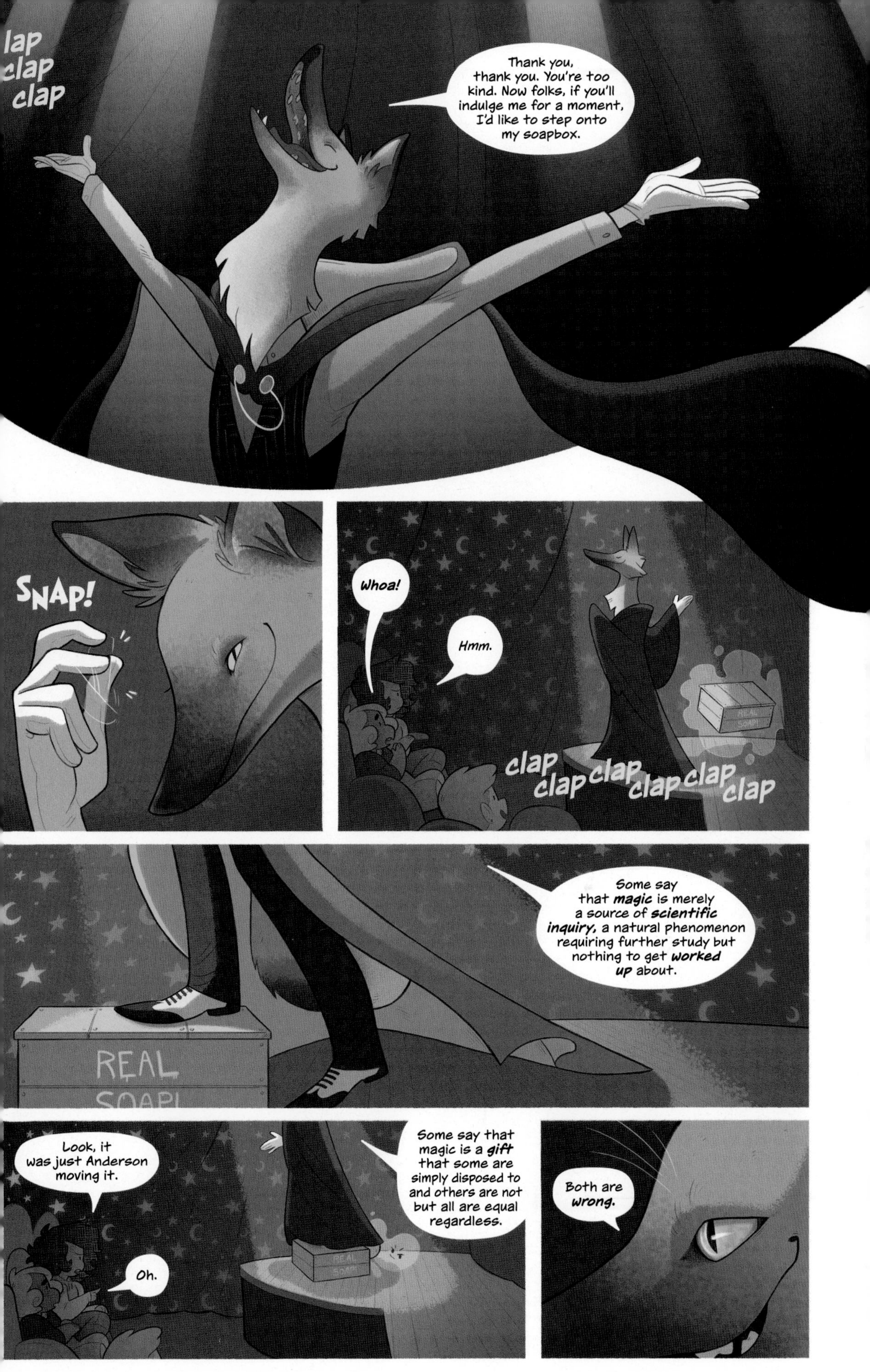
lap
clap
clap
Thank you, thank you. You're too kind. Now folks, if you'll indulge me for a moment, I'd like to step onto my soapbox.
SNAP!
Whoa!
Hmm.
clap clap clap clap clap clap
Some say that magic is merely a source of scientific inquiry, a natural phenomenon requiring further study but nothing to get worked up about.
REAL SOAP!
Look, it was just Anderson moving it.
Oh.
Some say that magic is a gift that some are simply disposed to and others are not but all are equal regardless.
Both are wrong.

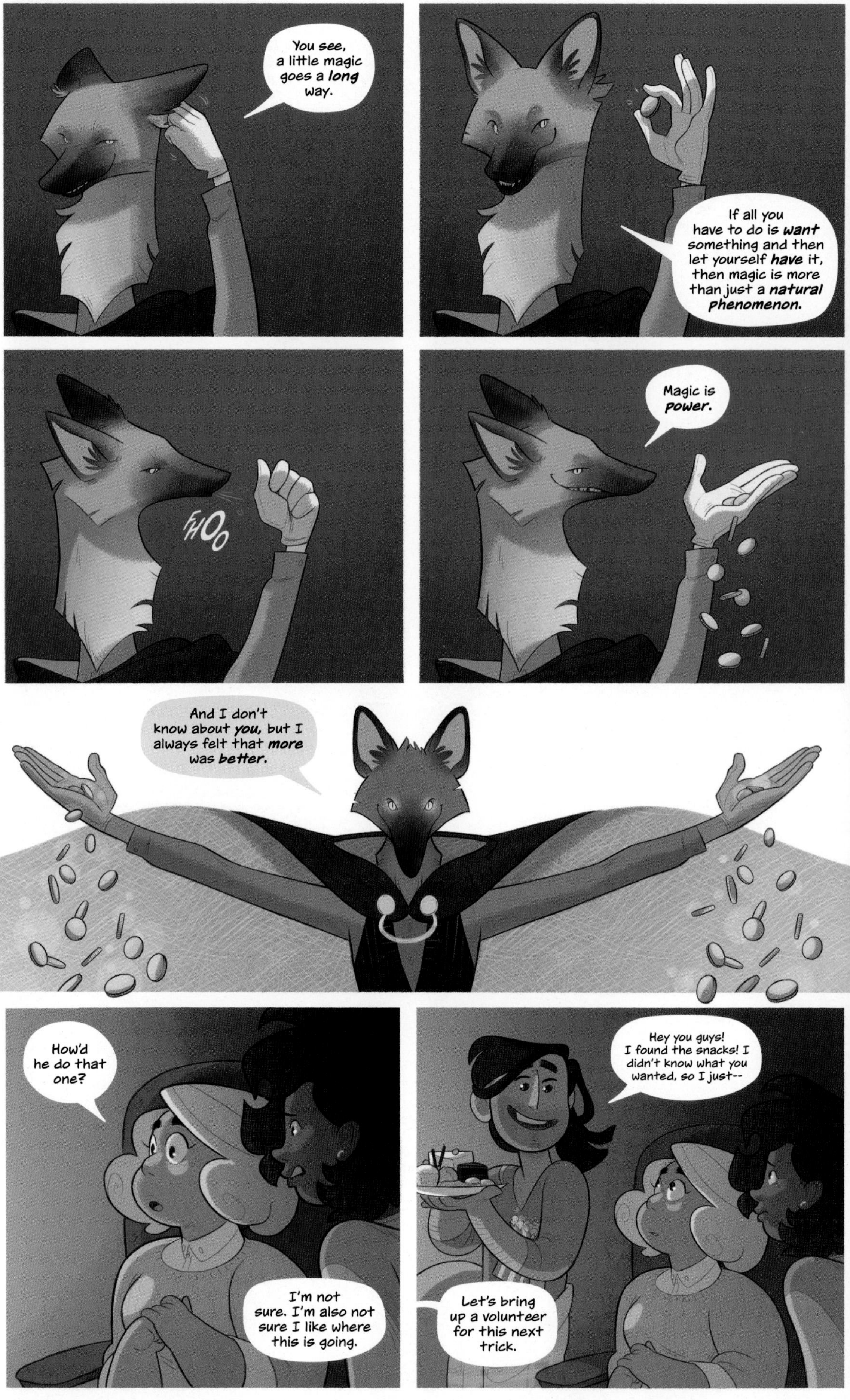
You see, a little magic goes a long way.
If all you have to do is want something and then let yourself have it, then magic is more than just a natural phenomenon.
FHOo
Magic is power.
And I don't know about you, but I always felt that more was better.
How'd he do that one?
I'm not sure. I'm also not sure I like where this is going.
Hey you guys! I found the snacks! I didn't know what you wanted, so I just--
Let's bring up a volunteer for this next trick.

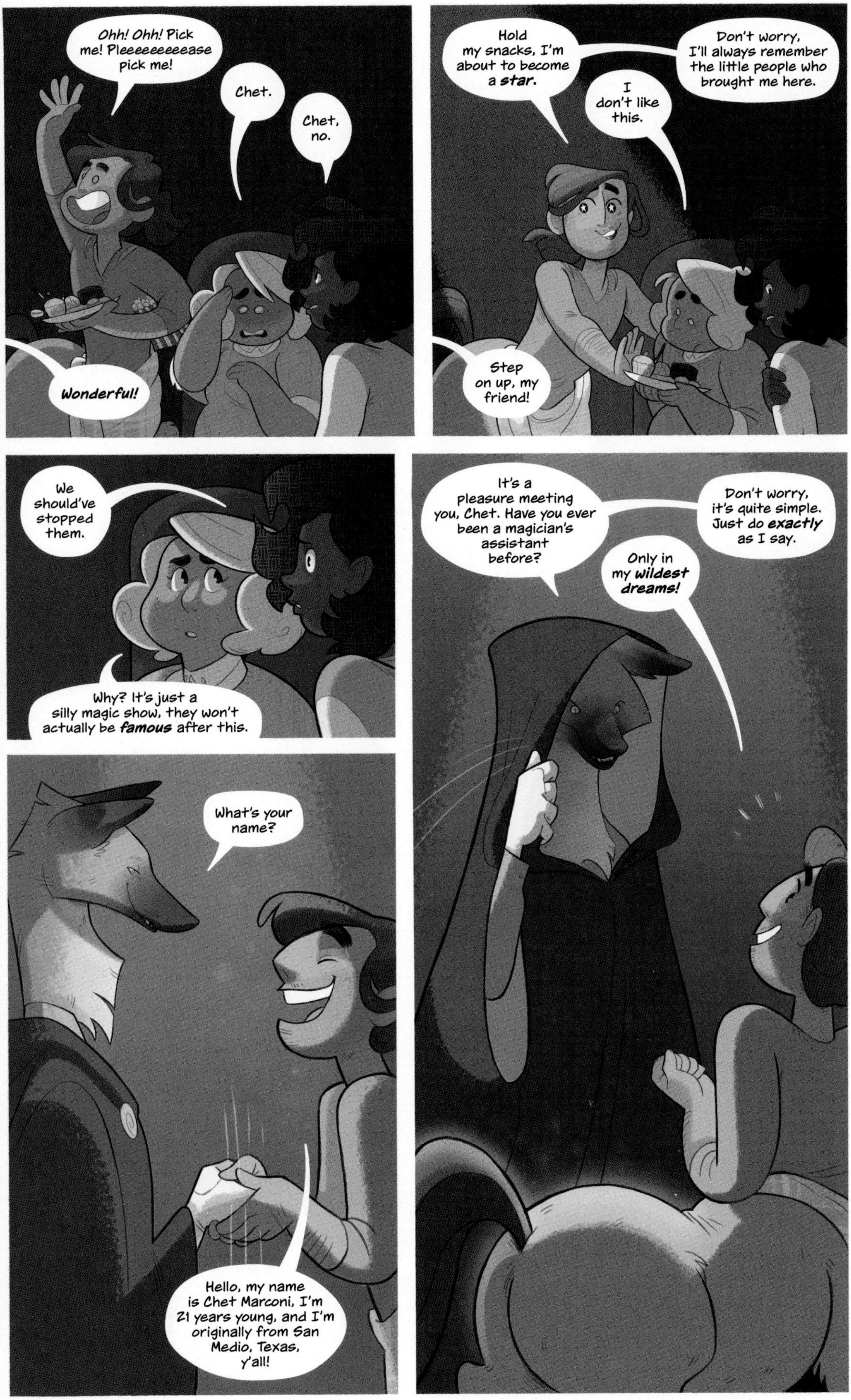
Ohh! Ohh! Pick me! Pleeeeeeeease pick me!
Chet.
Chet, no.
Wonderful!
Hold my snacks, I'm about to become a star.
Don't worry, I'll always remember the little people who brought me here.
I don't like this.
Step on up, my friend!
We should've stopped them.
Why? It's just a silly magic show, they won't actually be famous after this.
What's your name?
Hello, my name is Chet Marconi, I'm 21 years young, and I'm originally from San Medio, Texas, Y'all!
It's a pleasure meeting you, Chet. Have you ever been a magician's assistant before?
Don't worry, it's quite simple. Just do exactly as I say.
Only in my wildest dreams!

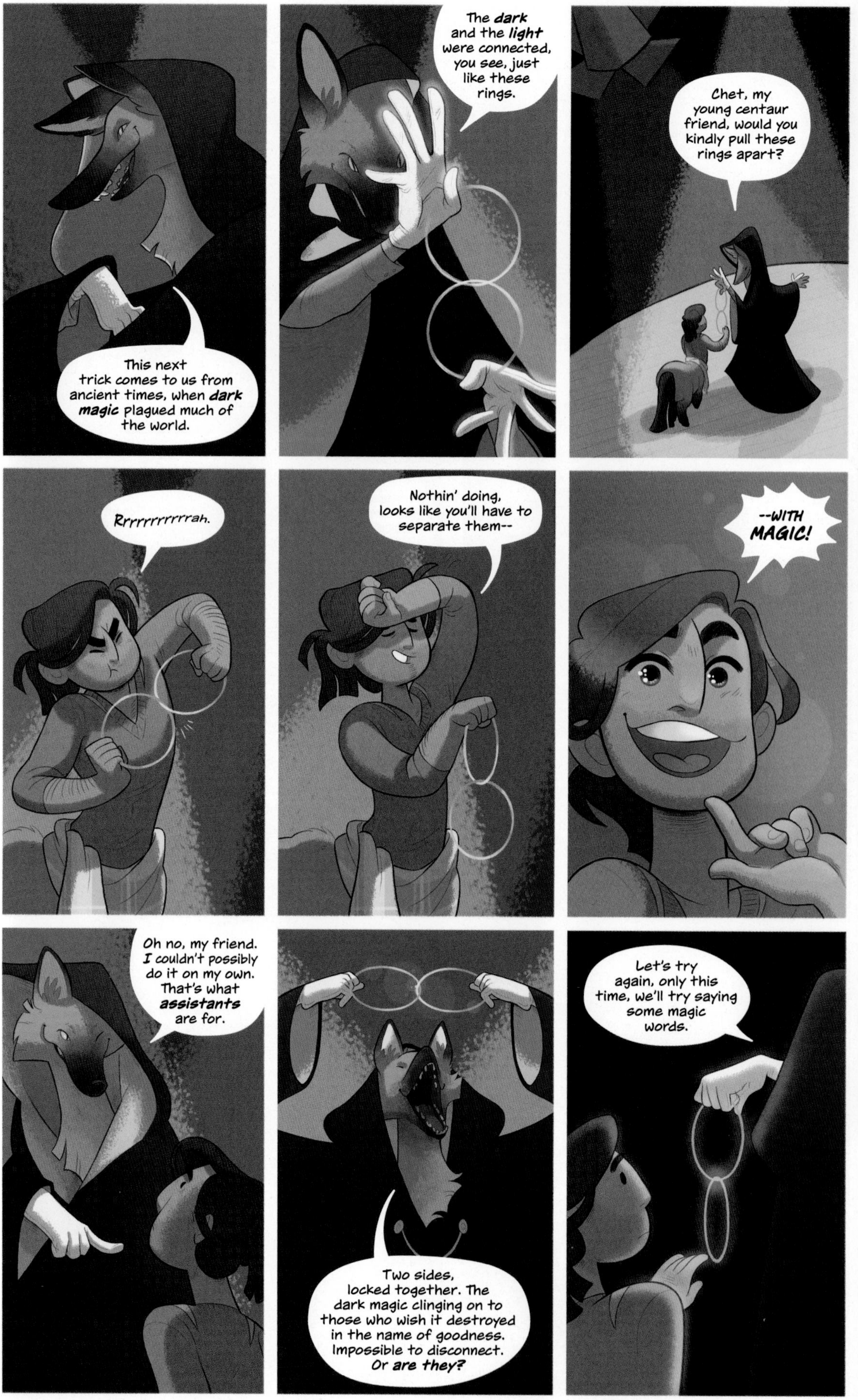
This next trick comes to us from ancient times, when dark magic plagued much of the world.
The dark and the light were connected, you see, just like these rings.
Chet, my young centaur friend, would you kindly pull these rings apart?
Rrrrrrrrrrrah.
Nothin' doing, looks like you'll have to separate them--
--WITH MAGIC!
Oh no, my friend. I couldn't possibly do it on my own. That's what assistants are for.
Two sides, locked together. The dark magic clinging on to those who wish it destroyed in the name of goodness. Impossible to disconnect. Or are they?
Let's try again, only this time, we'll try saying some magic words.

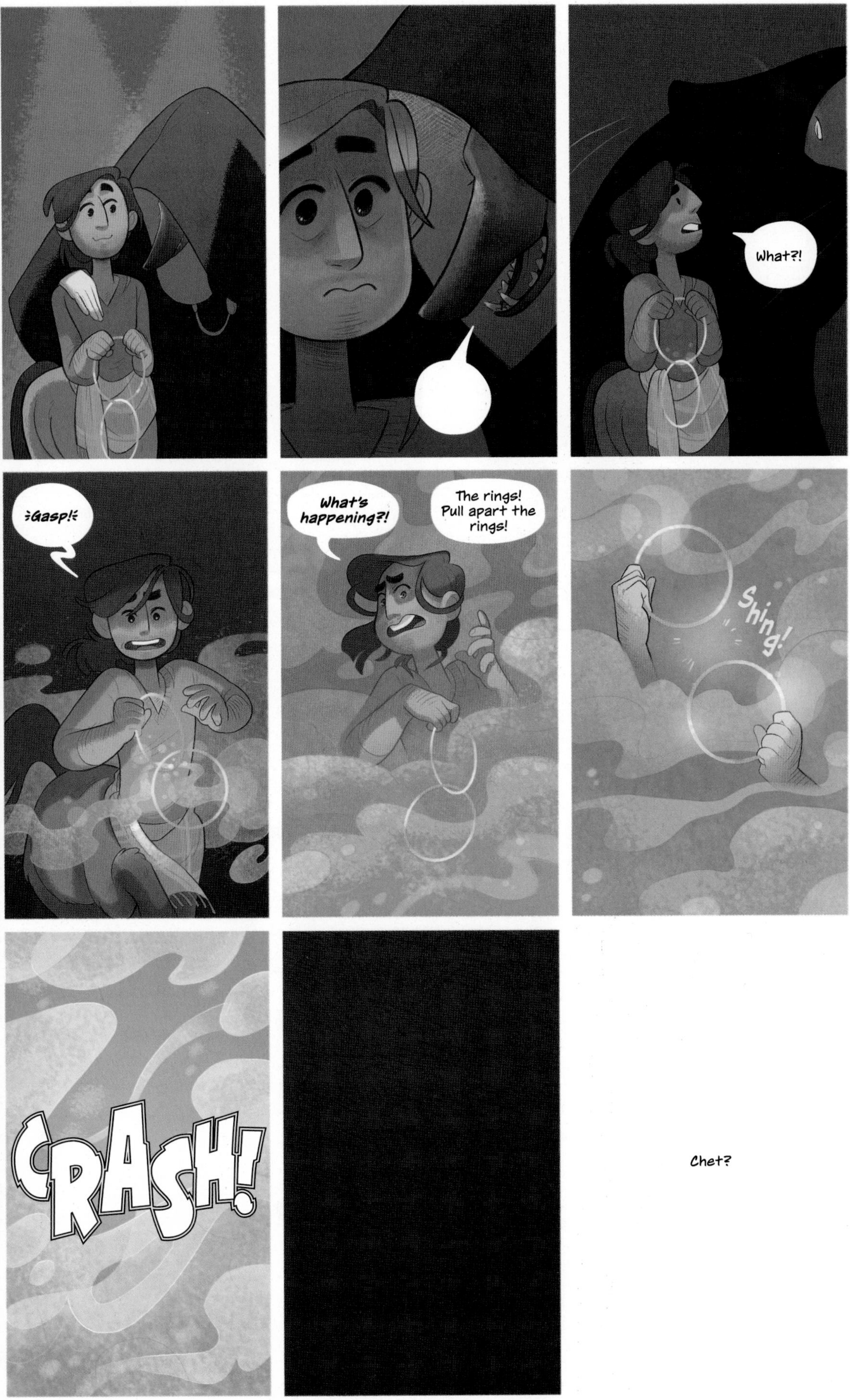
What?!
Gasp!
What's happening?!
The rings! Pull apart the rings!
Shing!
CRASH!
Chet?

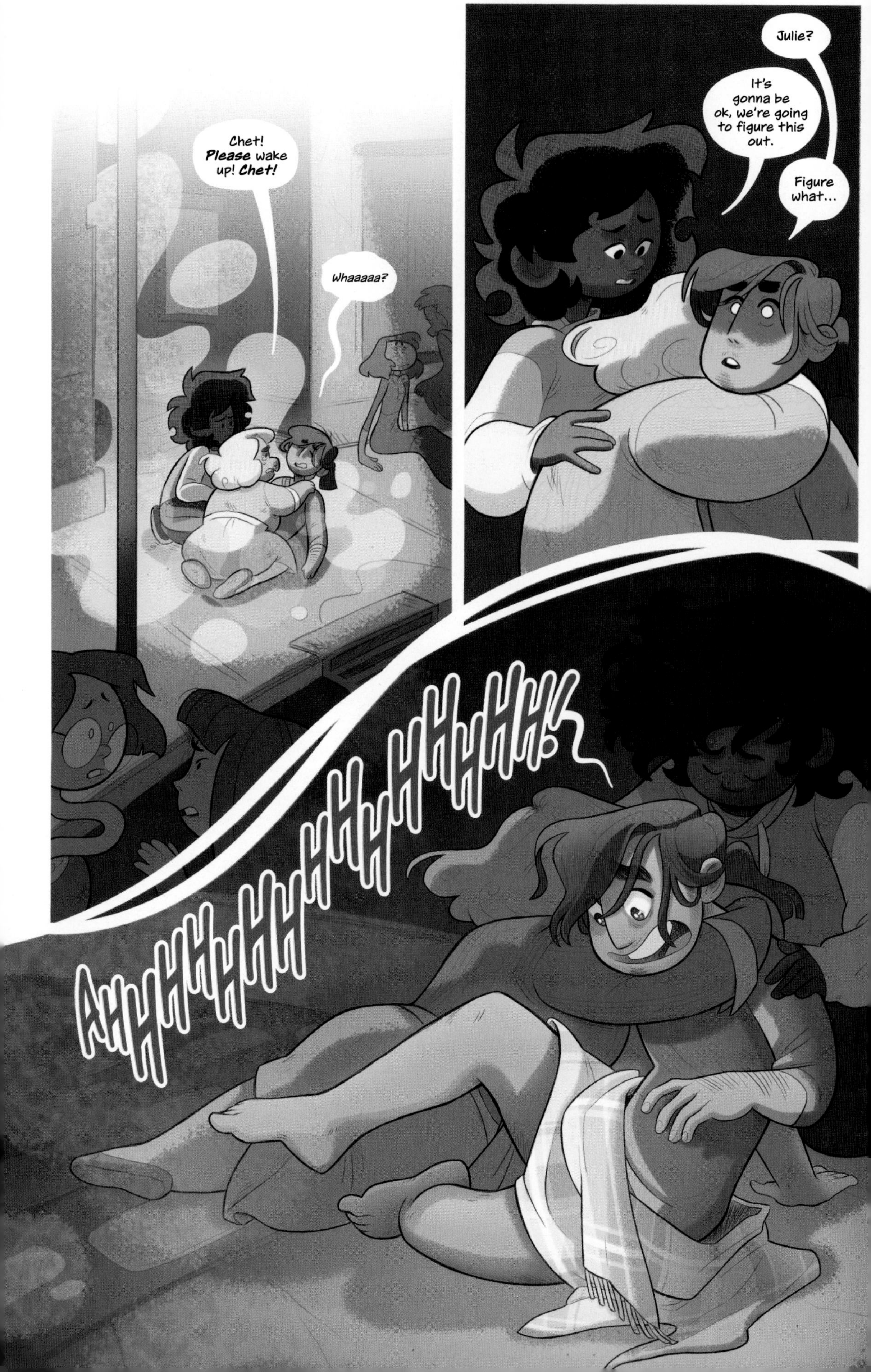
Chet! Please wake up! Chet!
Whaaaaa?
Julie?
It's gonna be ok, we're going to figure this out.
Figure what...
AHHHHHHHHHHHHHHHHHHHHK!

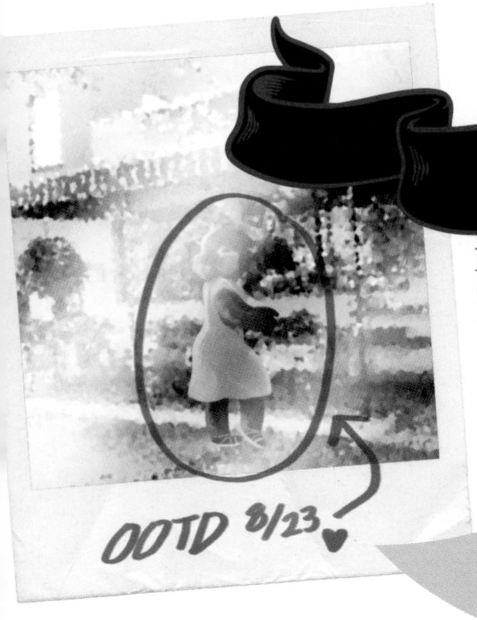
OOTD 8/23

ASK A KNOW-IT-ALL

Each month, we feature advice from a different local celebrity with a unique perspective.

This month's Know-It-All is Kiley Muller, a popular lifestyle and beauty vlogger better known by her sobriquet, Confyeti. Kiley is currently majoring in marketing at BSU and says to "like, comment, and subscribe."

Dear Know-It-All,
My boyfriend is totally perfect except for one thing: I love rollerblading, but he hates it! This is a total dealbreaker. How can I convince him to come blading with me?
- Inline for a Breakup

Hey Inline!
So what you wanna do is you wanna take your roller blades – I personally prefer derby skates because of their low ankles, but... wait, I'm sorry, is that a photographer? I was led to believe there would be no pictures.

Dear Know-It-All,
This guy I work with always calls me by the wrong name. It's really annoying. My coworkers think it's hilarious. Is there a way to politely correct him? We don't wear nametags.
- Evidently Evangeline

Hey Evangeline!
In the spirit of positivity, I like to see this as an opportunity to incorporate more of your personal brand – your name! – into your wardrobe. Consider spelling out your name in iron-on letters on a cute top, or... hmm. Can I just, like, give you guys a selfie? I have so many good ones, I'm sure there's one you'd like.

Dear Know-It-All,
Any advice on overthrowng the bourgeoisie?
- Proletariat in Peoria

Hey Proletariat!
Well, to be frank, our current economy may not allow for an outright overthrow, since the industrial... It's just that, whenever anyone other than me tries to take my picture, it never, uh, comes out quite right?

Dear Know-It-All,
I recently went on a date with a great girl, but I checked our astrological compatibility, and the results were apocalyptically bad. (I'm a Taurus, she's an Aries, need I say more?) Should I just call it quits and get it over with?
- Raging Bull

Hey Bull!
...I just feel like you guys aren't taking my lived experience as a bigfoot seriously? No no no, it's ok, I shouldn't assume everyone knows taking a picture of someone like me is like, metaphysically impossible? Yeah, ok, let's just keep going.

Dear Know-It-All,
My friends and family all say that I spoil my cat because I carry her around the neighborhood in a bjorn. I disagree. She loves it! She's a real gal about town! Am I being unreasonable?
- Don't Stop Meow

Hey Meow!
You know what? Go ahead, take as many pictures as you want. No, go ahead. But when they all turn out the same, don't say I didn't warn you.

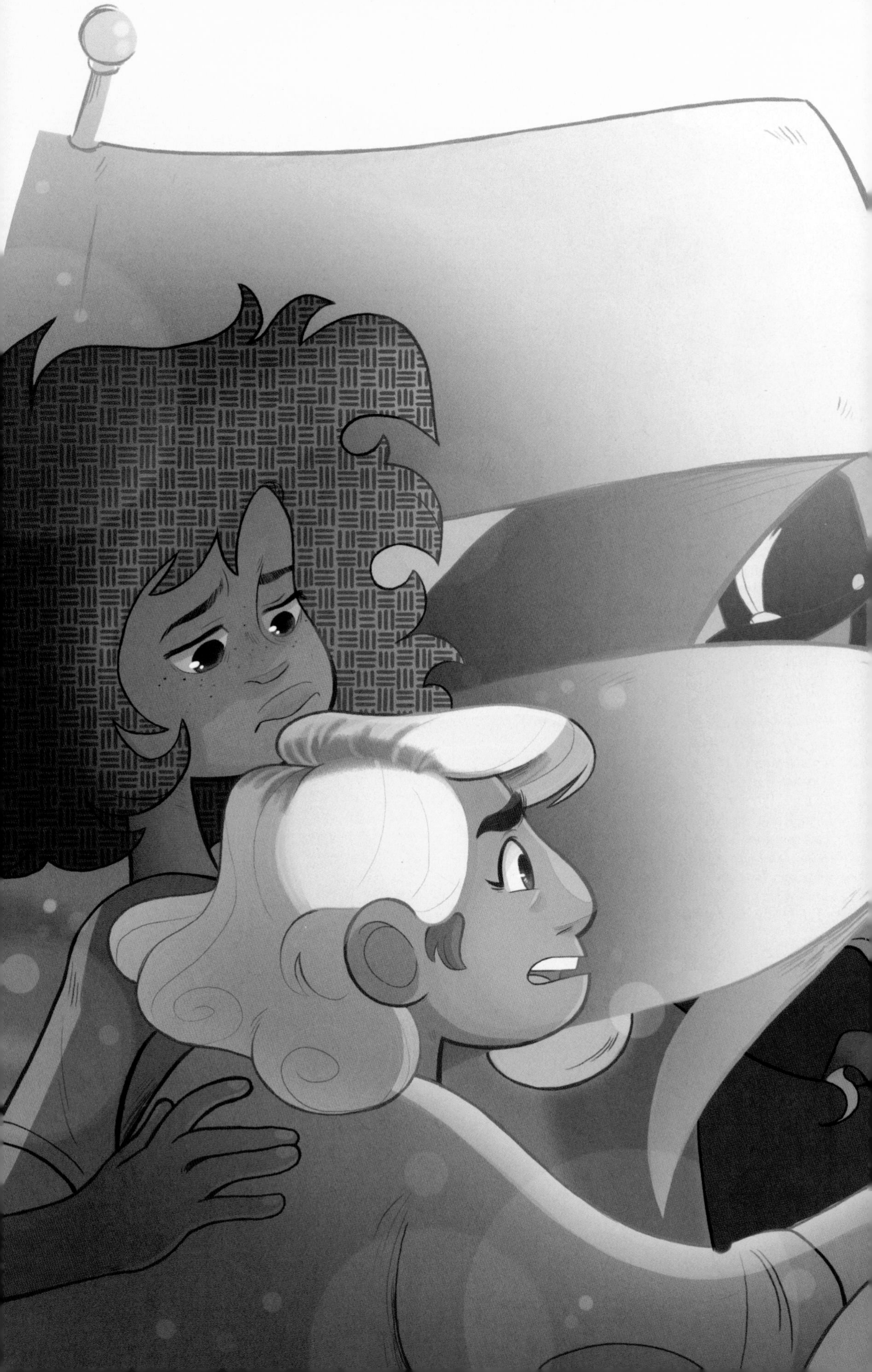

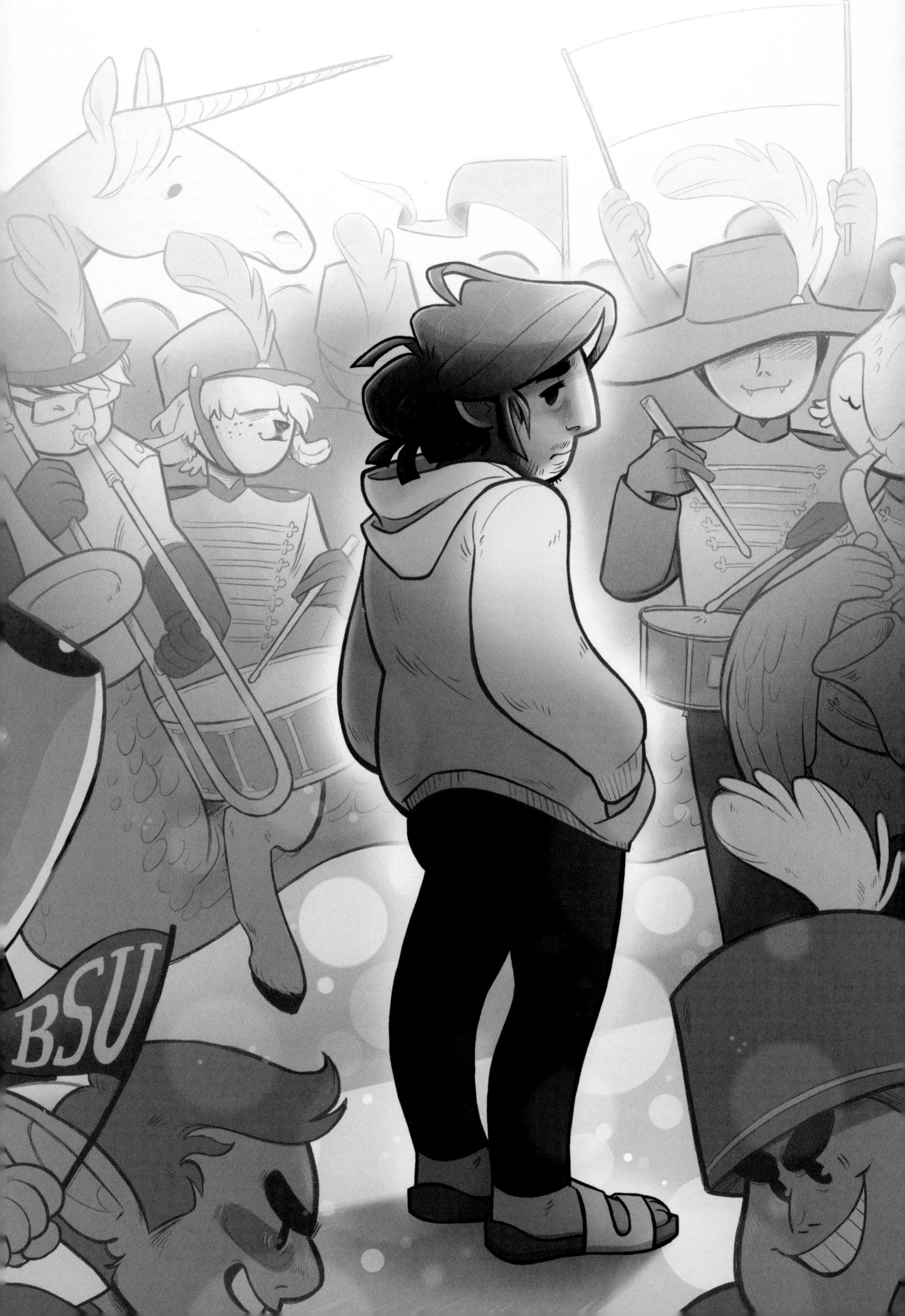
BSU

CHAPTER THREE

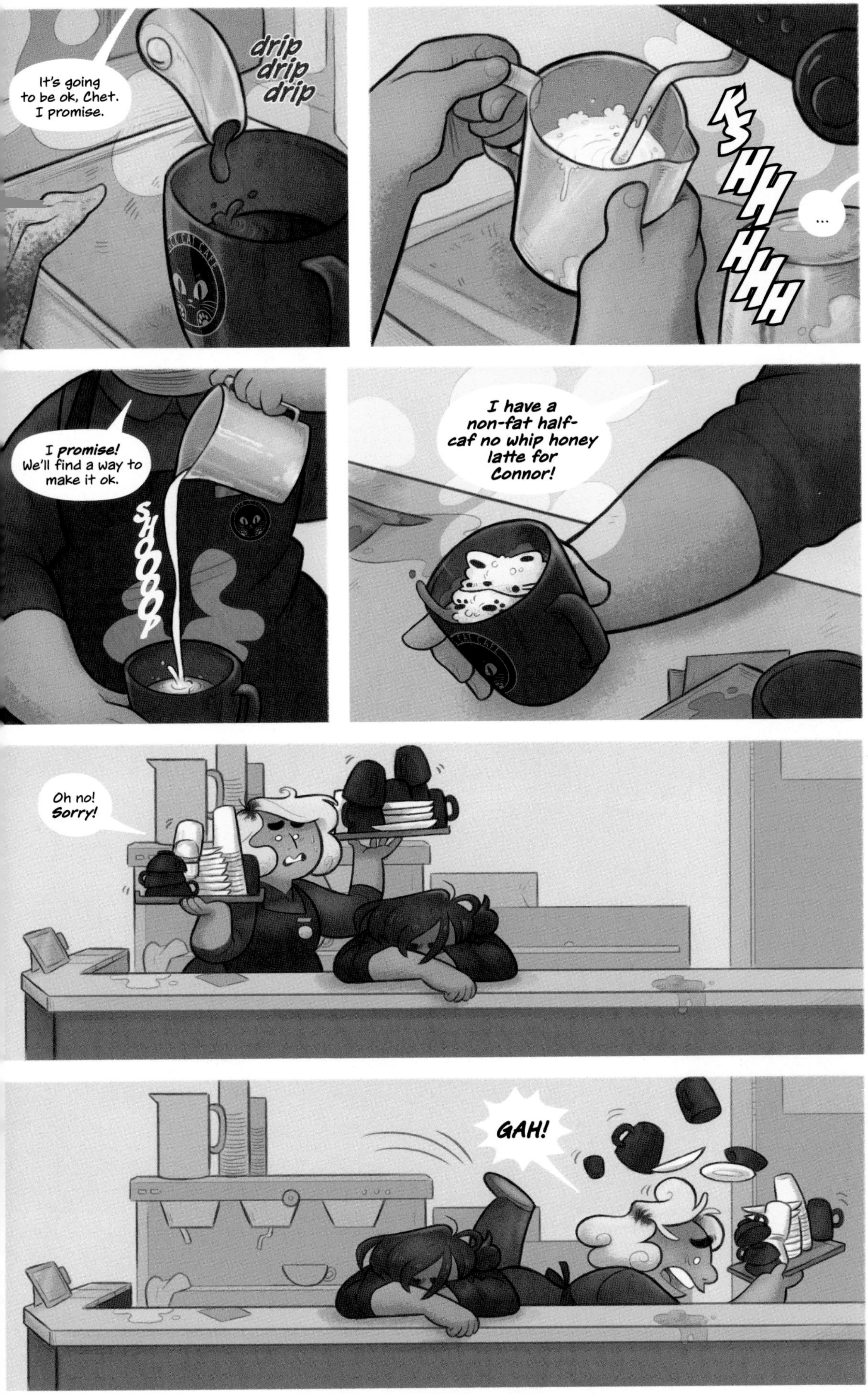

drip drip drip
It's going to be ok, Chet. I promise.
KSHHHHHHH
...
I promise! We'll find a way to make it ok.
SHOOOP
I have a non-fat half-caf no whip honey latte for Connor!
Oh no! Sorry!
GAH!

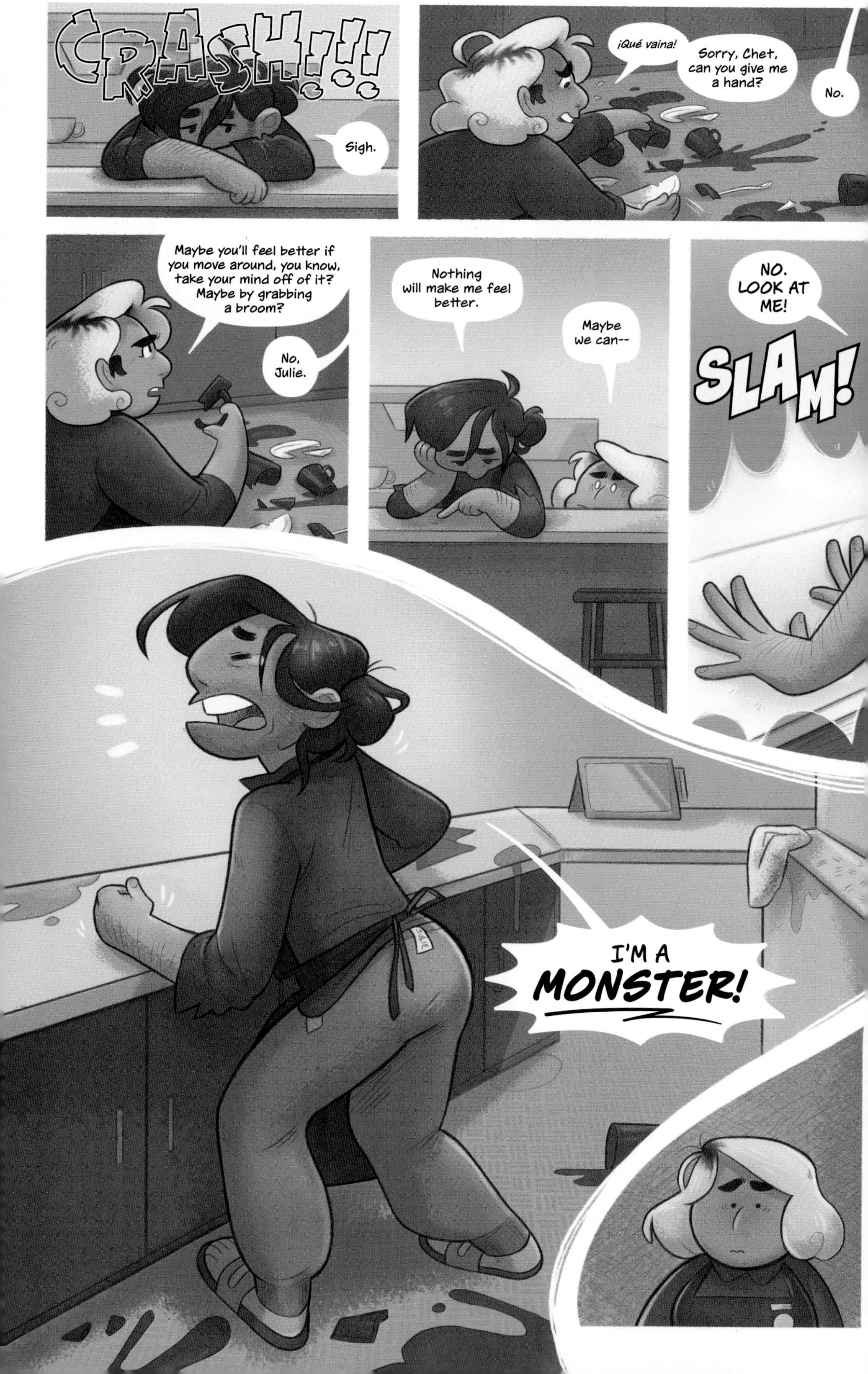
CRASH!!!
Sigh.
¡Qué vaina!
Sorry, Chet, can you give me a hand?
No.
Maybe you'll feel better if you move around, you know, take your mind off of it? Maybe by grabbing a broom?
No, Julie.
Nothing will make me feel better.
Maybe we can--
NO. LOOK AT ME!
SLAM!
I'M A MONSTER!

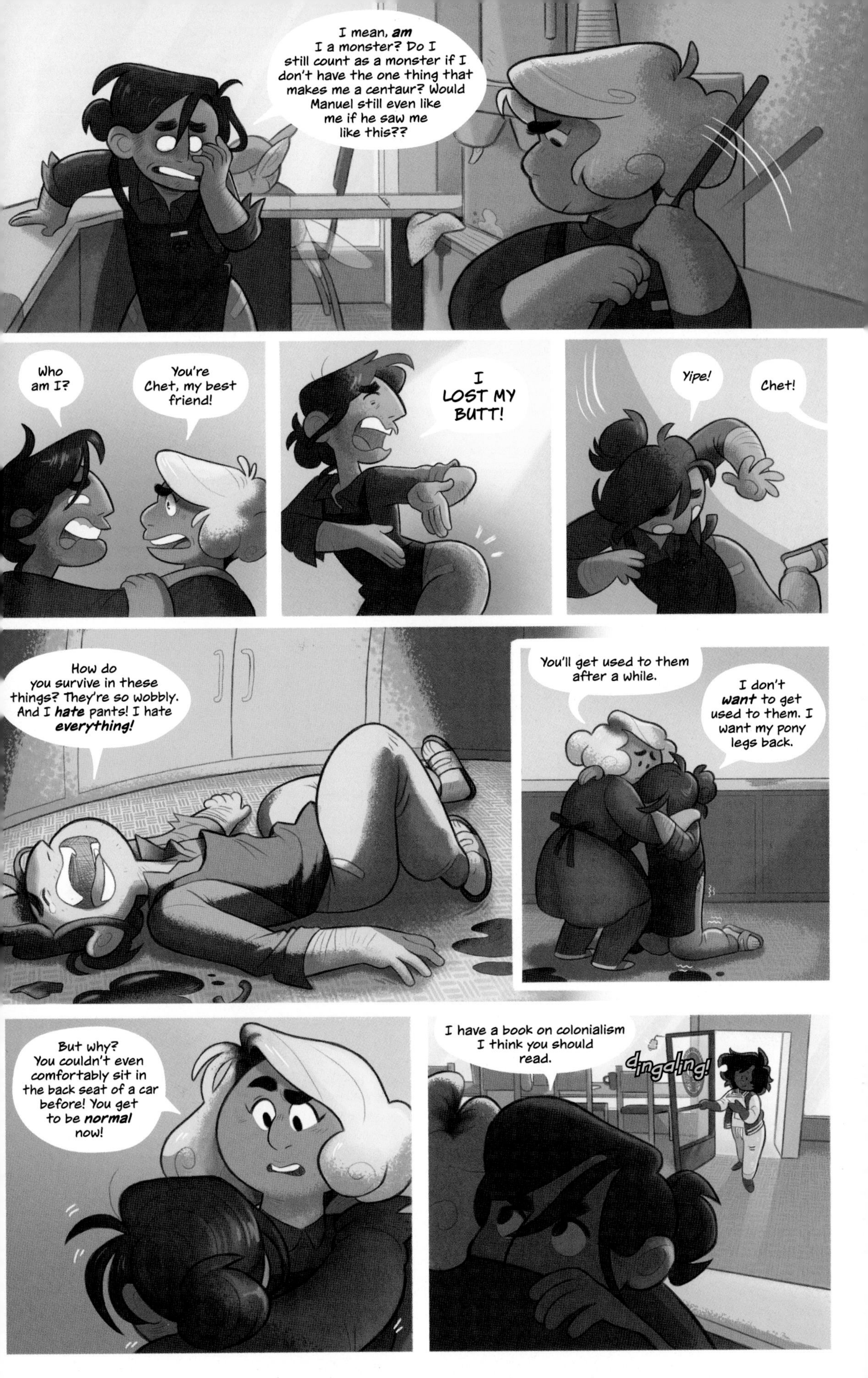
I mean, **am** I a monster? Do I still count as a monster if I don't have the one thing that makes me a centaur? Would Manuel still even like me if he saw me like this??
Who am I?
You're Chet, my best friend!
I LOST MY BUTT!
Yipe!
Chet!
How do you survive in these things? They're so wobbly. And I **hate** pants! I hate **everything!**
You'll get used to them after a while.
I don't **want** to get used to them. I want my pony legs back.
But why? You couldn't even comfortably sit in the back seat of a car before! You get to be **normal** now!
I have a book on colonialism I think you should read.
dingaling!

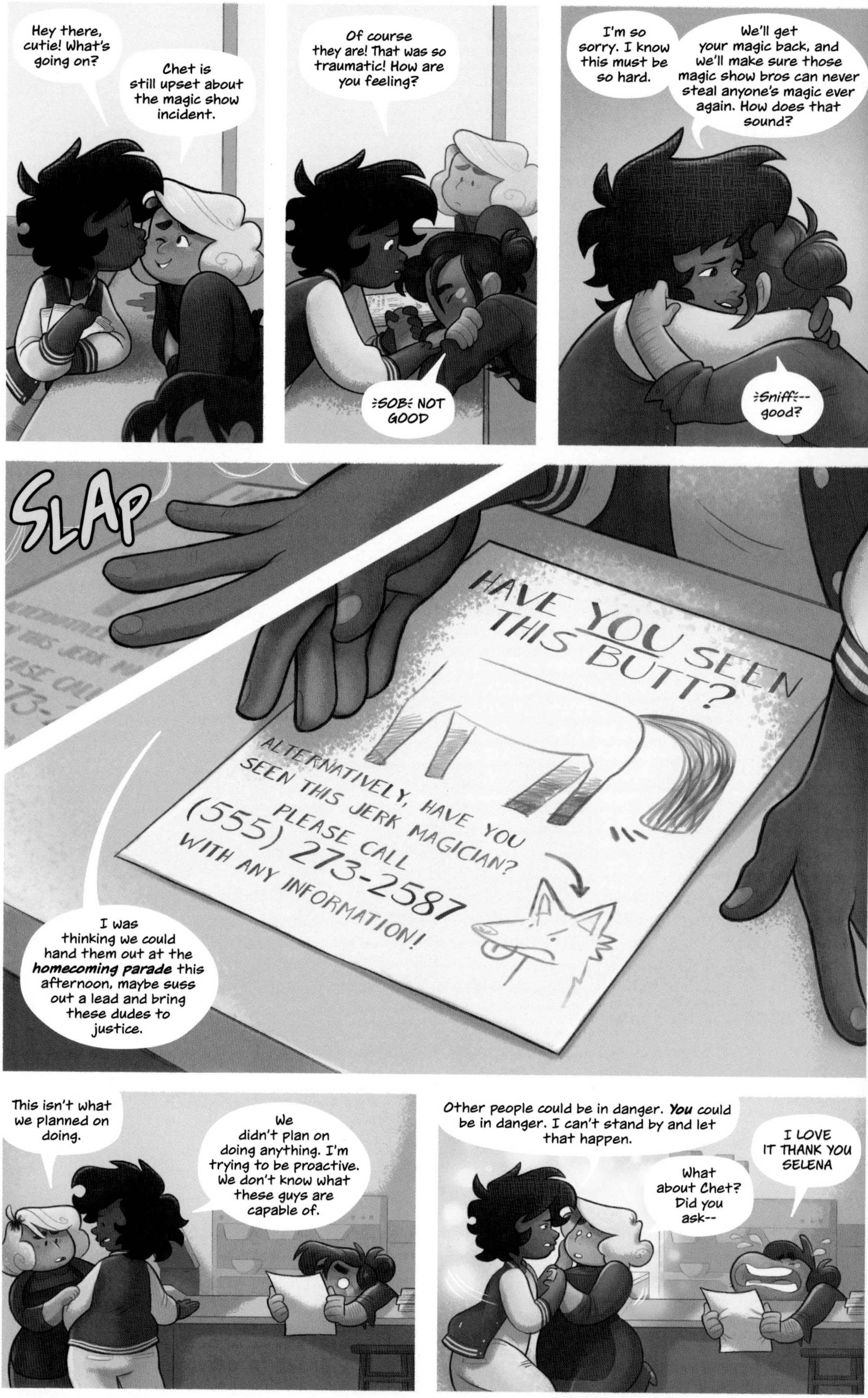
Hey there, cutie! What's going on?
Chet is still upset about the magic show incident.
Of course they are! That was so traumatic! How are you feeling?
SOB NOT GOOD
I'm so sorry. I know this must be so hard.
We'll get your magic back, and we'll make sure those magic show bros can never steal anyone's magic ever again. How does that sound?
Sniff-- good?
SLAP
HAVE YOU SEEN THIS BUTT?
ALTERNATIVELY, HAVE YOU SEEN THIS JERK MAGICIAN?
PLEASE CALL (555) 273-2587 WITH ANY INFORMATION!
I was thinking we could hand them out at the homecoming parade this afternoon, maybe suss out a lead and bring these dudes to justice.
This isn't what we planned on doing.
We didn't plan on doing anything. I'm trying to be proactive. We don't know what these guys are capable of.
Other people could be in danger. You could be in danger. I can't stand by and let that happen.
What about Chet? Did you ask--
I LOVE IT THANK YOU SELENA

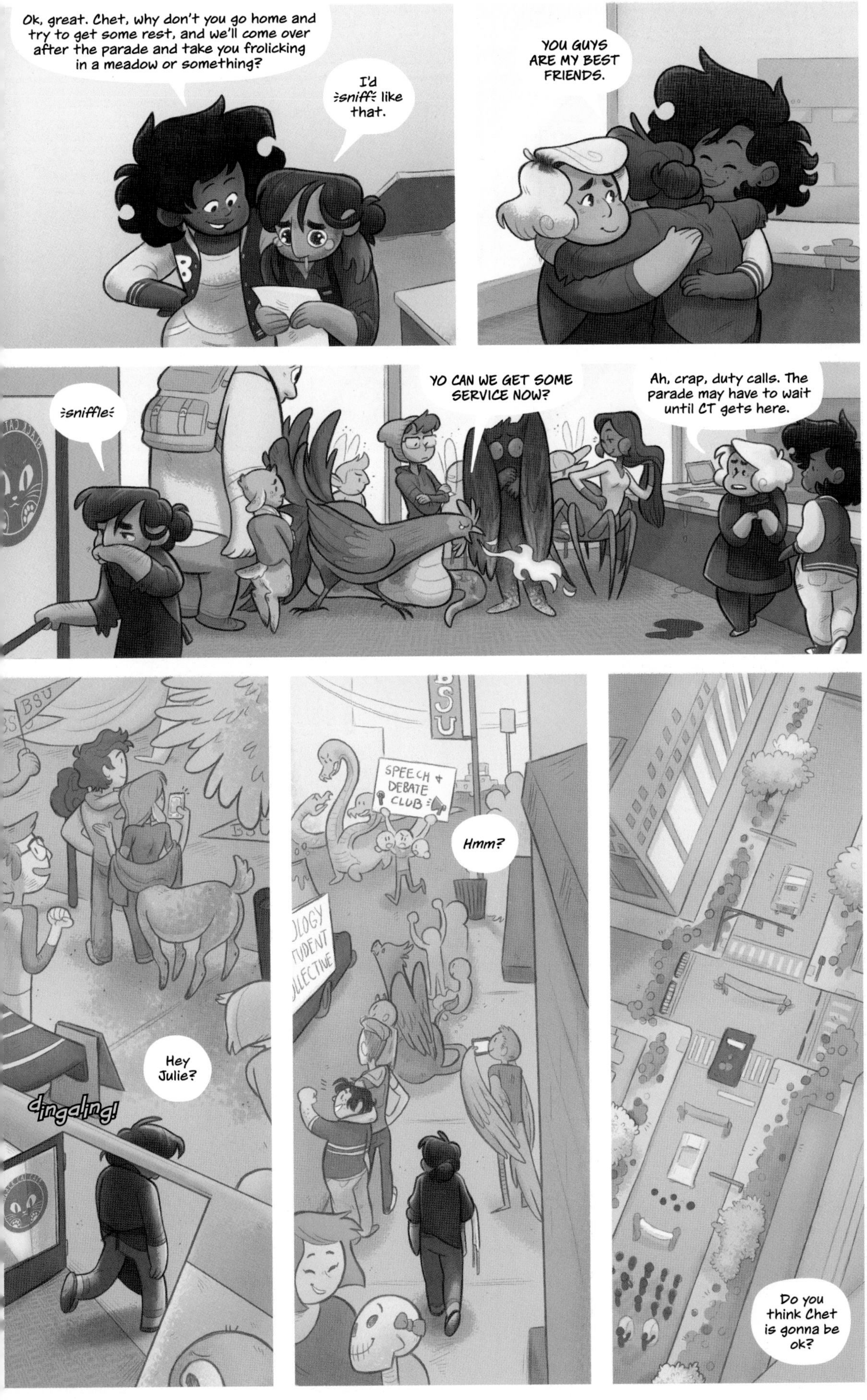

Ok, great. Chet, why don't you go home and try to get some rest, and we'll come over after the parade and take you frolicking in a meadow or something?
I'd *sniff* like that.
YOU GUYS ARE MY BEST FRIENDS.
sniffle
YO CAN WE GET SOME SERVICE NOW?
Ah, crap, duty calls. The parade may have to wait until CT gets here.
BSU
Hey Julie?
dingaling!
BSU
SPEECH + DEBATE CLUB
Hmm?
Do you think Chet is gonna be ok?

Pleasant Mountain Sisters

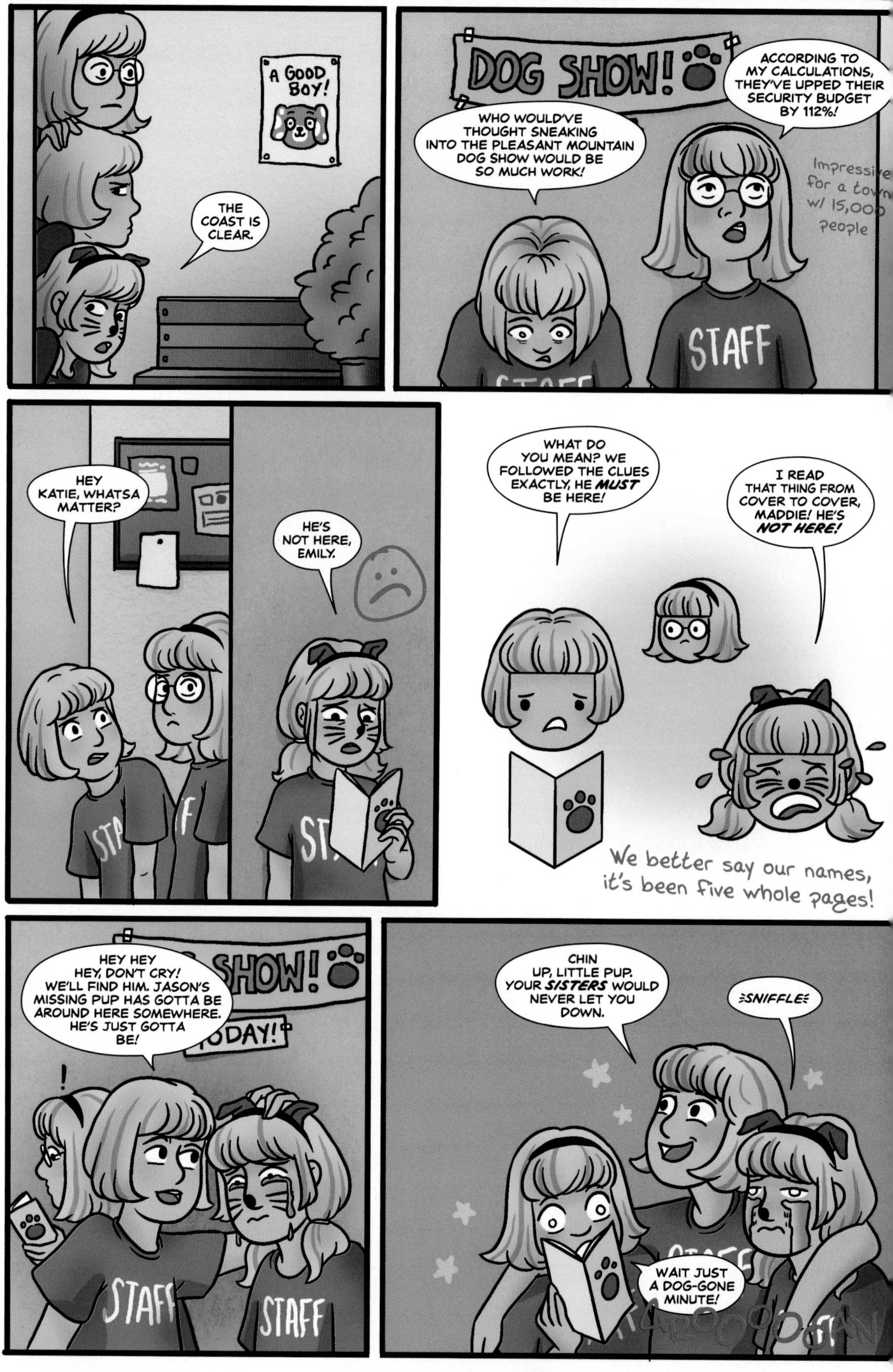

A GOOD BOY!
THE COAST IS CLEAR.
DOG SHOW!
WHO WOULD'VE THOUGHT SNEAKING INTO THE PLEASANT MOUNTAIN DOG SHOW WOULD BE SO MUCH WORK!
ACCORDING TO MY CALCULATIONS, THEY'VE UPPED THEIR SECURITY BUDGET BY 112%!
Impressive for a town w/ 15,000 people
STAFF
HEY KATIE, WHATSA MATTER?
HE'S NOT HERE, EMILY.
WHAT DO YOU MEAN? WE FOLLOWED THE CLUES EXACTLY, HE *MUST* BE HERE!
I READ THAT THING FROM COVER TO COVER, MADDIE! HE'S ***NOT HERE!***
We better say our names, it's been five whole pages!
HEY HEY HEY, DON'T CRY! WE'LL FIND HIM. JASON'S MISSING PUP HAS GOTTA BE AROUND HERE SOMEWHERE. HE'S JUST GOTTA BE!
TODAY!
!
CHIN UP, LITTLE PUP. YOUR ***SISTERS*** WOULD NEVER LET YOU DOWN.
SNIFFLE
WAIT JUST A DOG-GONE MINUTE!

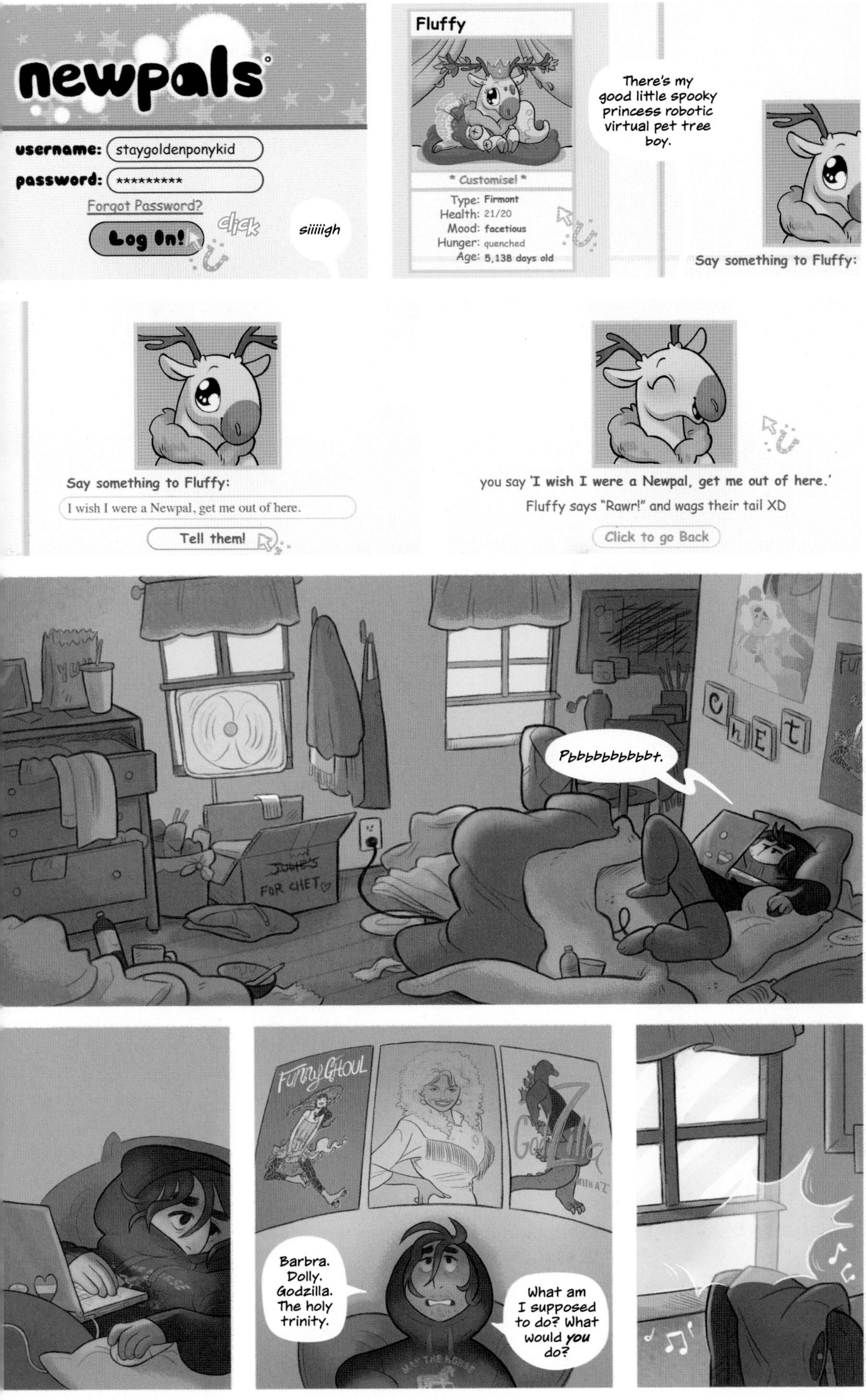
newpals
username: staygoldenponykid
password: *********
Forgot Password?
Log In!
click
siiiiigh
Fluffy
* Customise! *
Type: Firmont
Health: 21/20
Mood: facetious
Hunger: quenched
Age: 5,138 days old
There's my good little spooky princess robotic virtual pet tree boy.
Say something to Fluffy:
Say something to Fluffy:
I wish I were a Newpal, get me out of here.
Tell them!
you say 'I wish I were a Newpal, get me out of here.'
Fluffy says "Rawr!" and wags their tail XD
Click to go Back
FOR CHET
CHET
Pbbbbbbbbbbt.
FUNNY GIRL
GODZILLA WITH A "Z"
Barbra. Dolly. Godzilla. The holy trinity.
What am I supposed to do? What would *you* do?

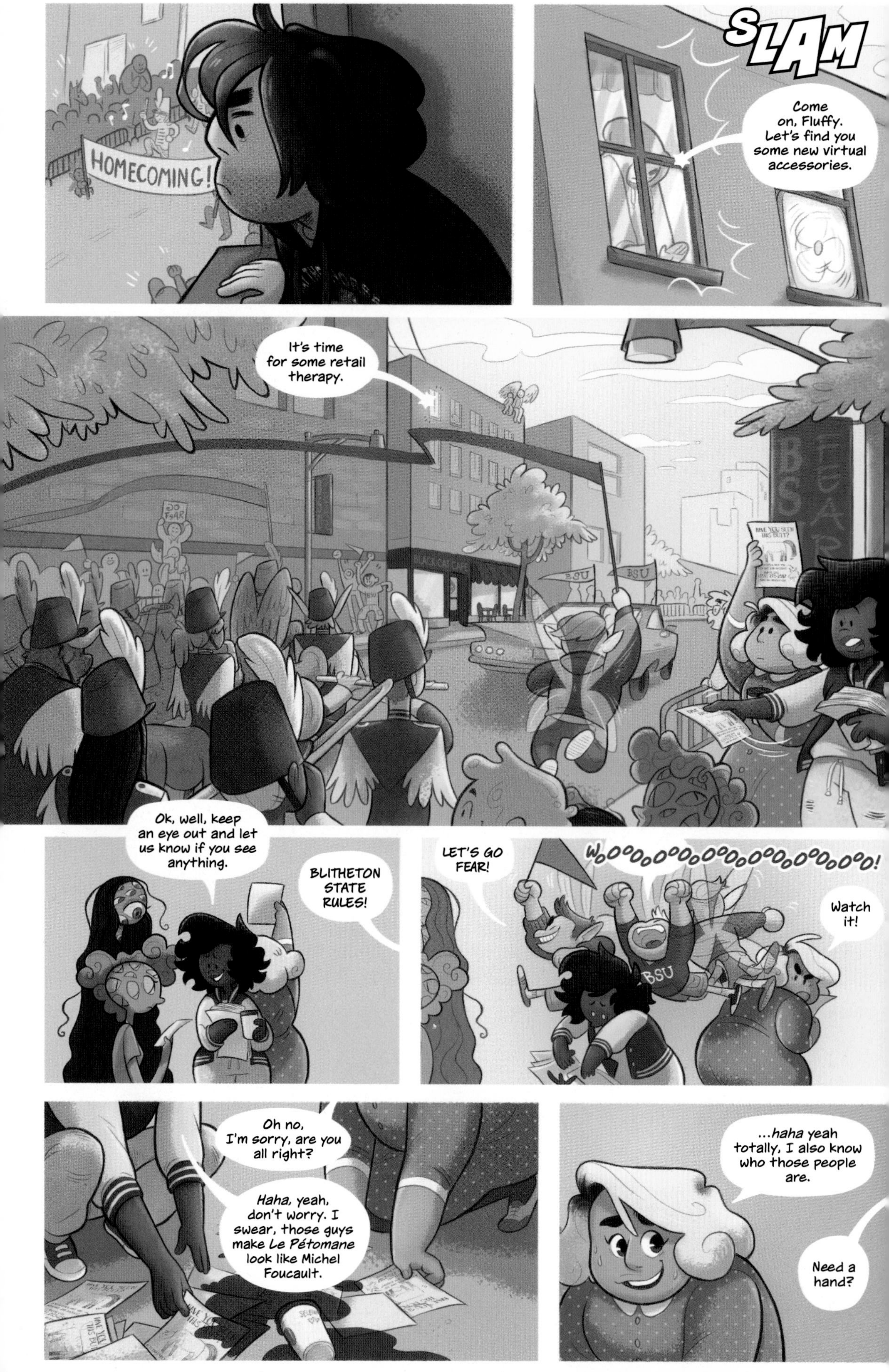
HOMECOMING!
SLAM
Come on, Fluffy. Let's find you some new virtual accessories.
It's time for some retail therapy.
BSU
BSU
BLACK CAT CAFE
GO FEAR
Ok, well, keep an eye out and let us know if you see anything.
BLITHETON STATE RULES!
LET'S GO FEAR!
WoOoOoOoOoOoOoOoOoOoOoO!
Watch it!
BSU
Oh no, I'm sorry, are you all right?
Haha, yeah, don't worry. I swear, those guys make *Le Pétomane* look like Michel Foucault.
...*haha* yeah totally, I also know who those people are.
Need a hand?

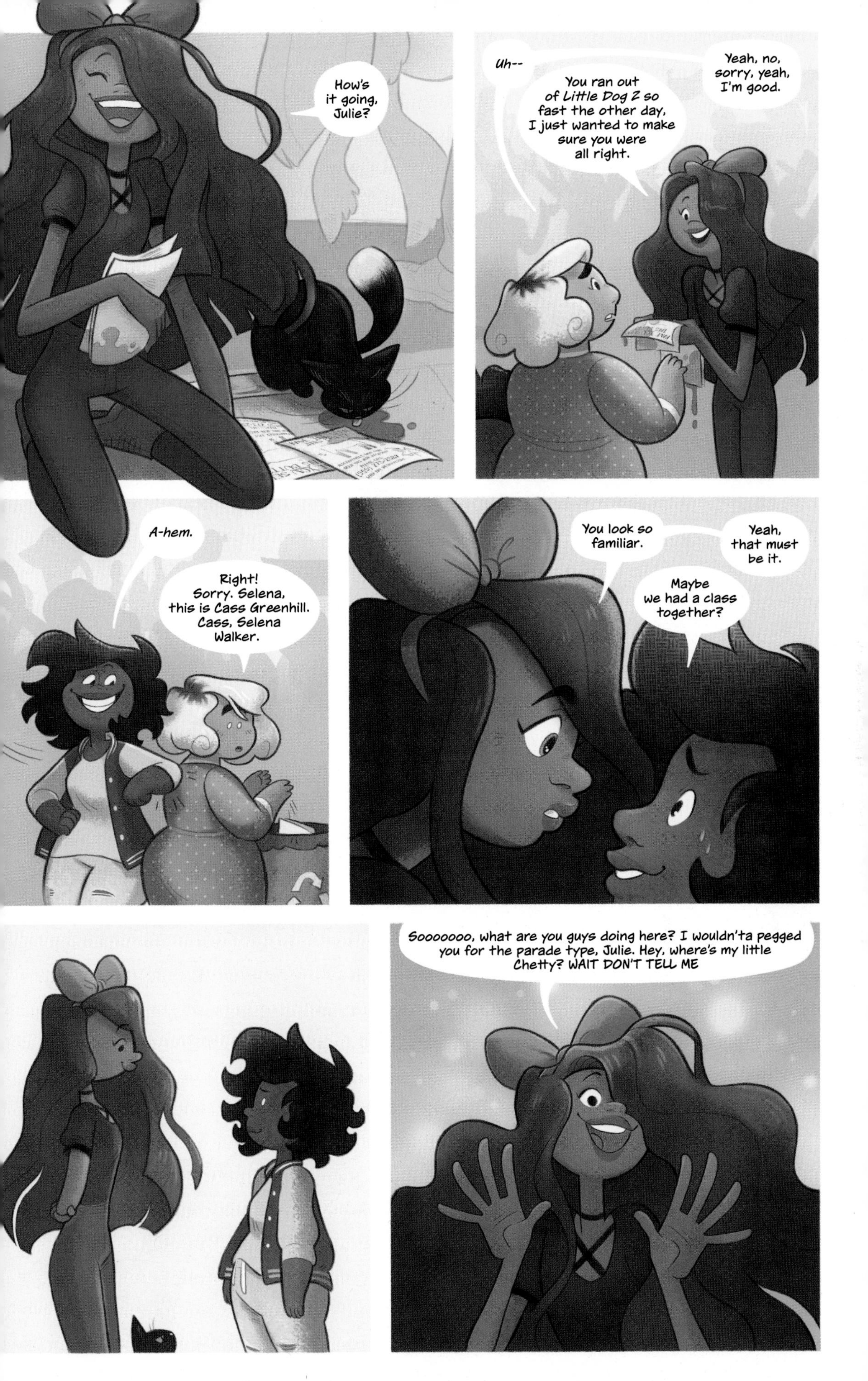
How's it going, Julie?
Uh--
You ran out of Little Dog 2 so fast the other day, I just wanted to make sure you were all right.
Yeah, no, sorry, yeah, I'm good.
A-hem.
Right! Sorry. Selena, this is Cass Greenhill. Cass, Selena Walker.
You look so familiar.
Maybe we had a class together?
Yeah, that must be it.
Sooooooo, what are you guys doing here? I wouldn't'a pegged you for the parade type, Julie. Hey, where's my little Chetty? WAIT DON'T TELL ME

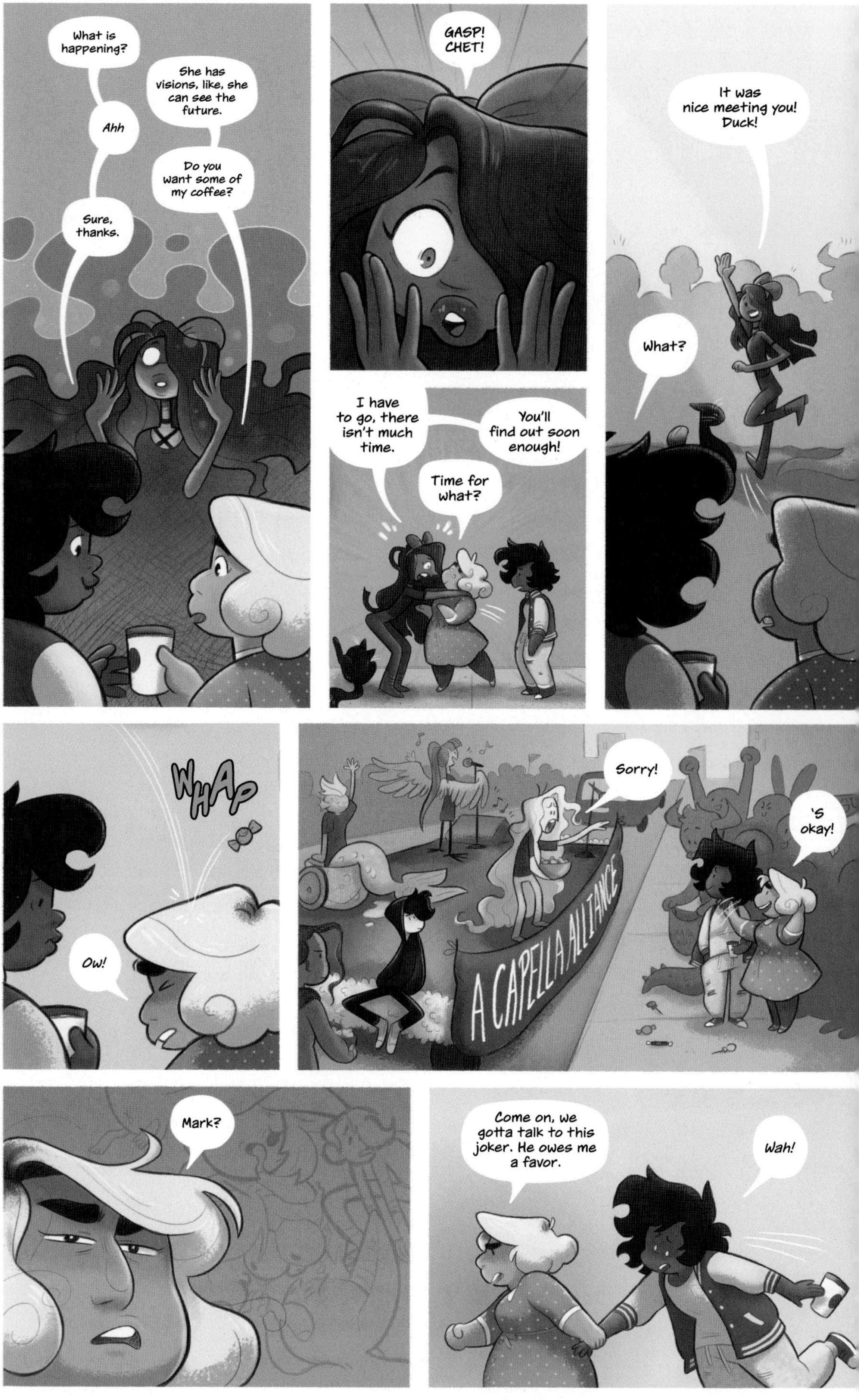
What is happening?
She has visions, like, she can see the future.
Ahh
Do you want some of my coffee?
Sure, thanks.
GASP! CHET!
I have to go, there isn't much time.
You'll find out soon enough!
Time for what?
It was nice meeting you! Duck!
What?
WHAP
Ow!
A CAPELLA ALLIANCE
Sorry!
'S okay!
Mark?
Come on, we gotta talk to this joker. He owes me a favor.
Wah!

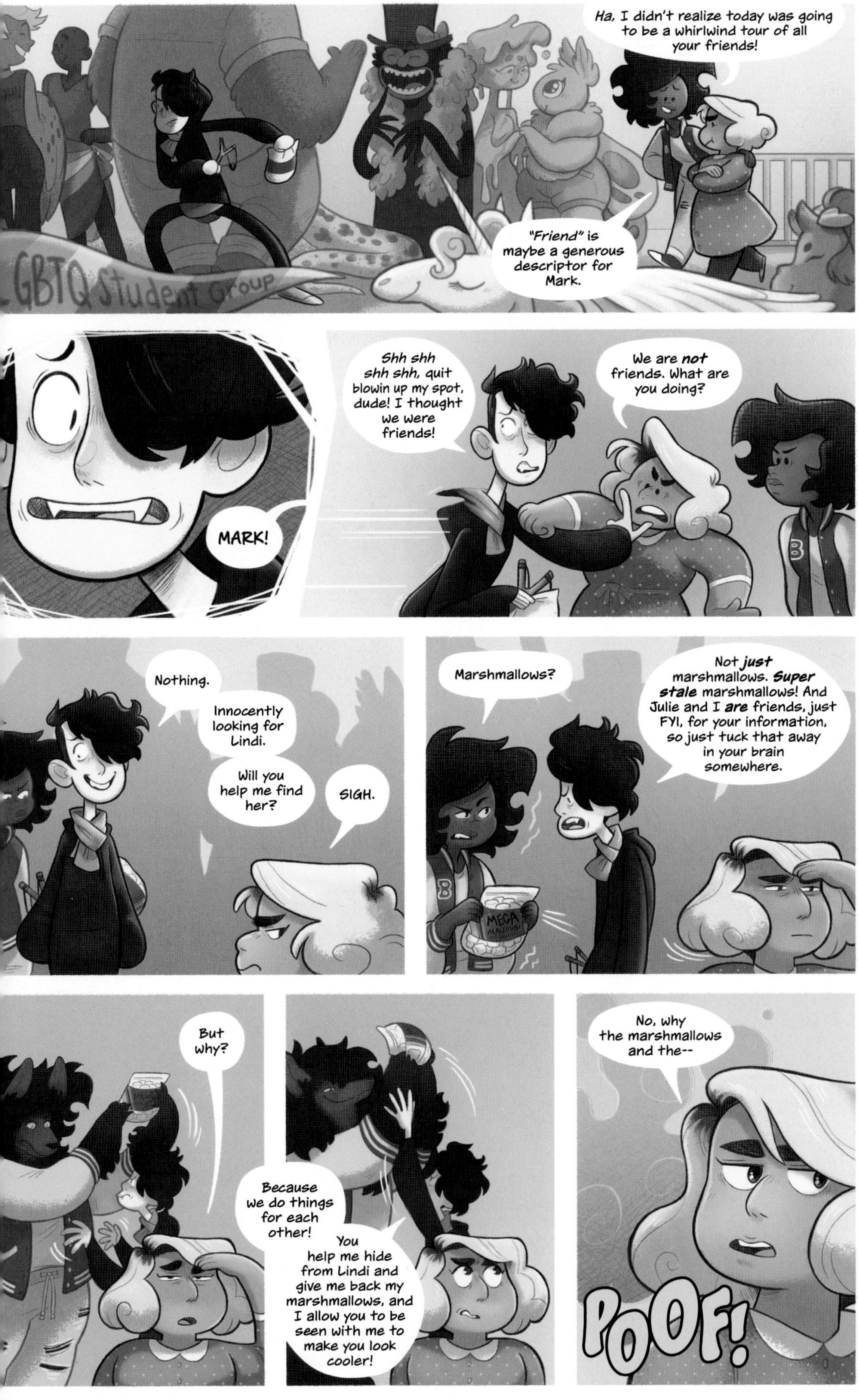

LGBTQ Student Group
Ha, I didn't realize today was going to be a whirlwind tour of all your friends!
"Friend" is maybe a generous descriptor for Mark.
MARK!
Shh shh shh shh, quit blowin up my spot, dude! I thought we were friends!
We are not friends. What are you doing?
Nothing.
Innocently looking for Lindi.
Will you help me find her?
SIGH.
Marshmallows?
Not just marshmallows. Super stale marshmallows! And Julie and I are friends, just FYI, for your information, so just tuck that away in your brain somewhere.
MEGA MALLOWS!
But why?
Because we do things for each other!
You help me hide from Lindi and give me back my marshmallows, and I allow you to be seen with me to make you look cooler!
No, why the marshmallows and the--
POOF!

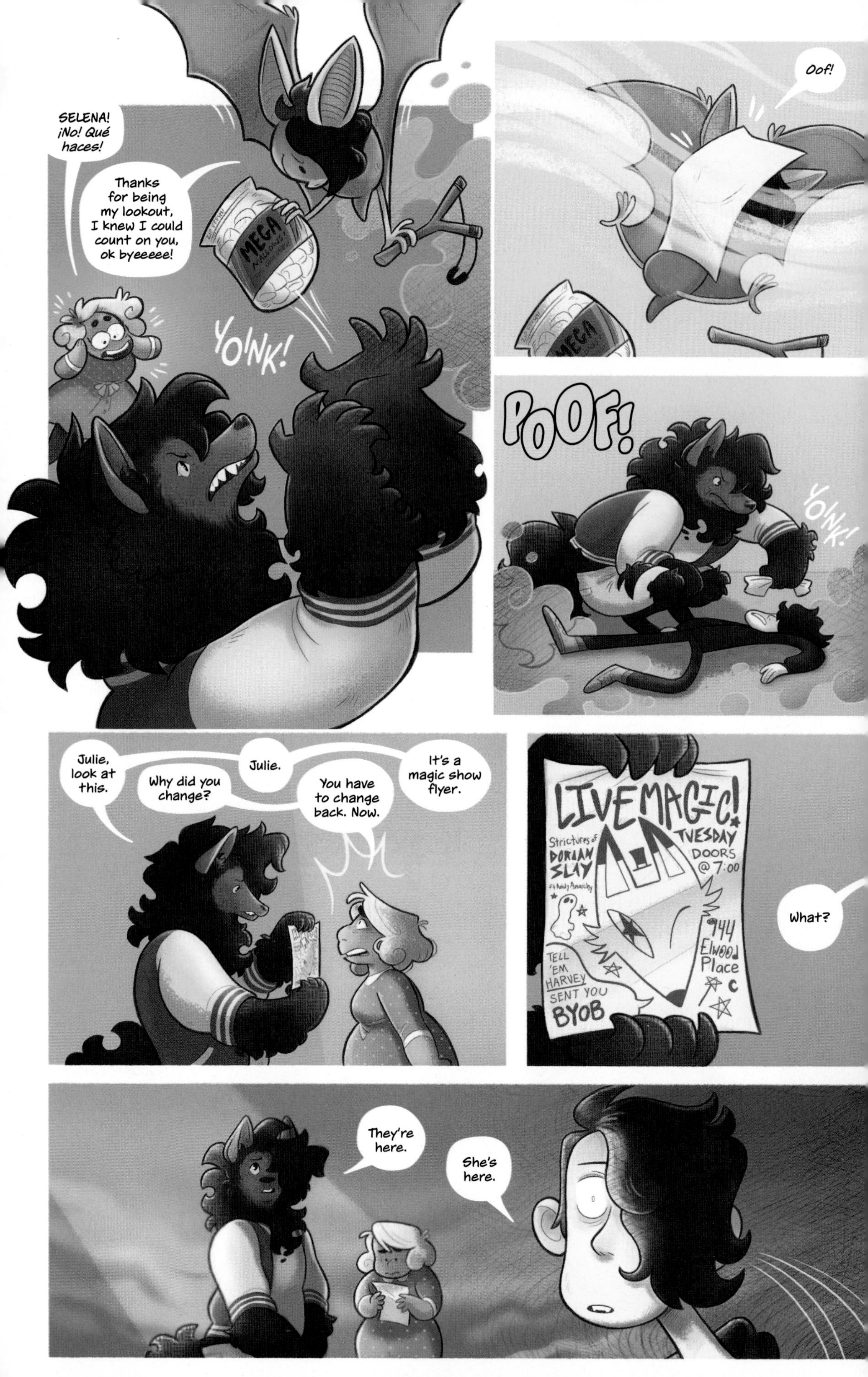
SELENA! ¡No! Qué haces!
Thanks for being my lookout, I knew I could count on you, ok byeeeee!
MEGA
YOINK!
Oof!
POOF!
YOINK!
Julie, look at this.
Why did you change?
Julie.
You have to change back. Now.
It's a magic show flyer.
LIVE MAGIC!
Strictures of DORIAN SLAY ft Andy Anarchy
TUESDAY DOORS @ 7:00
944 Elwood Place
TELL 'EM HARVEY SENT YOU
BYOB
What?
They're here.
She's here.

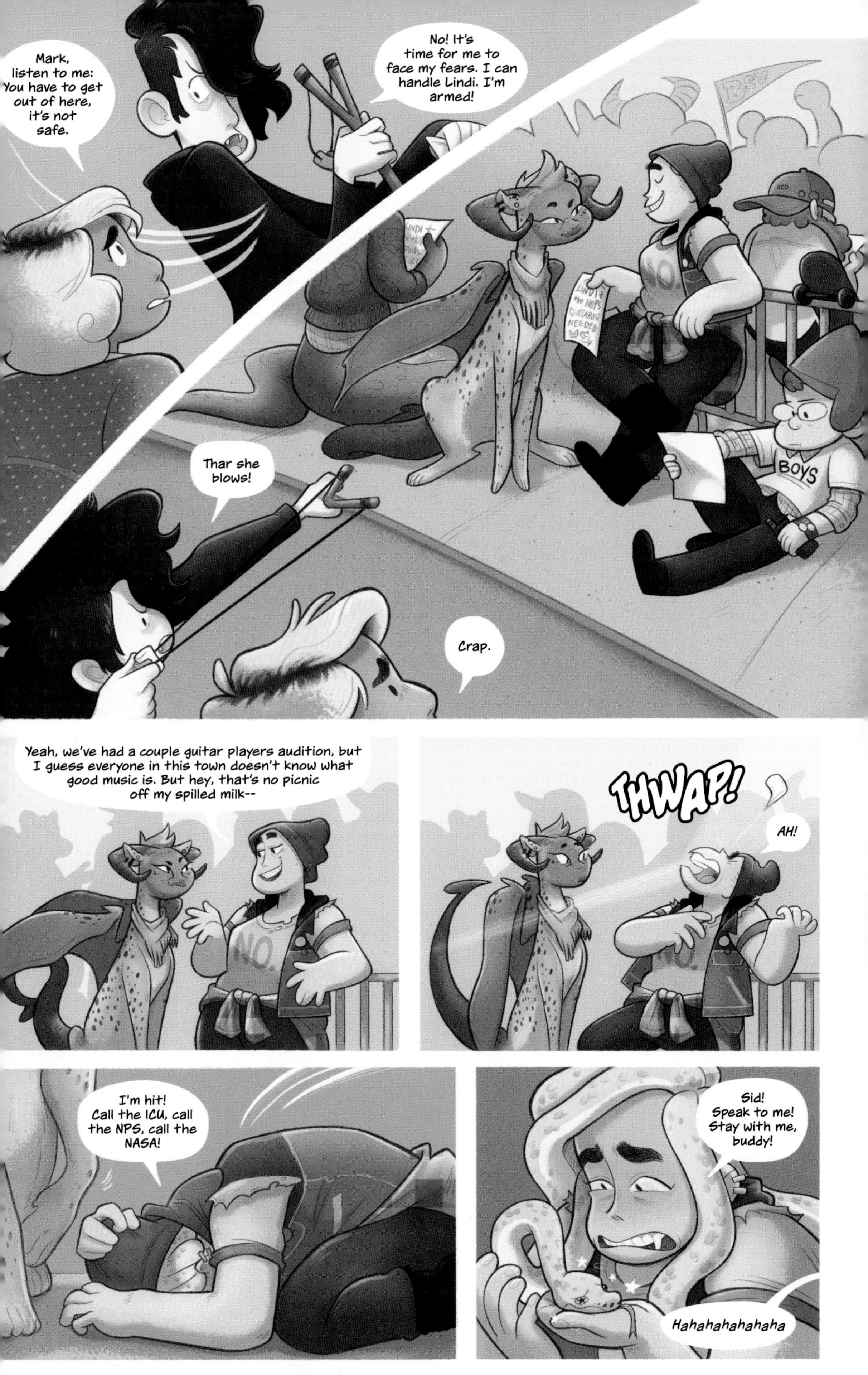
Mark, listen to me: You have to get out of here, it's not safe.
No! It's time for me to face my fears. I can handle Lindi. I'm armed!
BSU
RED.
LINDI + the HOPS GUITARIST NEEDED
BOYS
Thar she blows!
Crap.
Yeah, we've had a couple guitar players audition, but I guess everyone in this town doesn't know what good music is. But hey, that's no picnic off my spilled milk--
THWAP!
AH!
I'm hit! Call the ICU, call the NPS, call the NASA!
Sid! Speak to me! Stay with me, buddy!
Hahahahahahaha

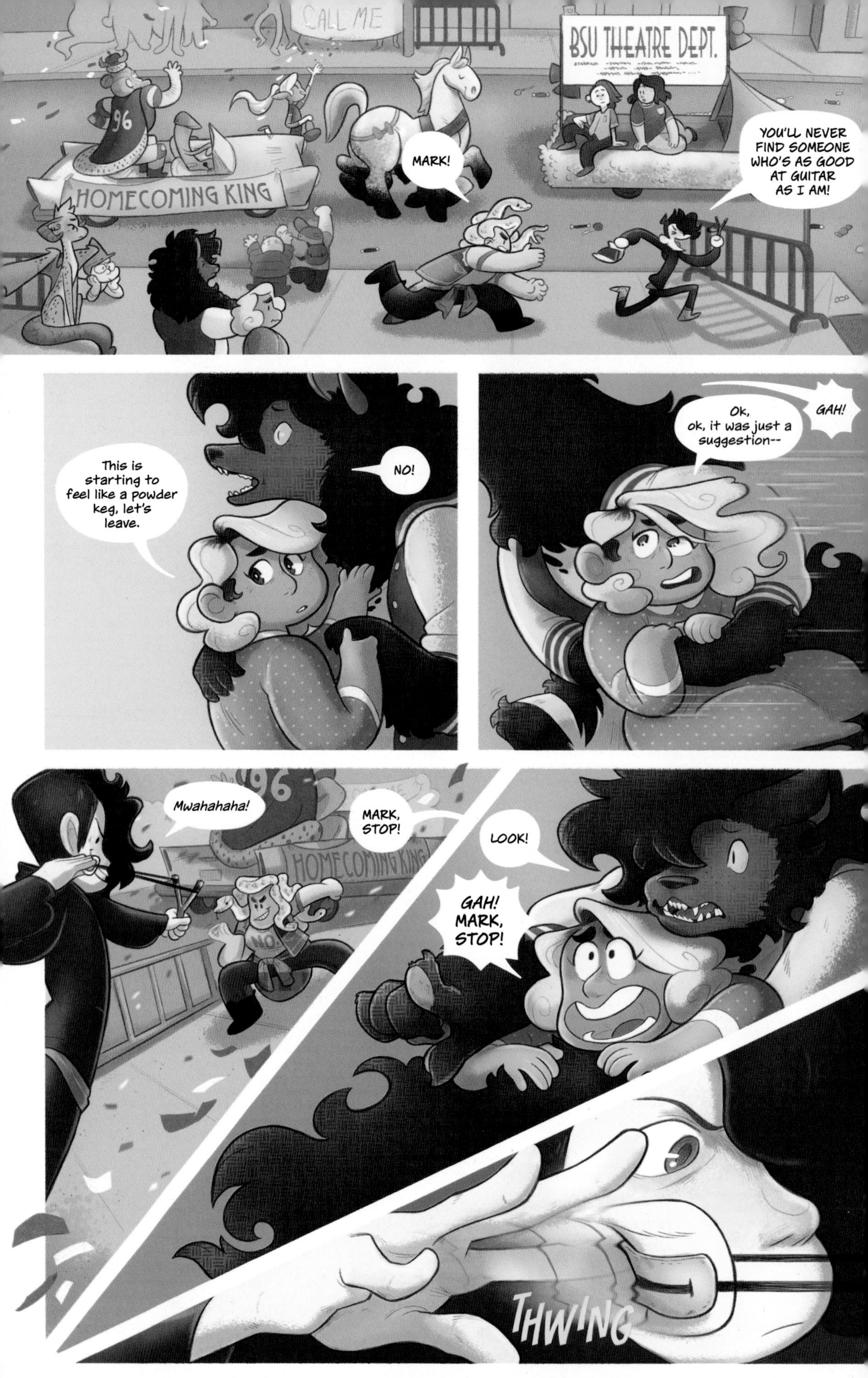
CALL ME
BSU THEATRE DEPT.
96
HOMECOMING KING
MARK!
YOU'LL NEVER FIND SOMEONE WHO'S AS GOOD AT GUITAR AS I AM!
This is starting to feel like a powder keg, let's leave.
NO!
Ok, ok, it was just a suggestion--
GAH!
Mwahahaha!
MARK, STOP!
HOMECOMING KING
NO.
LOOK!
GAH! MARK, STOP!
THWING

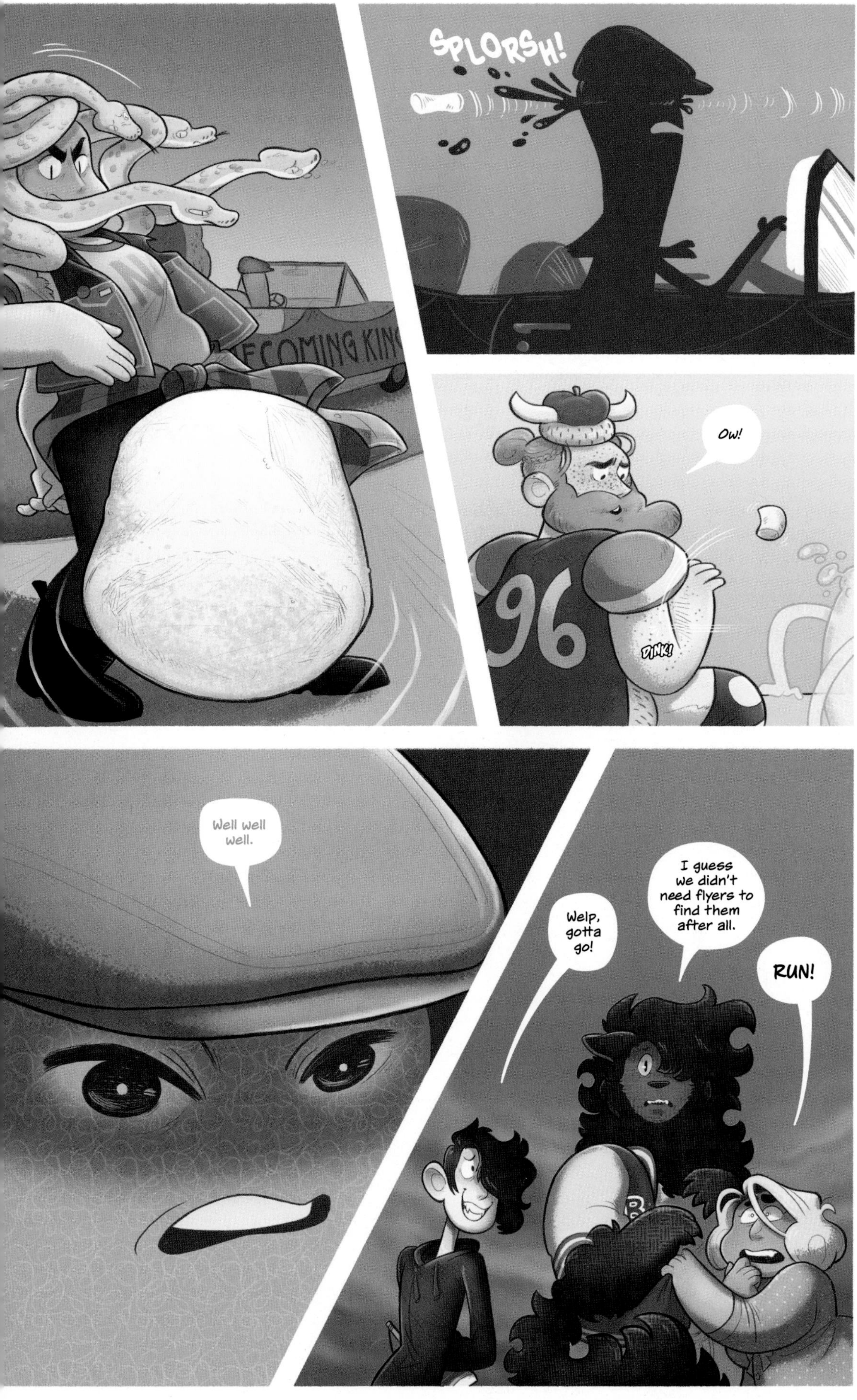
SPLORSH!
Ow!
DINK!
Well well well.
I guess we didn't need flyers to find them after all.
Welp, gotta go!
RUN!

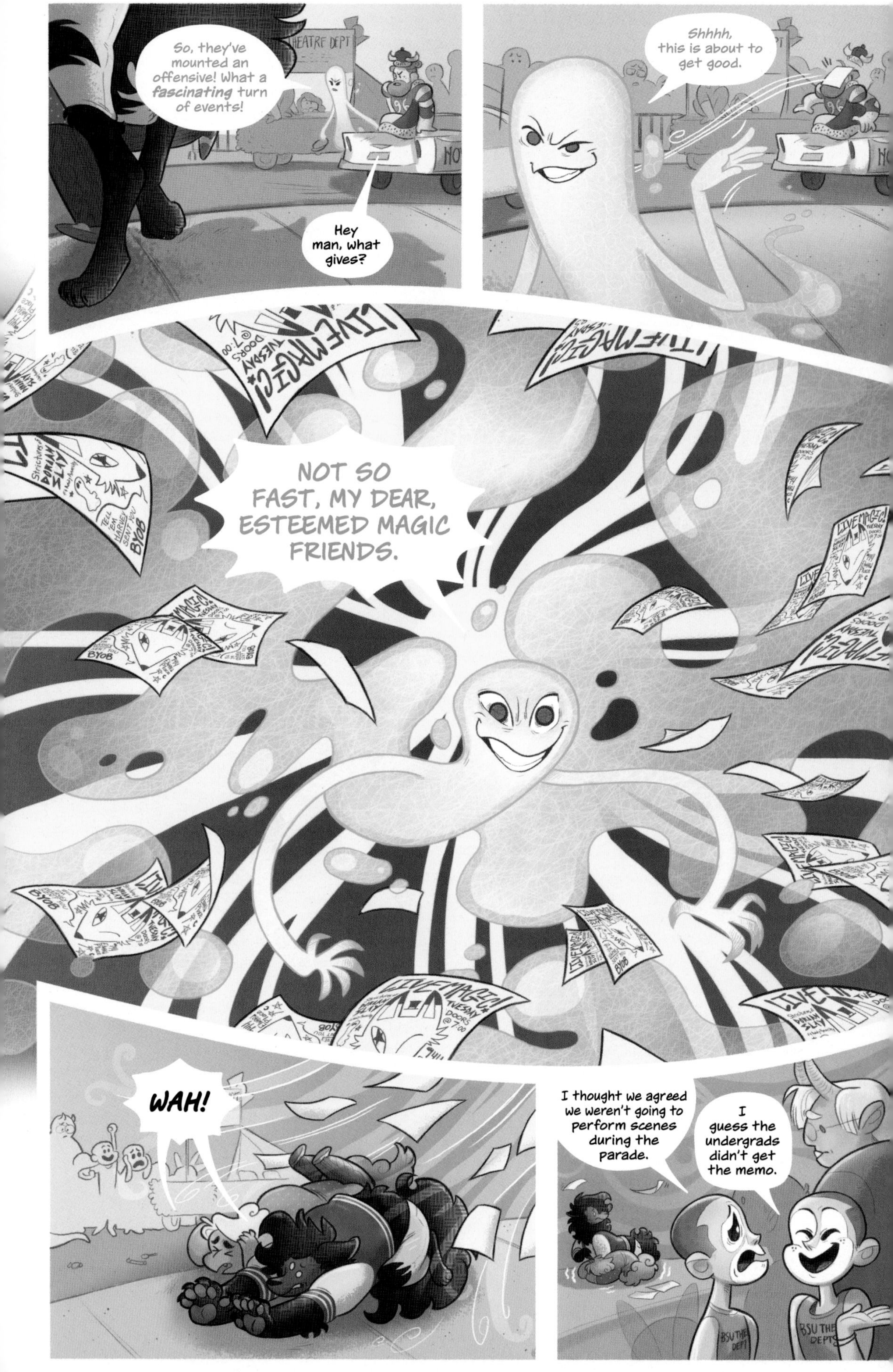

THEATRE DEPT
So, they've mounted an offensive! What a *fascinating* turn of events!
Hey man, what gives?
Shhhh, this is about to get good.
LIVE MAGIC! TUESDAY DOORS @ 7:00
NOT SO FAST, MY DEAR, ESTEEMED MAGIC FRIENDS.
WAH!
I thought we agreed we weren't going to perform scenes during the parade.
I guess the undergrads didn't get the memo.

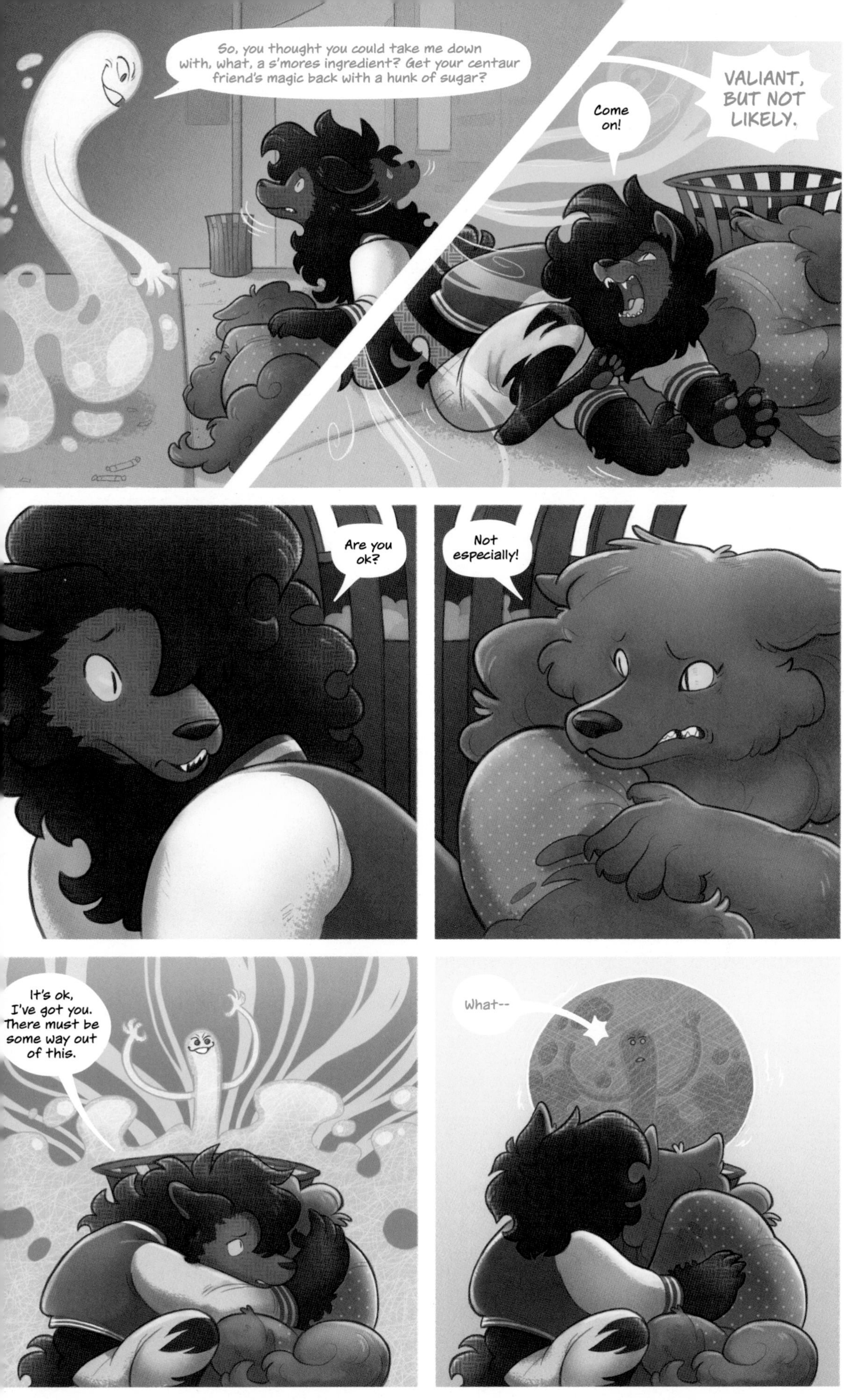
So, you thought you could take me down with, what, a s'mores ingredient? Get your centaur friend's magic back with a hunk of sugar?
VALIANT, BUT NOT LIKELY.
Come on!
Are you ok?
Not especially!
It's ok, I've got you. There must be some way out of this.
What--

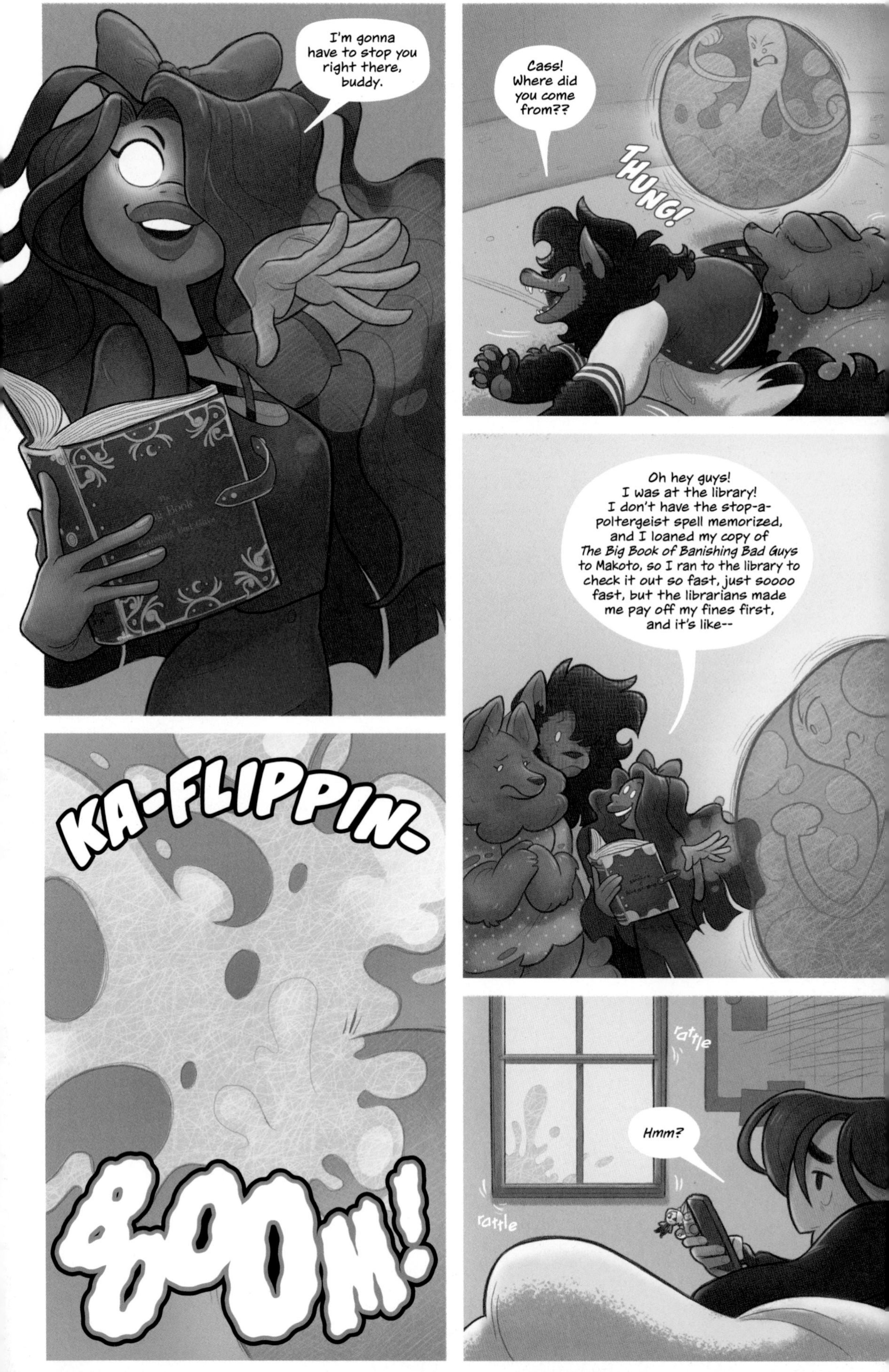
I'm gonna have to stop you right there, buddy.
Cass! Where did you come from??
THUNG!
KA-FLIPPIN-
BOOM!
Oh hey guys! I was at the library! I don't have the stop-a-poltergeist spell memorized, and I loaned my copy of *The Big Book of Banishing Bad Guys* to Makoto, so I ran to the library to check it out so fast, just soooo fast, but the librarians made me pay off my fines first, and it's like--
rattle
Hmm?
rattle

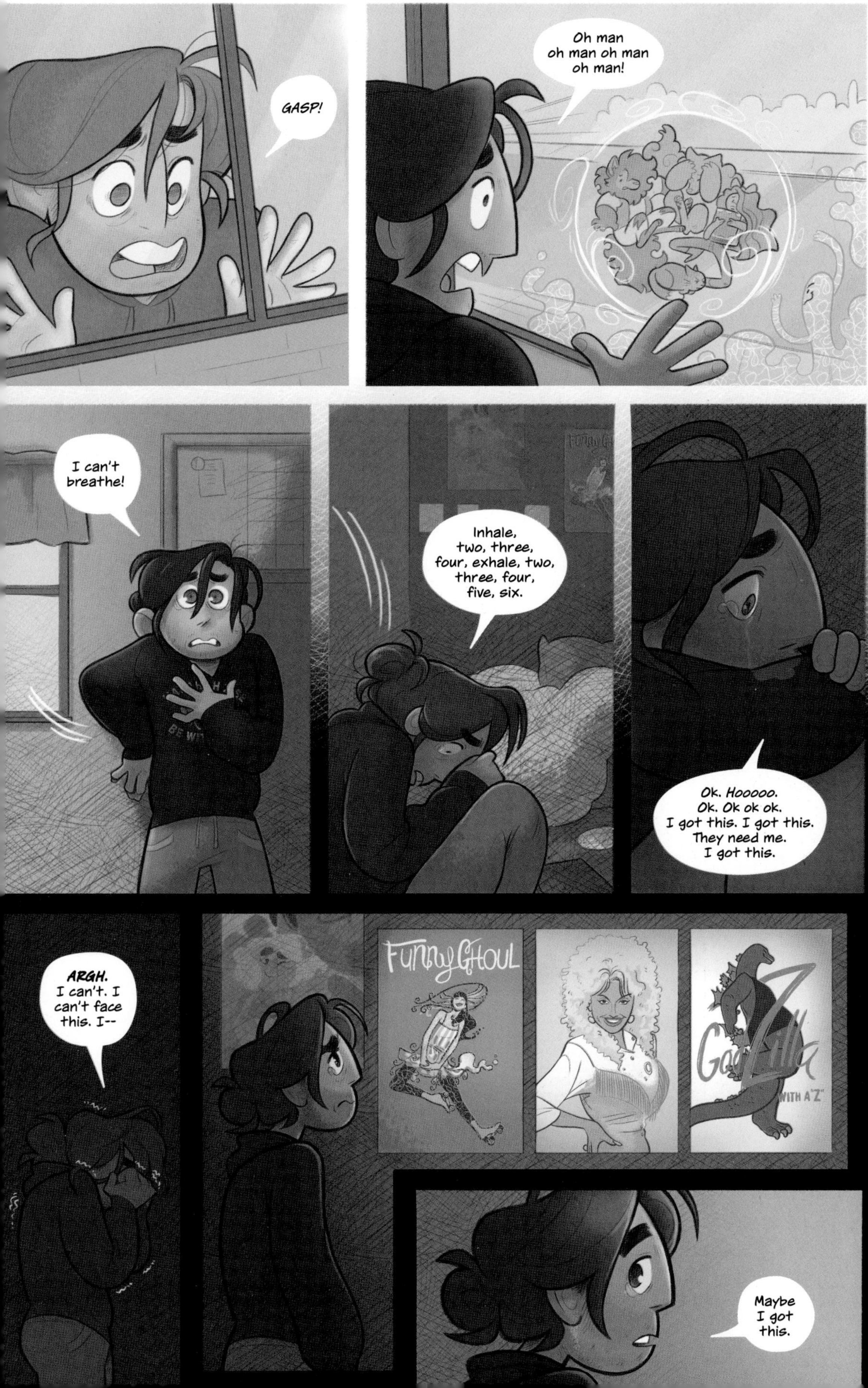
GASP!
Oh man oh man oh man oh man!
I can't breathe!
Inhale, two, three, four, exhale, two, three, four, five, six.
Ok. Hooooo. Ok. Ok ok ok. I got this. I got this. They need me. I got this.
ARGH. I can't. I can't face this. I--
FUNNY GHOUL
GODZILLA
WITH A "Z"
Maybe I got this.

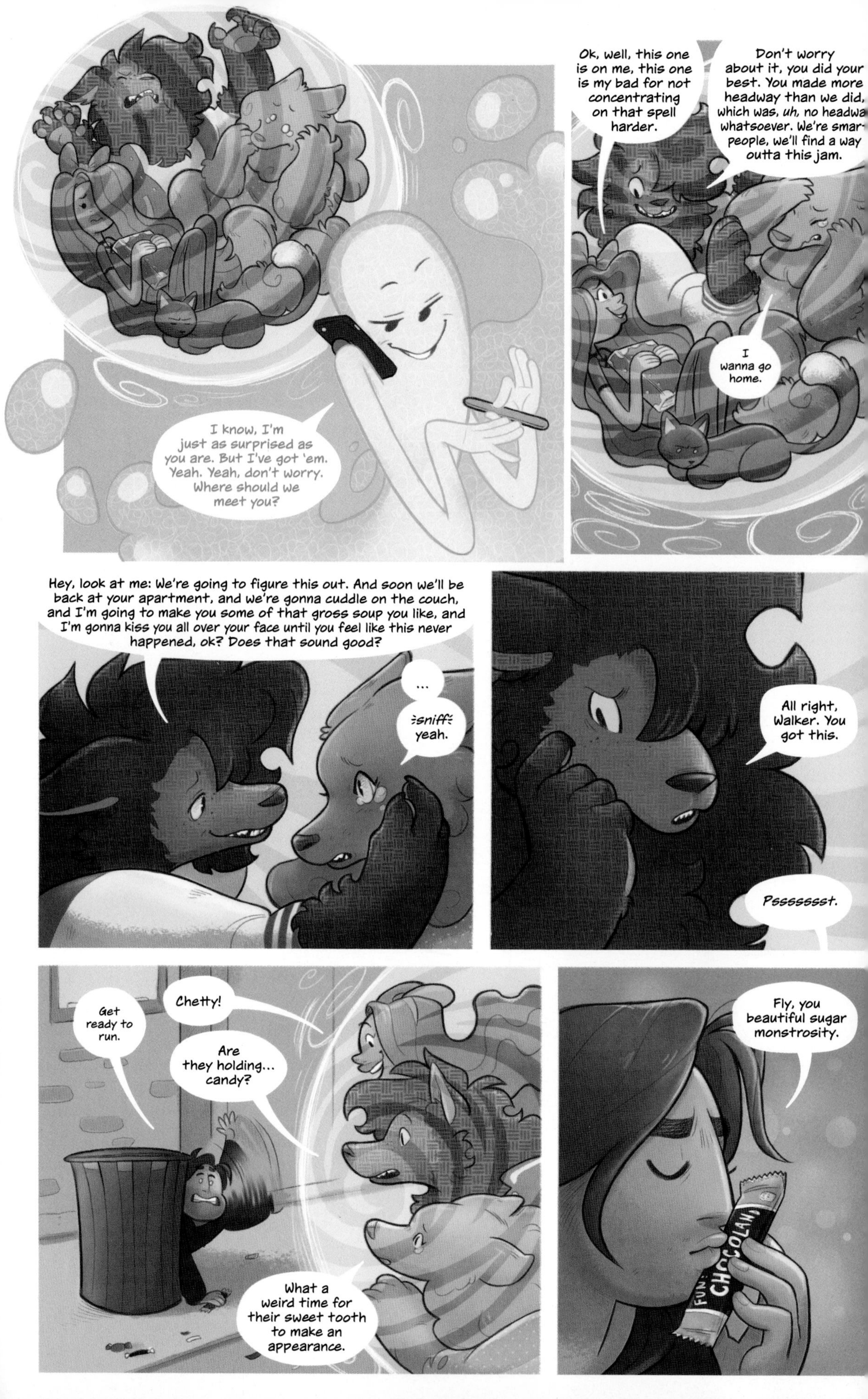
I know, I'm just as surprised as you are. But I've got 'em. Yeah. Yeah, don't worry. Where should we meet you?
Ok, well, this one is on me, this one is my bad for not concentrating on that spell harder.
Don't worry about it, you did your best. You made more headway than we did, which was, *uh*, no headwa whatsoever. We're smar- people, we'll find a way outta this jam.
I wanna go home.
Hey, look at me: We're going to figure this out. And soon we'll be back at your apartment, and we're gonna cuddle on the couch, and I'm going to make you some of that gross soup you like, and I'm gonna kiss you all over your face until you feel like this never happened, ok? Does that sound good?
...
sniff yeah.
All right, Walker. You got this.
Pssssssst.
Get ready to run.
Chetty!
Are they holding... candy?
What a weird time for their sweet tooth to make an appearance.
Fly, you beautiful sugar monstrosity.
CHOCOLAN

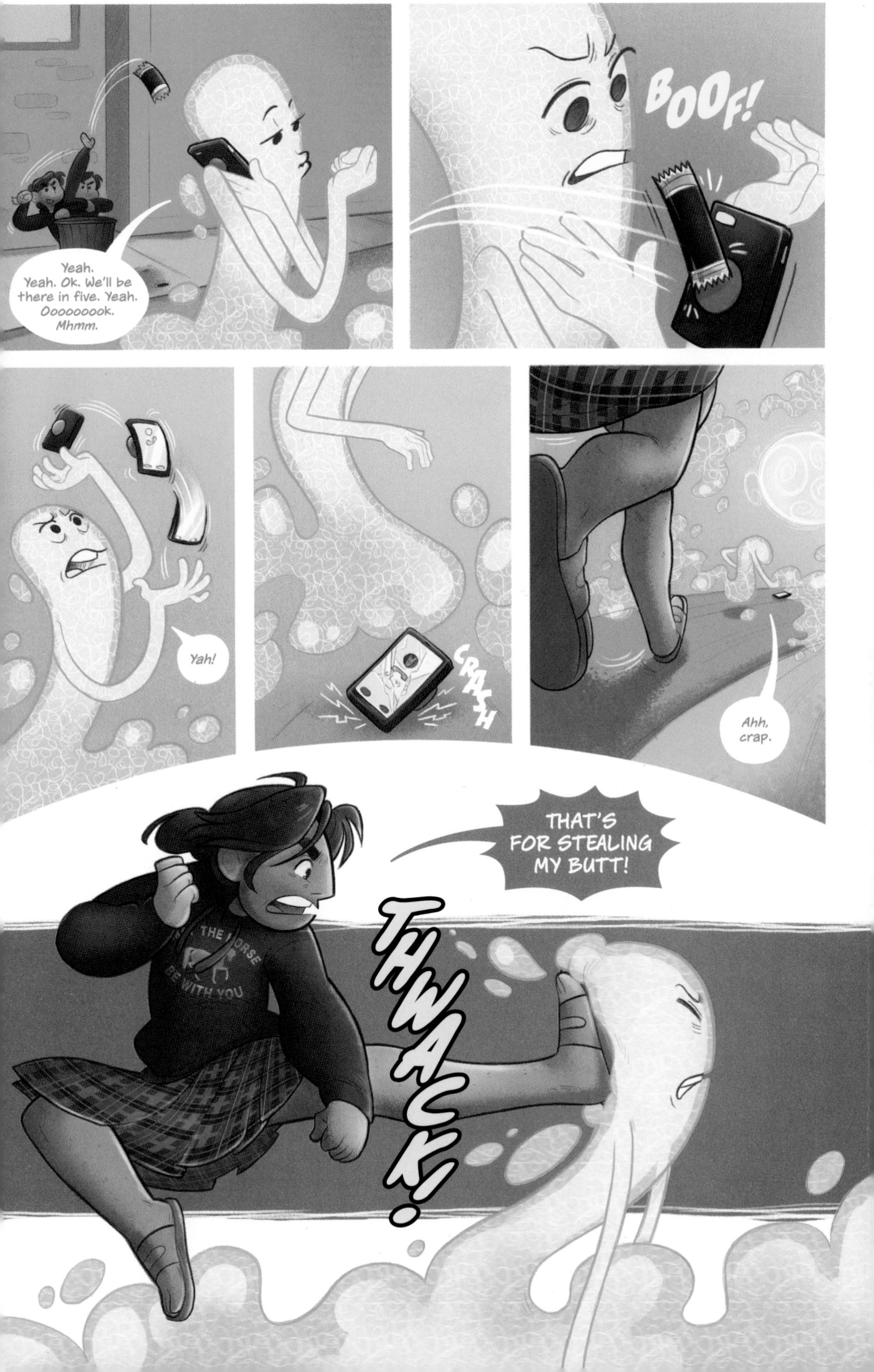
Yeah.
Yeah. Ok. We'll be there in five. Yeah. Oooooooook. Mhmm.
BOOF!
Yah!
CRASH
Ahh, crap.
THAT'S FOR STEALING MY BUTT!
THWACK!

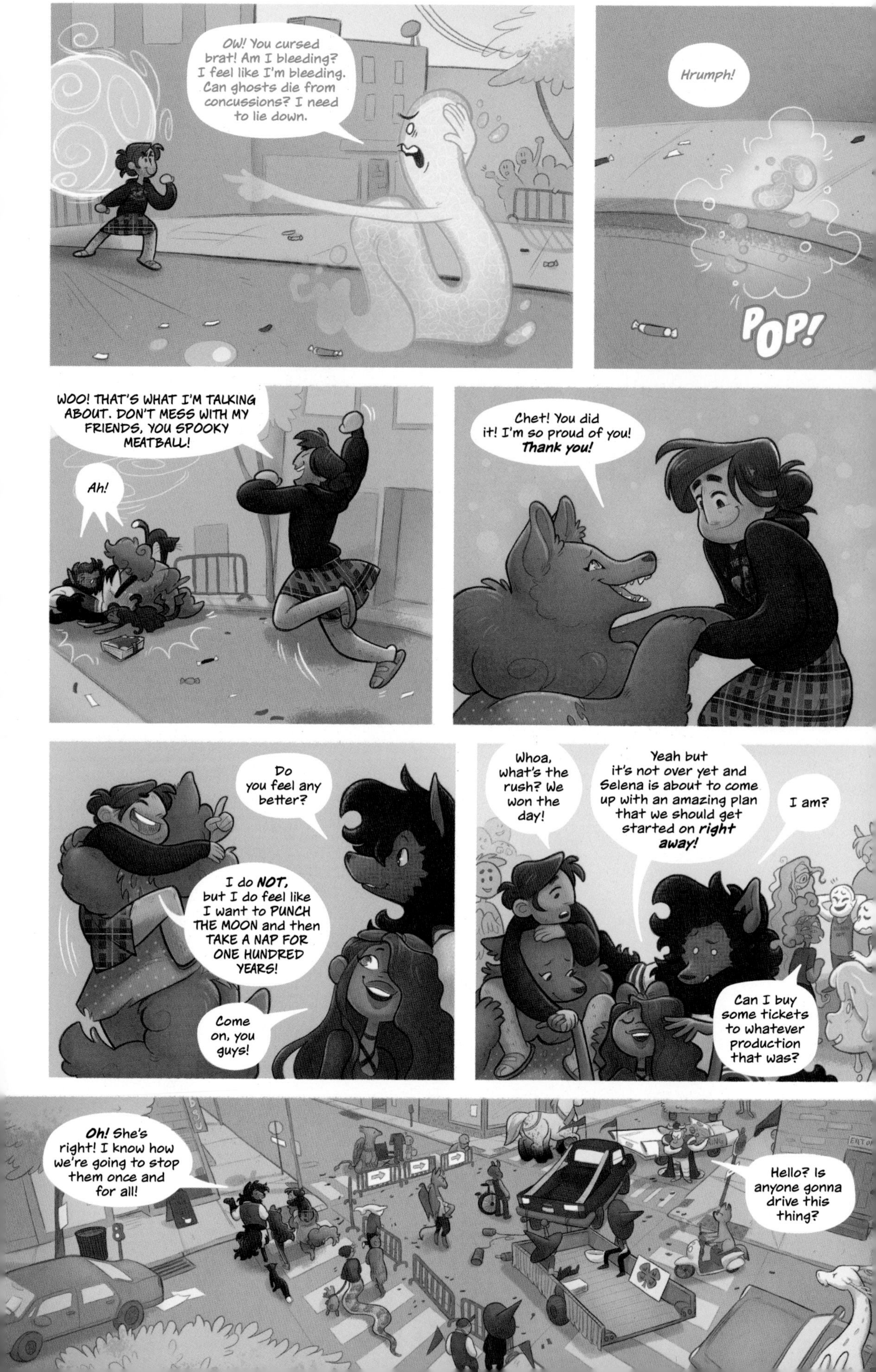
OW! You cursed brat! Am I bleeding? I feel like I'm bleeding. Can ghosts die from concussions? I need to lie down.
Hrumph!
POP!
WOO! THAT'S WHAT I'M TALKING ABOUT. DON'T MESS WITH MY FRIENDS, YOU SPOOKY MEATBALL!
Ah!
Chet! You did it! I'm so proud of you! Thank you!
Do you feel any better?
I do NOT, but I do feel like I want to PUNCH THE MOON and then TAKE A NAP FOR ONE HUNDRED YEARS!
Come on, you guys!
Whoa, what's the rush? We won the day!
Yeah but it's not over yet and Selena is about to come up with an amazing plan that we should get started on right away!
I am?
Can I buy some tickets to whatever production that was?
Oh! She's right! I know how we're going to stop them once and for all!
Hello? Is anyone gonna drive this thing?

ASK A KNOW-IT-ALL

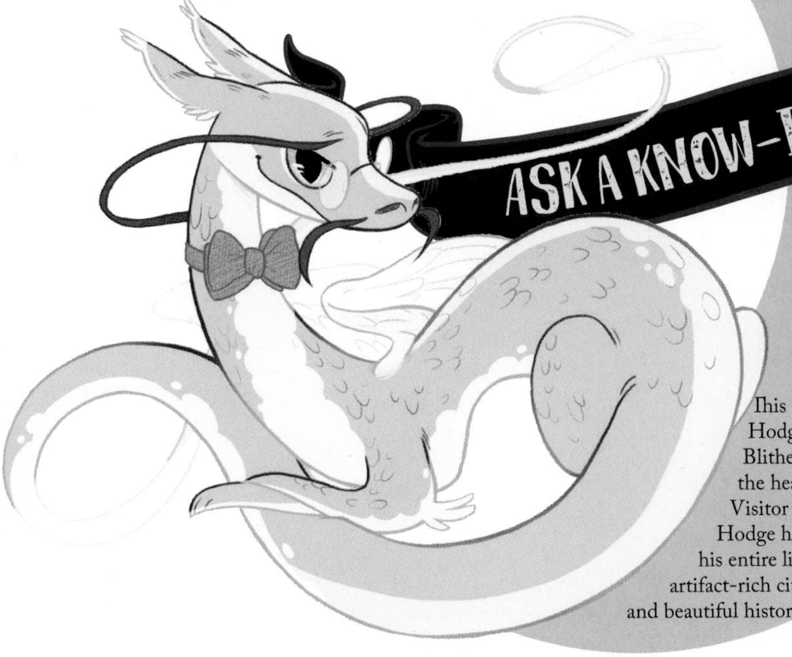

Each month, we feature advice from a different local celebrity with a unique perspective.

This month's Know-It-All is Hodge Ranford, president of the Blitheton Historical Society and the head curator for the Blitheton Visitor Center and Museum. Hodge has lived in Blitheton his entire life and calls it "the most artifact-rich city on earth, full of precious and beautiful history, hmm, so precious, yes."

Dear Know-It-All,
A young woman who I asked out told me that she'd prefer to be friends. I totally respect her decision and really do want to be friends with her, but my romantic feelings won't go away. What do I do?
-Conflicted in Columbus

Conflicted:
What a happy day, Conflicted, as I have the perfect advice for you: Bring your Romantic Feelings to the Blitheton Visitor Center and Museum. We're always looking to expand our horde- I mean, collection. "Collection," not "horde." We'll just, uh, cut that out and move on, ok? Ahem. And although our museum boasts one of the largest collections of Feelings in the tristate area, I would encourage you to remember that we are making history every day and that your unwanted Romantic Feelings may prove instructive for future generations. No reason for them to go to waste, right?

Dear Know-It-All,
If you were my lost watch, where would you be?
-Concerned Citizen

Concerned:
Well, it's not at the Blitheton Visitor Center and Museum, if that's what you're asking! Haha! So don't even bother looking there! Haha! Because it's NOT THERE! HAHA!

Dear Know-It-All,
Meow meow meow meow meow! Meow meow meow meow meow meow meow; meow, meow meow meow meow. Meow meow meow meow meow meow, meow meow meow meow. Meow meow meow meow meow meow meow meow meow?
-Meow meow

Meow:
I must confess, I don't know much about the particulars of labor laws, but as with all else, perhaps the answer lies in history: In the early twentieth century, Blitheton experienced its own workers rights revolution! It's true! And the only place to find out more is the Blitheton Visitor Center and Museum! If you stop in, I can show you some artifacts that I think you might find instructive; we have everything from newspapers and strike signs to an old boot worn by a scab, not to mention our collection of actual bodily scabs from that time period! What could be more informative than that!

Dear Know-It-All,
No matter what I do, I can't keep my room clean! My roommates think I'm a pig, but I'm doing the best I can. Every time I try to organize, somehow everything ends up messier than before. Help!
-Drowning in Clutter

Drowning:
First and foremost, there is nothing wrong with clutter. Clutter is a sign of a large collection of items, which we all know is the universal ideal. However, if your roommates are truly so barbaric as to not appreciate your penchant for preserving history, your many wondrous items will certainly find a welcome home at the Blitheton Visitor Center and Museum. Don't hesitate to bring 'em by! Please. Bring them here. Give them to me. I'll hang onto them for you. Just let me have them. Please.

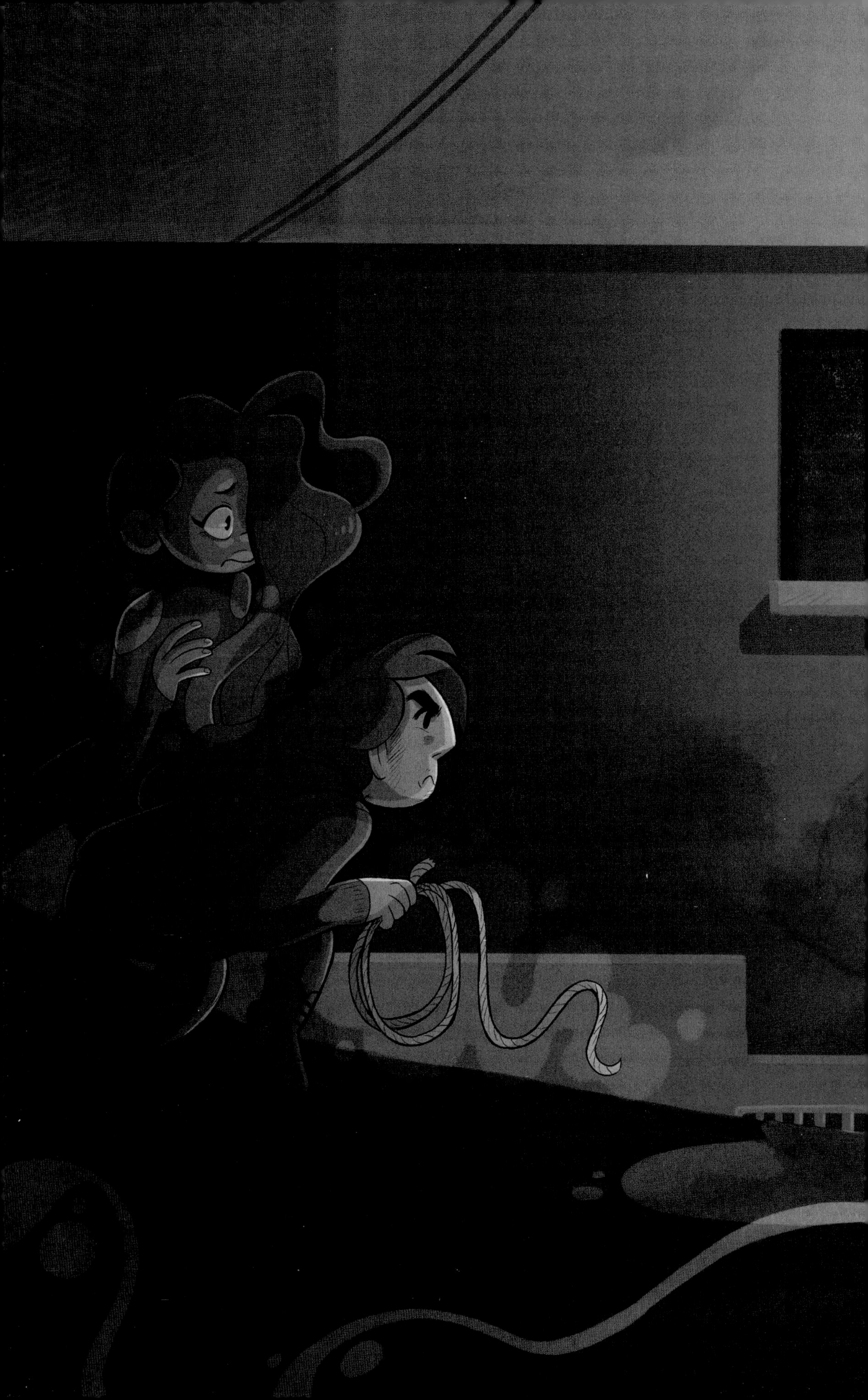

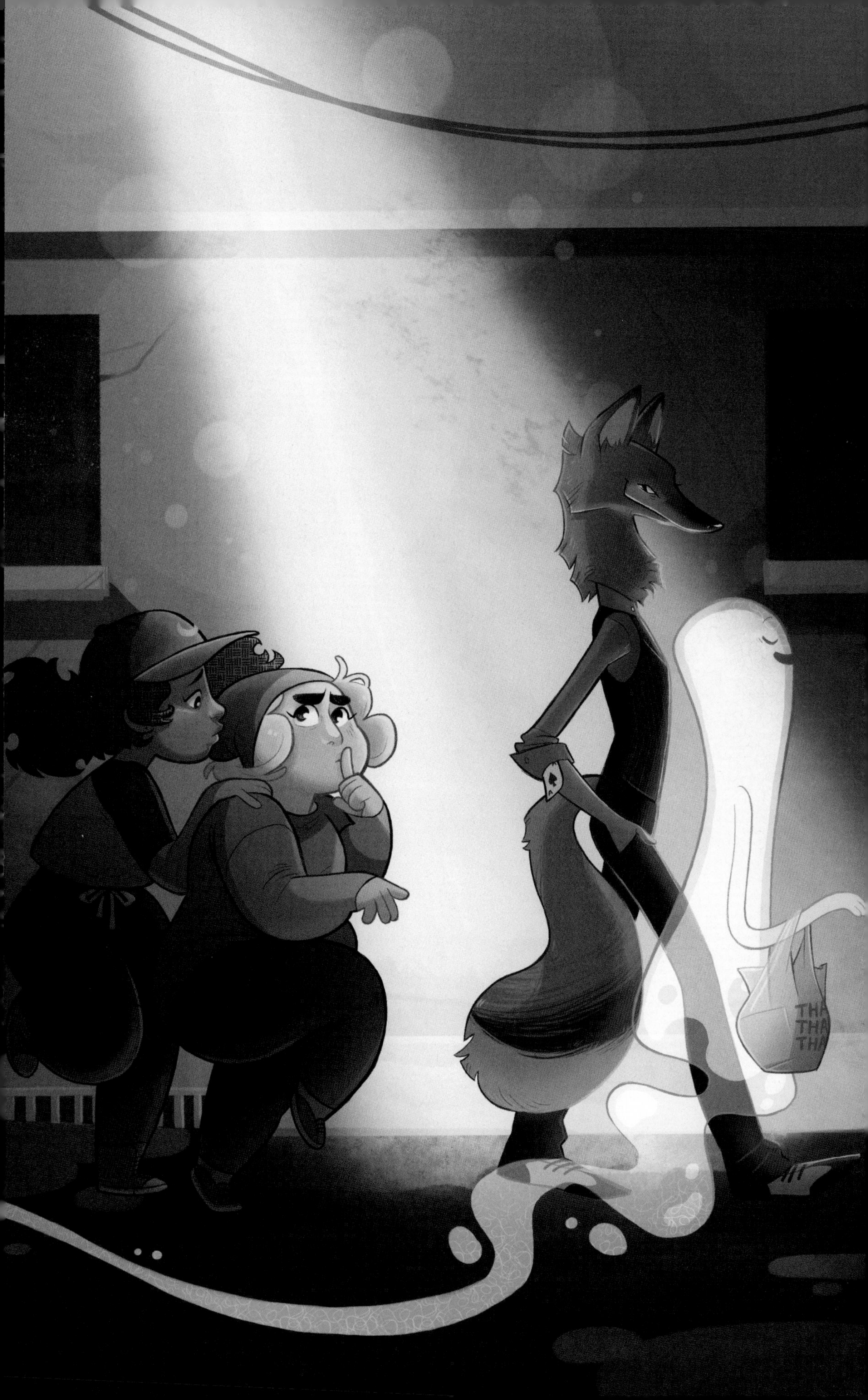
THA
THA
THA

CHAPTER FOUR

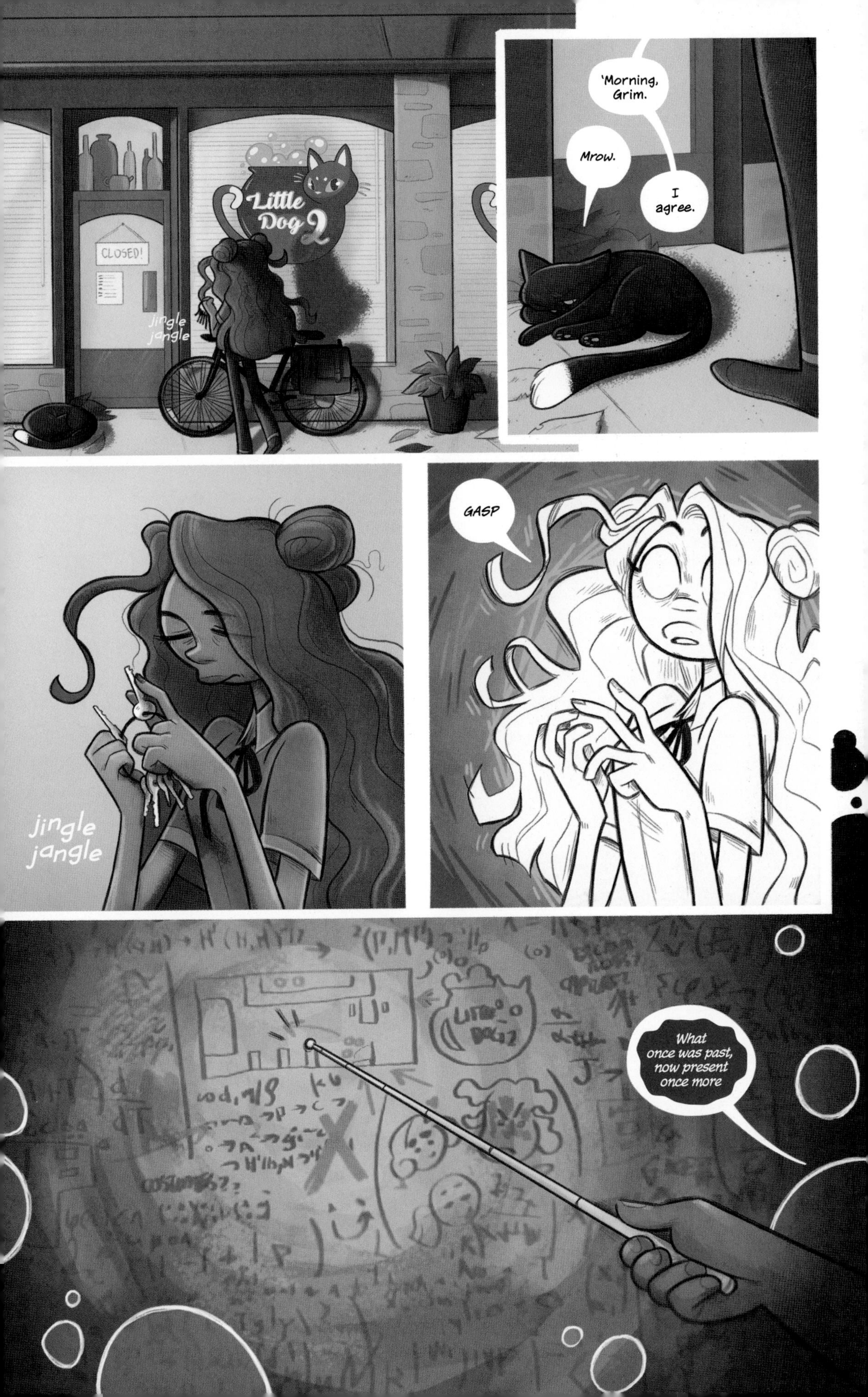
Little Dog 2
CLOSED!
jingle jangle
'Morning, Grim.
Mrow.
I agree.
jingle jangle
GASP
What once was past, now present once more

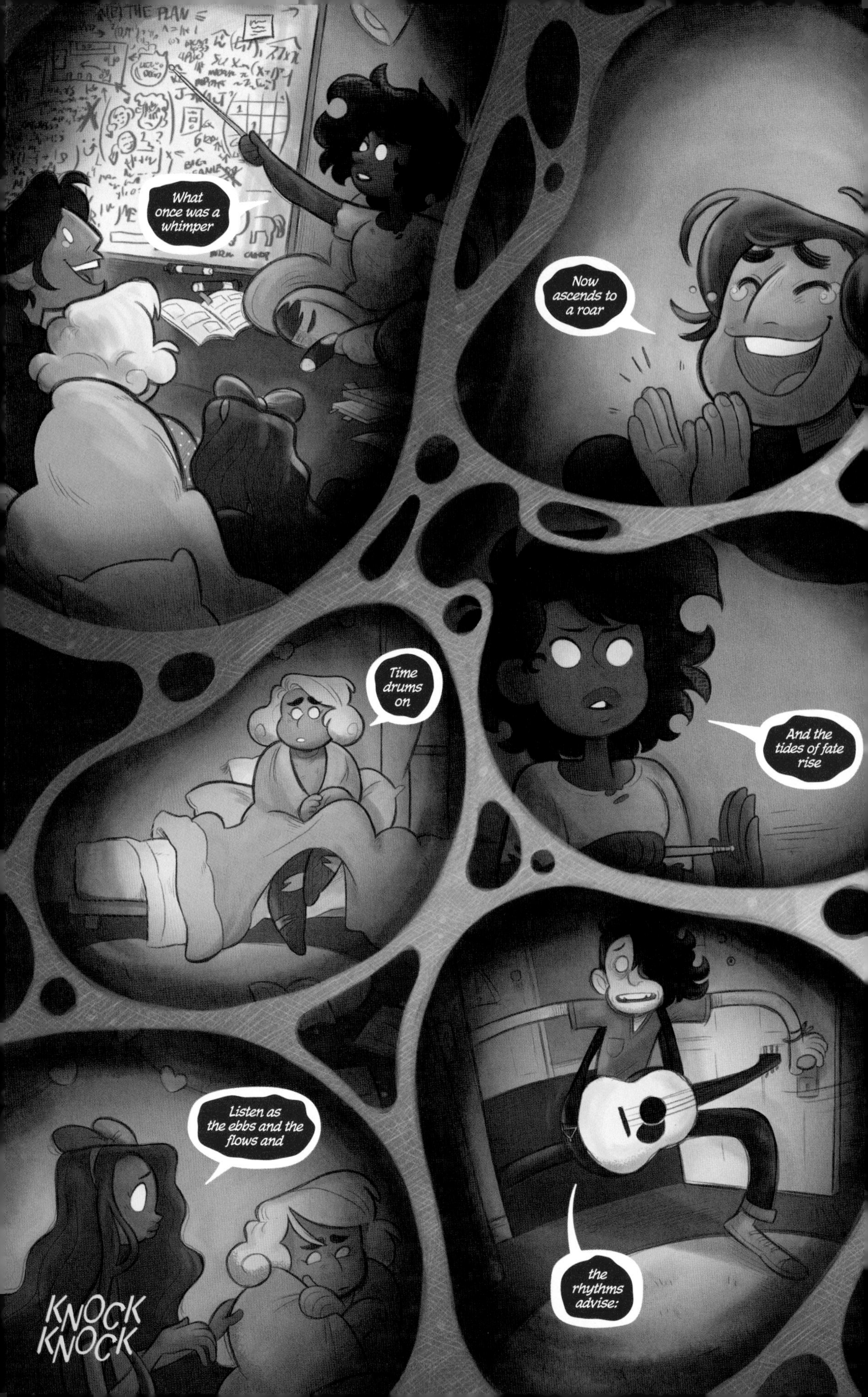
What once was a whimper
Now ascends to a roar
Time drums on
And the tides of fate rise
Listen as the ebbs and the flows and
the rhythms advise:
KNOCK KNOCK

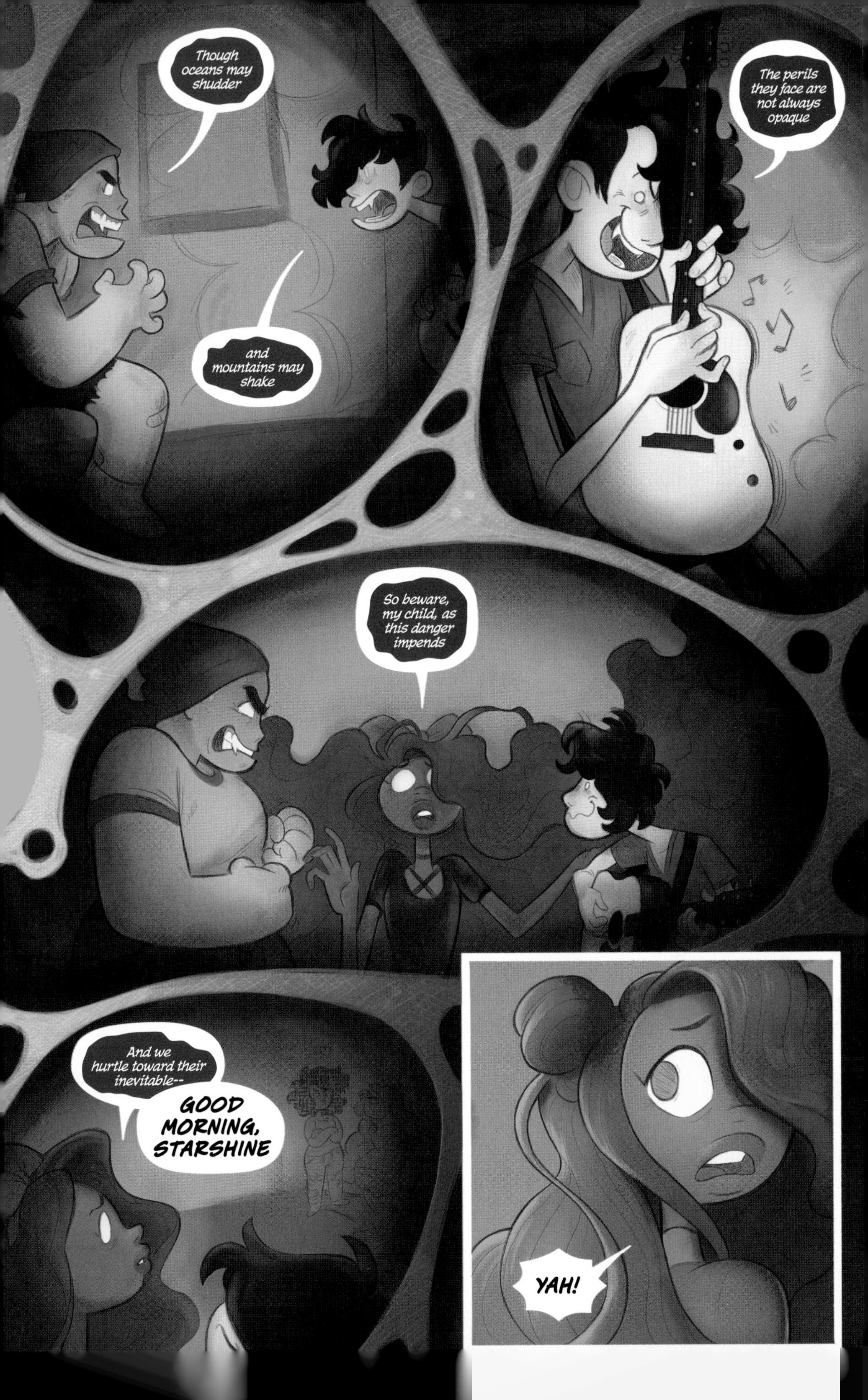
Though oceans may shudder
and mountains may shake
The perils they face are not always opaque
So beware, my child, as this danger impends
And we hurtle toward their inevitable--
GOOD MORNING, STARSHINE
YAH!

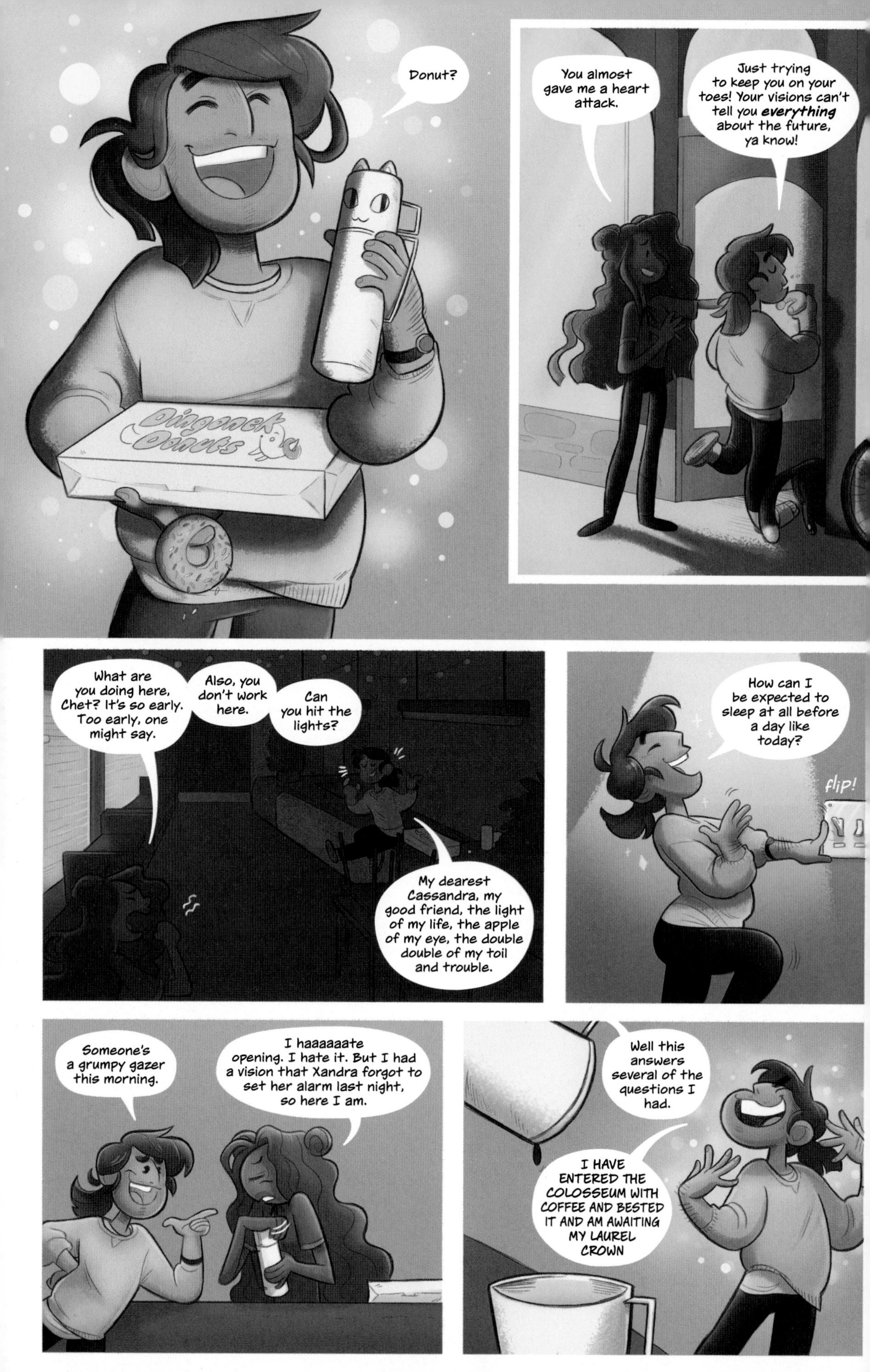
Donut?
You almost gave me a heart attack.
Just trying to keep you on your toes! Your visions can't tell you ***everything*** about the future, ya know!
What are you doing here, Chet? It's so early. Too early, one might say.
Also, you don't work here.
Can you hit the lights?
My dearest Cassandra, my good friend, the light of my life, the apple of my eye, the double double of my toil and trouble.
How can I be expected to sleep at all before a day like today?
flip!
Someone's a grumpy gazer this morning.
I haaaaaate opening. I hate it. But I had a vision that Xandra forgot to set her alarm last night, so here I am.
Well this answers several of the questions I had.
I HAVE ENTERED THE COLOSSEUM WITH COFFEE AND BESTED IT AND AM AWAITING MY LAUREL CROWN

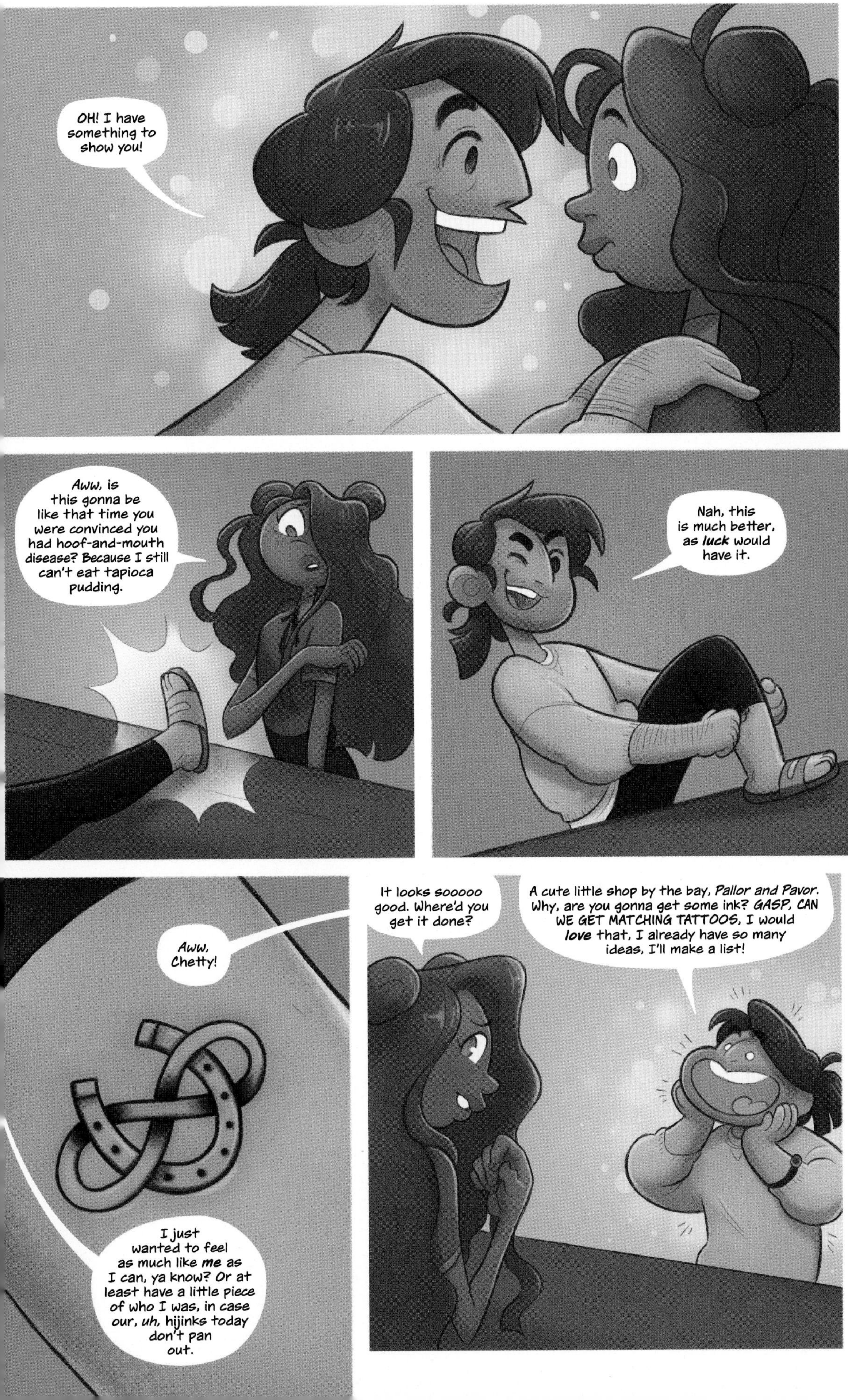
OH! I have something to show you!
Aww, is this gonna be like that time you were convinced you had hoof-and-mouth disease? Because I still can't eat tapioca pudding.
Nah, this is much better, as *luck* would have it.
Aww, Chetty!
I just wanted to feel as much like *me* as I can, ya know? Or at least have a little piece of who I was, in case our, *uh*, hijinks today don't pan out.
It looks sooooo good. Where'd you get it done?
A cute little shop by the bay, *Pallor and Pavor*.
Why, are you gonna get some ink? *GASP*, CAN WE GET MATCHING TATTOOS, I would *love* that, I already have so many ideas, I'll make a list!

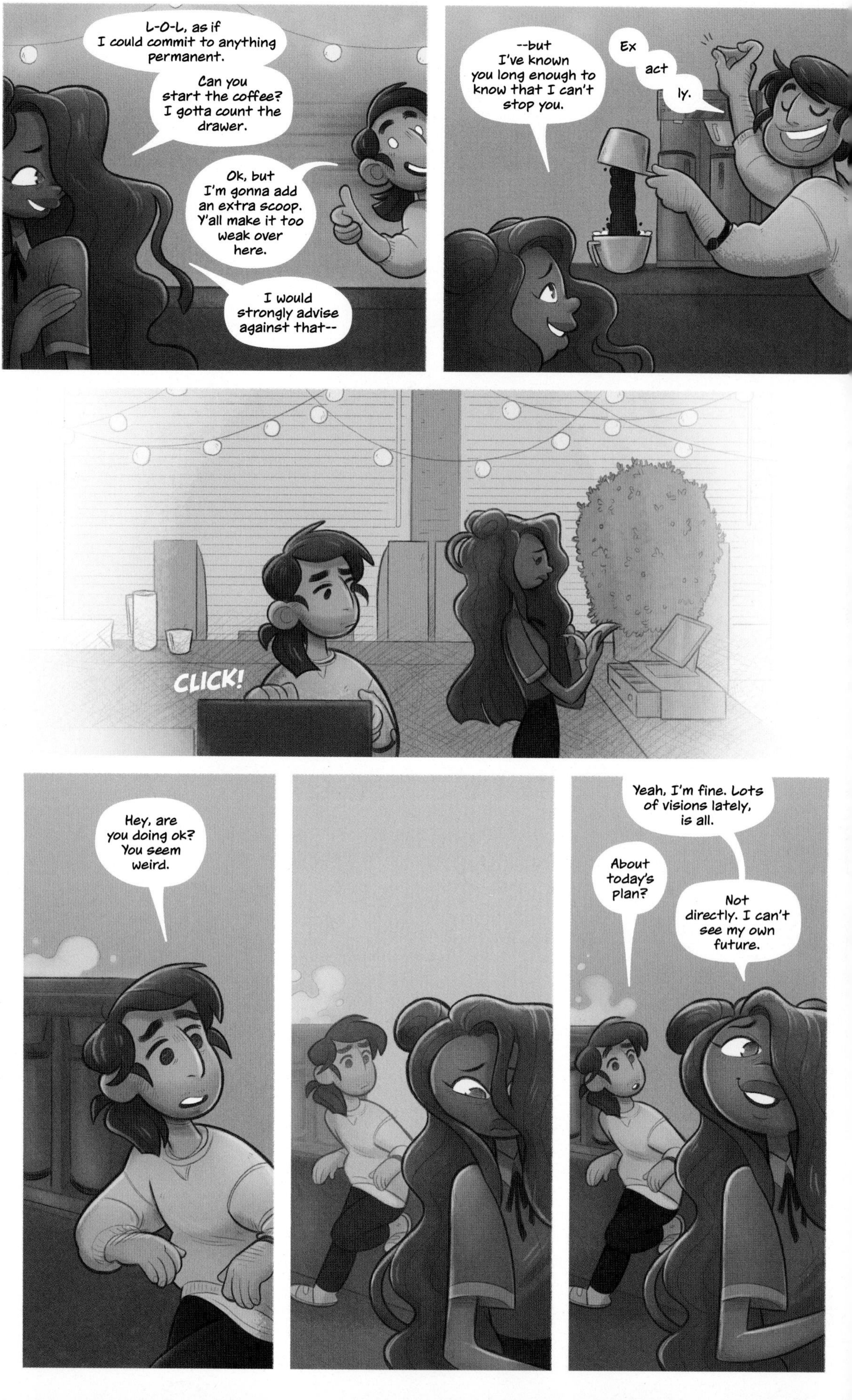
L-O-L, as if I could commit to anything permanent.
Can you start the coffee? I gotta count the drawer.
Ok, but I'm gonna add an extra scoop. Y'all make it too weak over here.
I would strongly advise against that--
--but I've known you long enough to know that I can't stop you.
Ex
act
ly.
CLICK!
Hey, are you doing ok? You seem weird.
Yeah, I'm fine. Lots of visions lately, is all.
About today's plan?
Not directly. I can't see my own future.

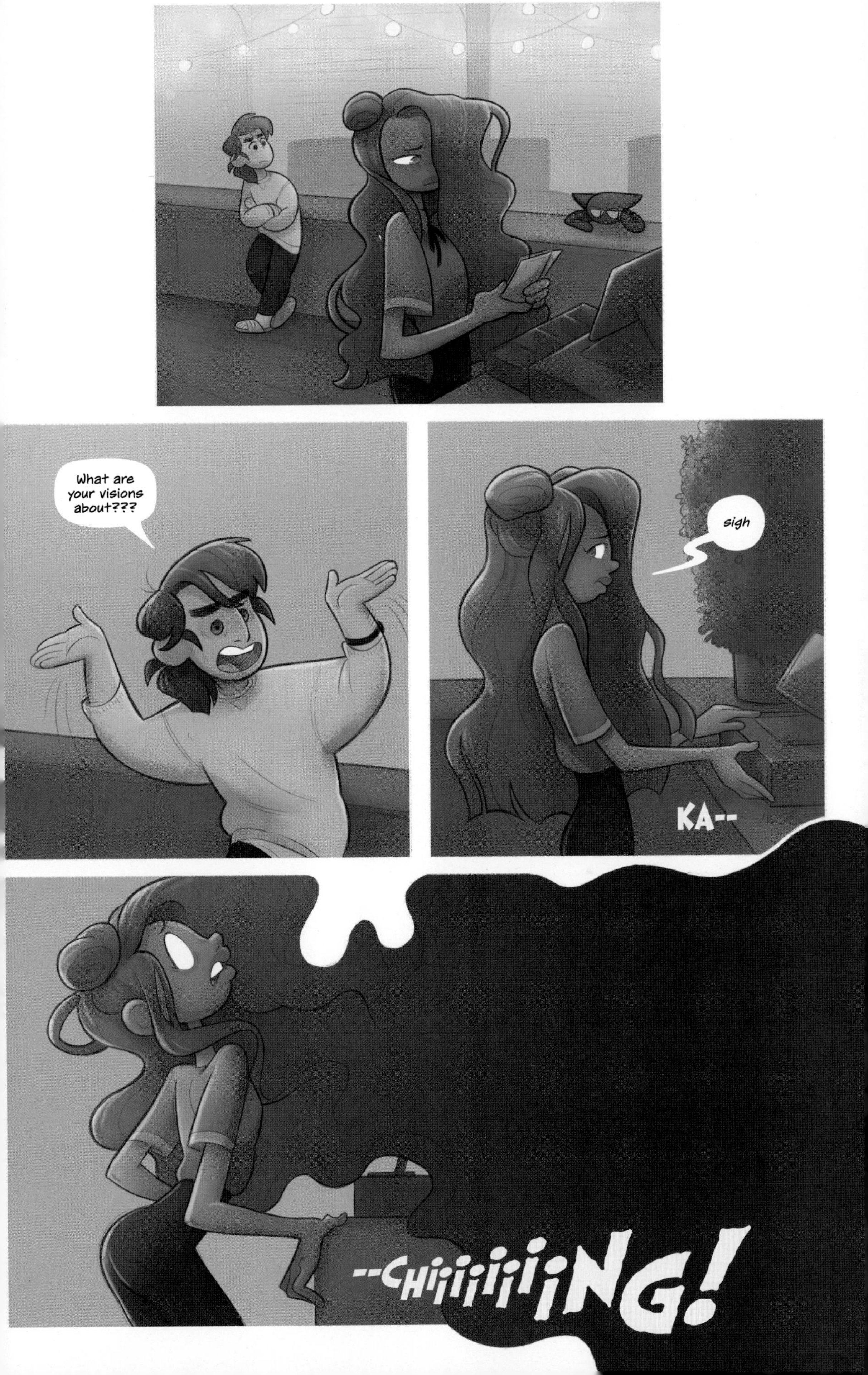
What are your visions about???
sigh
KA--
--CHiiiiiiiiNG!

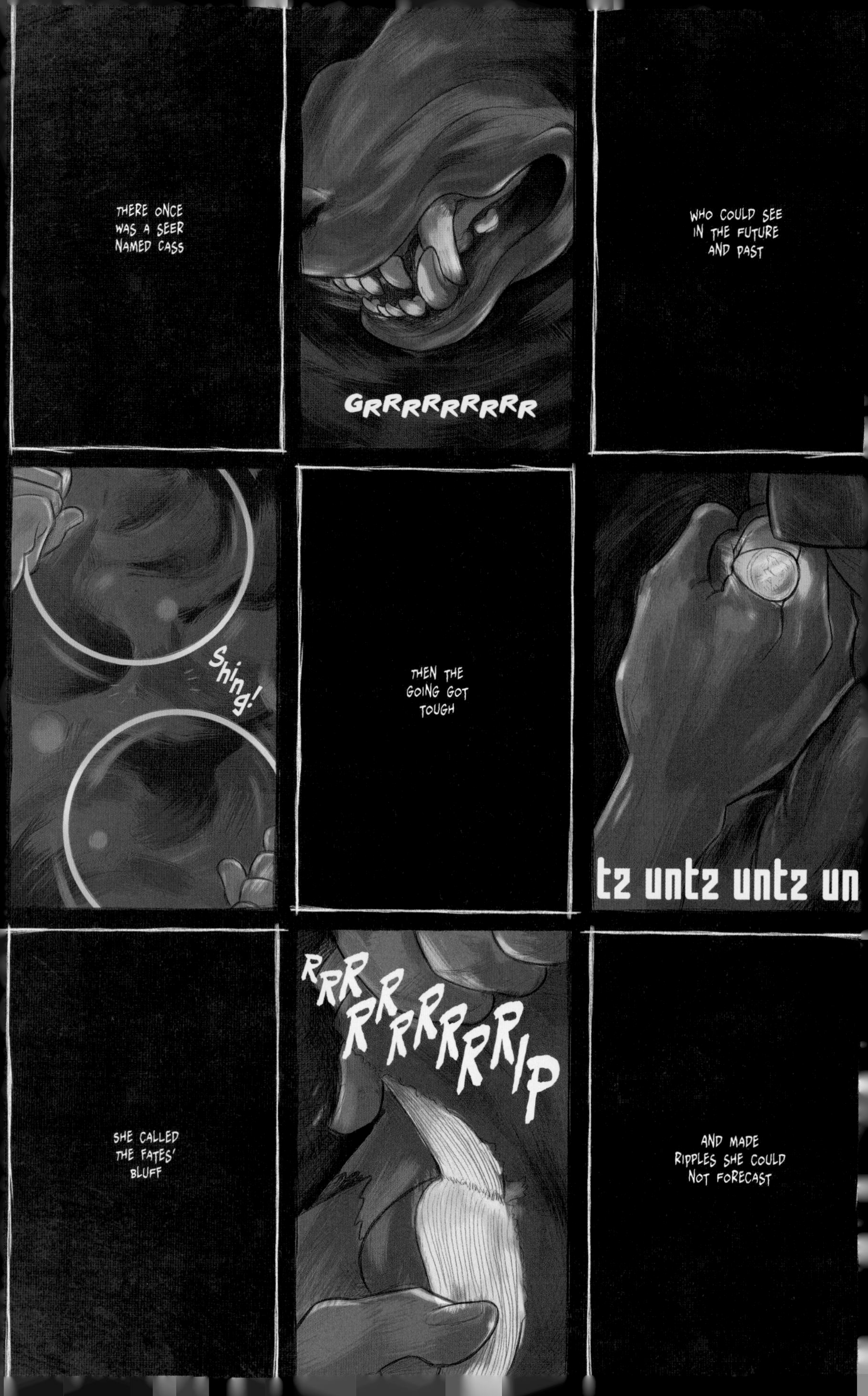
THERE ONCE WAS A SEER NAMED CASS
GRRRRRRRRR
WHO COULD SEE IN THE FUTURE AND PAST
Shing!
THEN THE GOING GOT TOUGH
tz untz untz un
SHE CALLED THE FATES' BLUFF
RRR RR RRRRRRIP
AND MADE RIPPLES SHE COULD NOT FORECAST

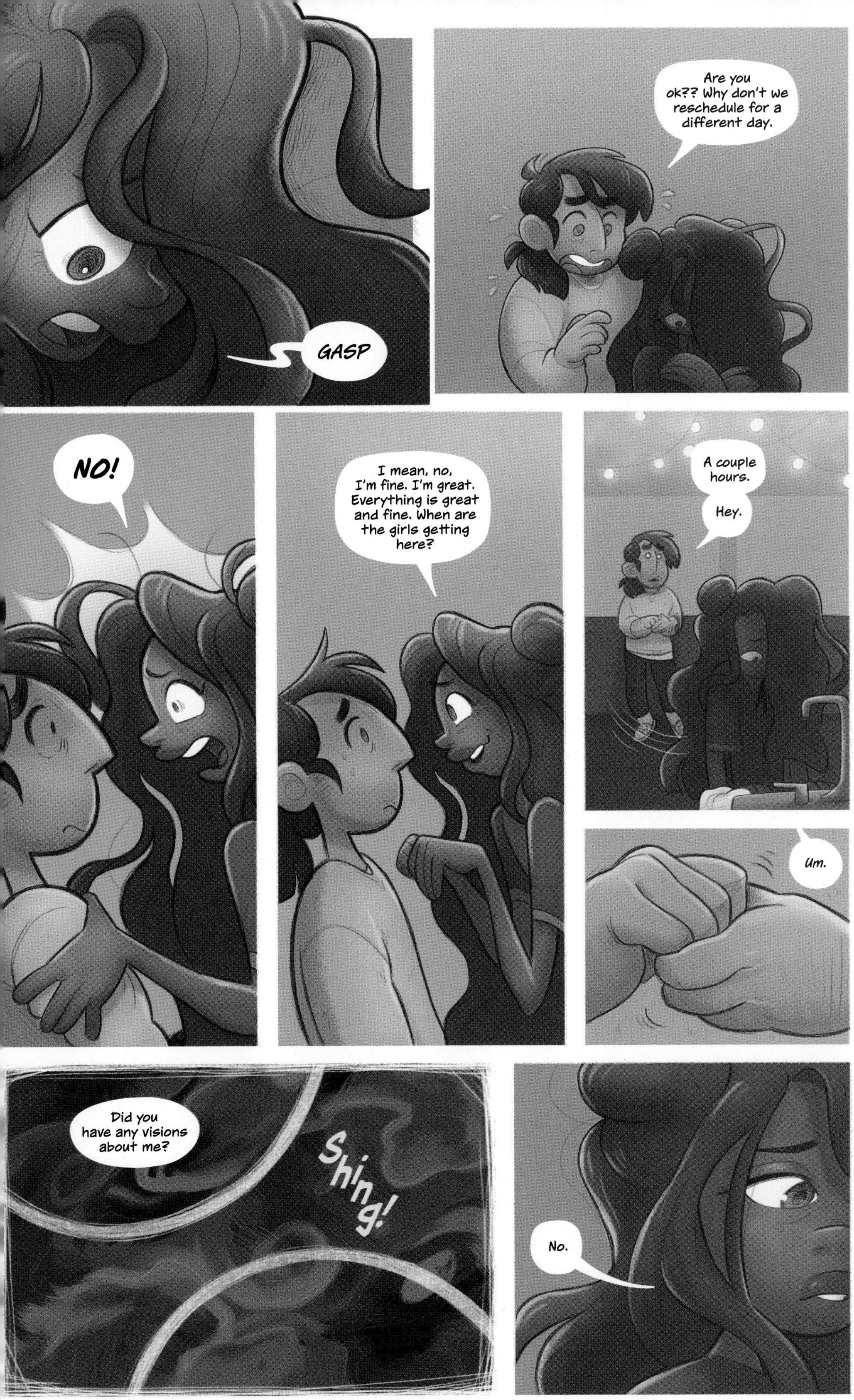
GASP
Are you ok?? Why don't we reschedule for a different day.
NO!
I mean, no, I'm fine. I'm great. Everything is great and fine. When are the girls getting here?
A couple hours.
Hey.
Um.
Did you have any visions about me?
Shing!
No.

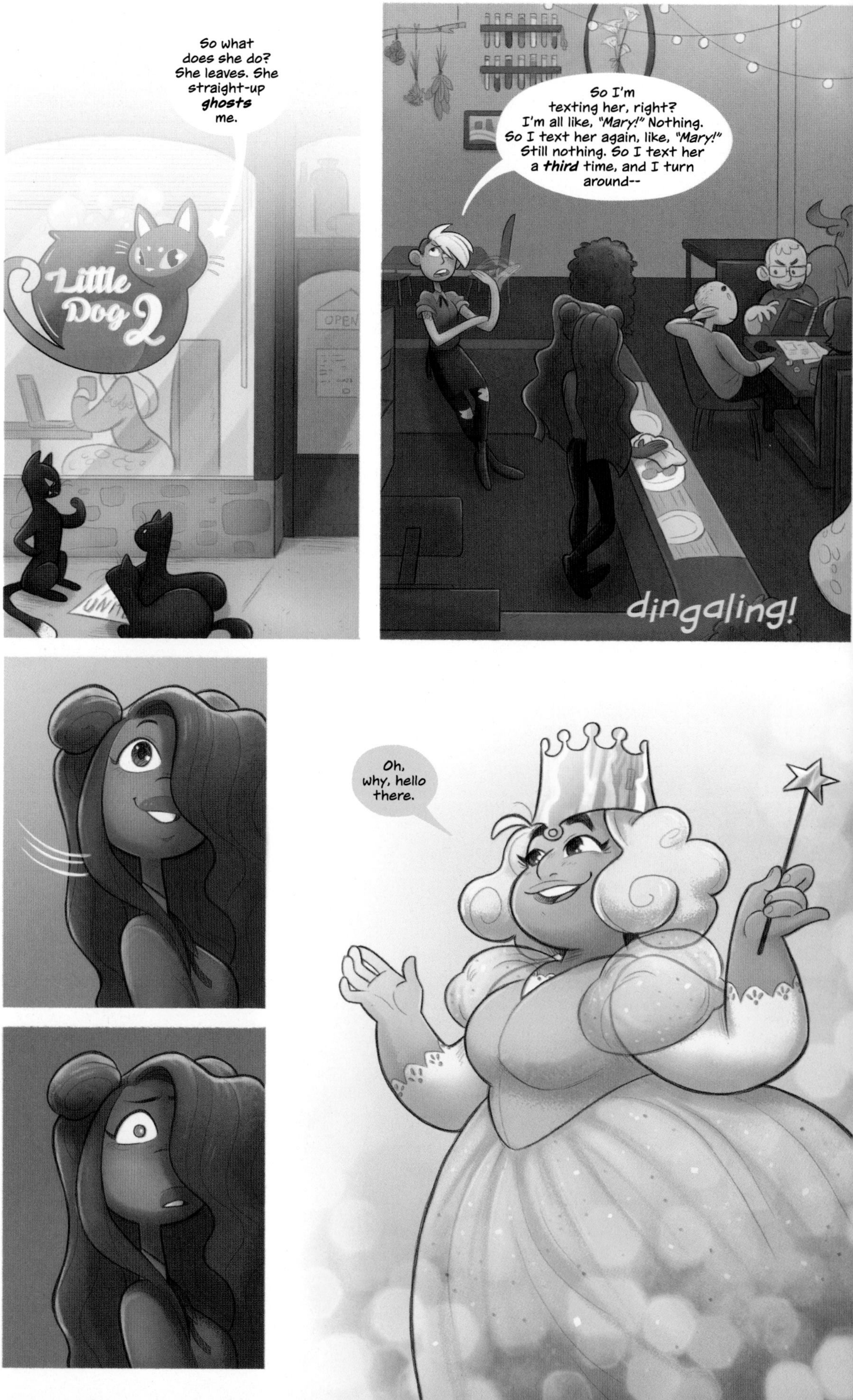
So what does she do? She leaves. She straight-up ghosts me.
Little Dog 2
OPEN
So I'm texting her, right? I'm all like, "Mary!" Nothing. So I text her again, like, "Mary!" Still nothing. So I text her a third time, and I turn around--
dingaling!
Oh, why, hello there.

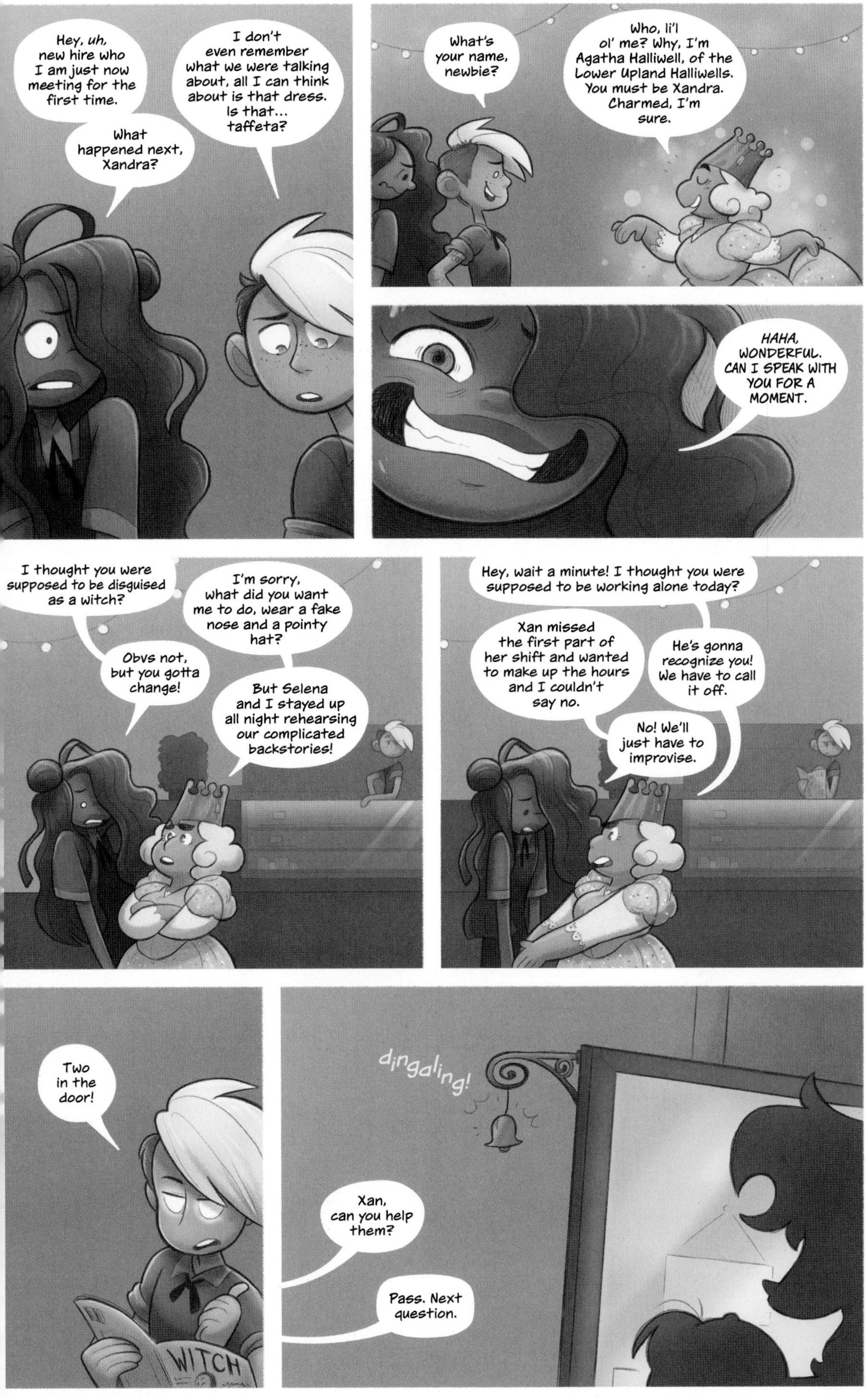
Hey, uh, new hire who I am just now meeting for the first time.
What happened next, Xandra?
I don't even remember what we were talking about, all I can think about is that dress. Is that... taffeta?
What's your name, newbie?
Who, li'l ol' me? Why, I'm Agatha Halliwell, of the Lower Upland Halliwells. You must be Xandra. Charmed, I'm sure.
HAHA, WONDERFUL. CAN I SPEAK WITH YOU FOR A MOMENT.
I thought you were supposed to be disguised as a witch?
Obvs not, but you gotta change!
I'm sorry, what did you want me to do, wear a fake nose and a pointy hat?
But Selena and I stayed up all night rehearsing our complicated backstories!
Hey, wait a minute! I thought you were supposed to be working alone today?
Xan missed the first part of her shift and wanted to make up the hours and I couldn't say no.
He's gonna recognize you! We have to call it off.
No! We'll just have to improvise.
Two in the door!
WITCH
Xan, can you help them?
Pass. Next question.
dingaling!

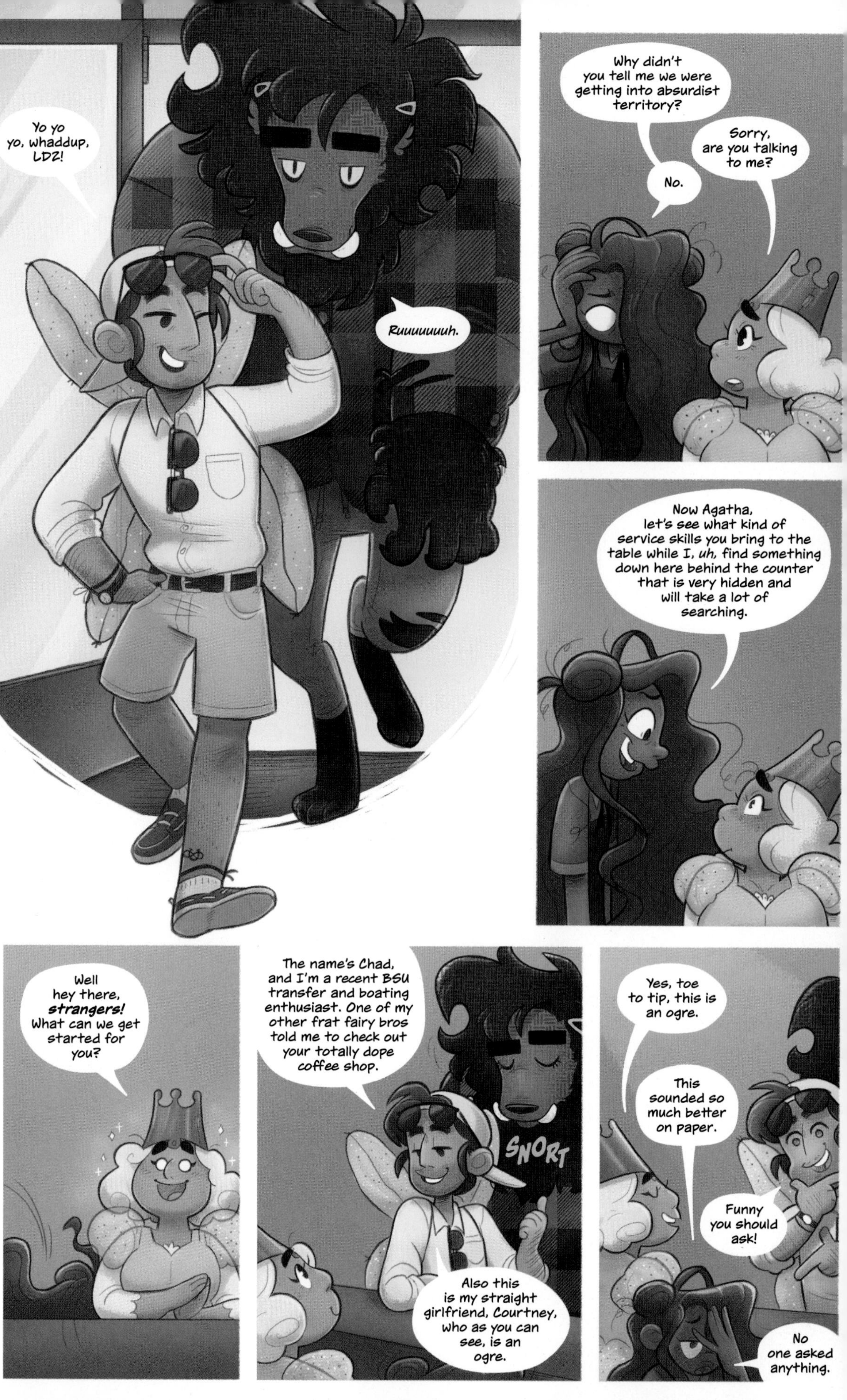

Yo yo yo, whaddup, LDZ!
Ruuuuuuuh.
Why didn't you tell me we were getting into absurdist territory?
No.
Sorry, are you talking to me?
Now Agatha, let's see what kind of service skills you bring to the table while I, *uh,* find something down here behind the counter that is very hidden and will take a lot of searching.
Well hey there, ***strangers!*** What can we get started for you?
The name's Chad, and I'm a recent BSU transfer and boating enthusiast. One of my other frat fairy bros told me to check out your totally dope coffee shop.
SNORT
Also this is my straight girlfriend, Courtney, who as you can see, is an ogre.
Yes, toe to tip, this is an ogre.
This sounded so much better on paper.
Funny you should ask!
No one asked anything.

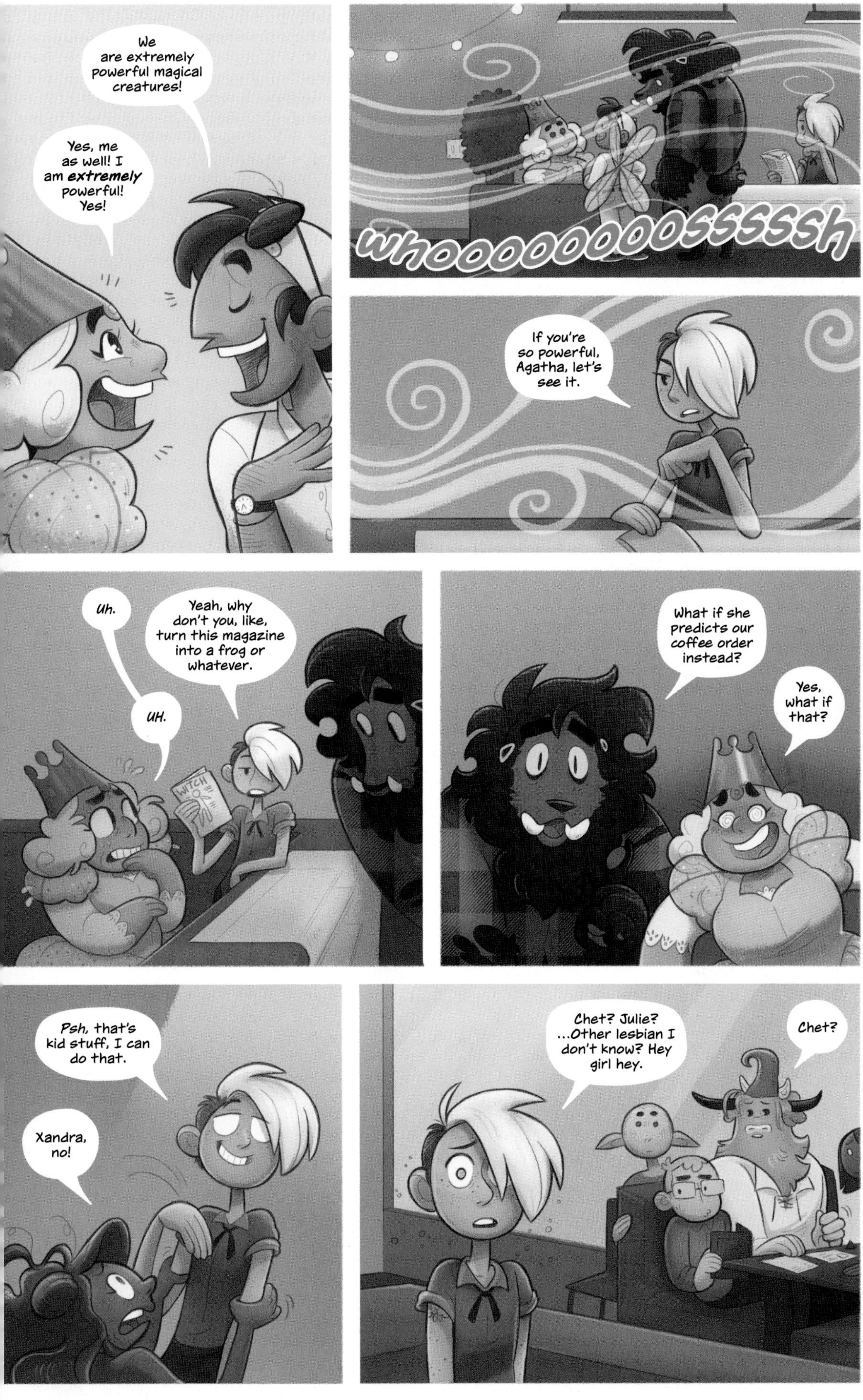
We are extremely powerful magical creatures!
Yes, me as well! I am *extremely* powerful! Yes!
whoooooooosssssh
If you're so powerful, Agatha, let's see it.
Uh.
Yeah, why don't you, like, turn this magazine into a frog or whatever.
UH.
WITCH
What if she predicts our coffee order instead?
Yes, what if that?
Psh, that's kid stuff, I can do that.
Xandra, no!
Chet? Julie? ...Other lesbian I don't know? Hey girl hey.
Chet?

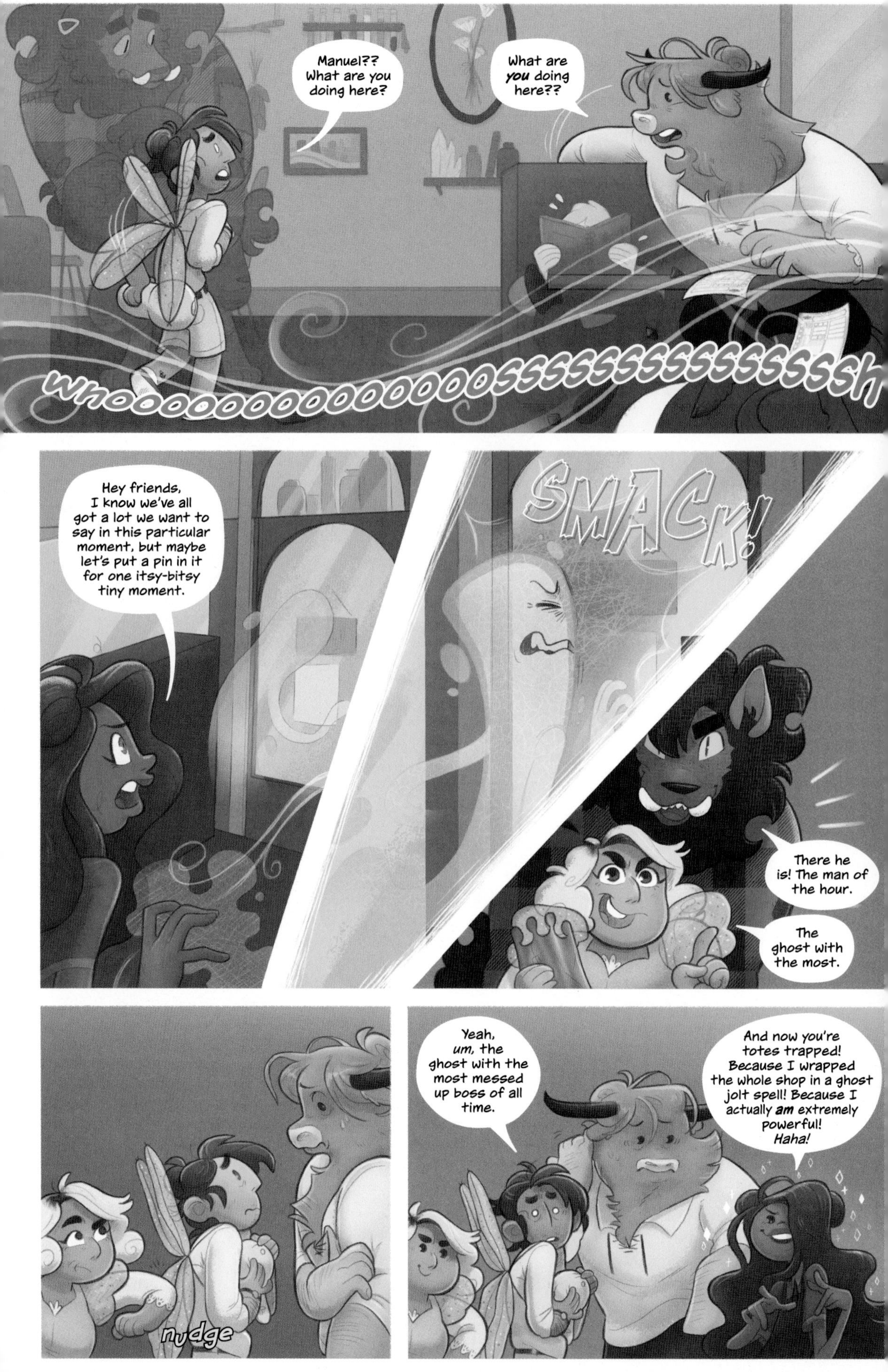
Manuel?? What are you doing here?
What are *you* doing here??
WHOOOOOOOOOOOOOOOOSSSSSSSSSSSSSSSSH
Hey friends, I know we've all got a lot we want to say in this particular moment, but maybe let's put a pin in it for one itsy-bitsy tiny moment.
SMACK!
There he is! The man of the hour.
The ghost with the most.
nudge
Yeah, *um*, the ghost with the most messed up boss of all time.
And now you're totes trapped! Because I wrapped the whole shop in a ghost jolt spell! Because I actually ***am*** extremely powerful! *Haha!*

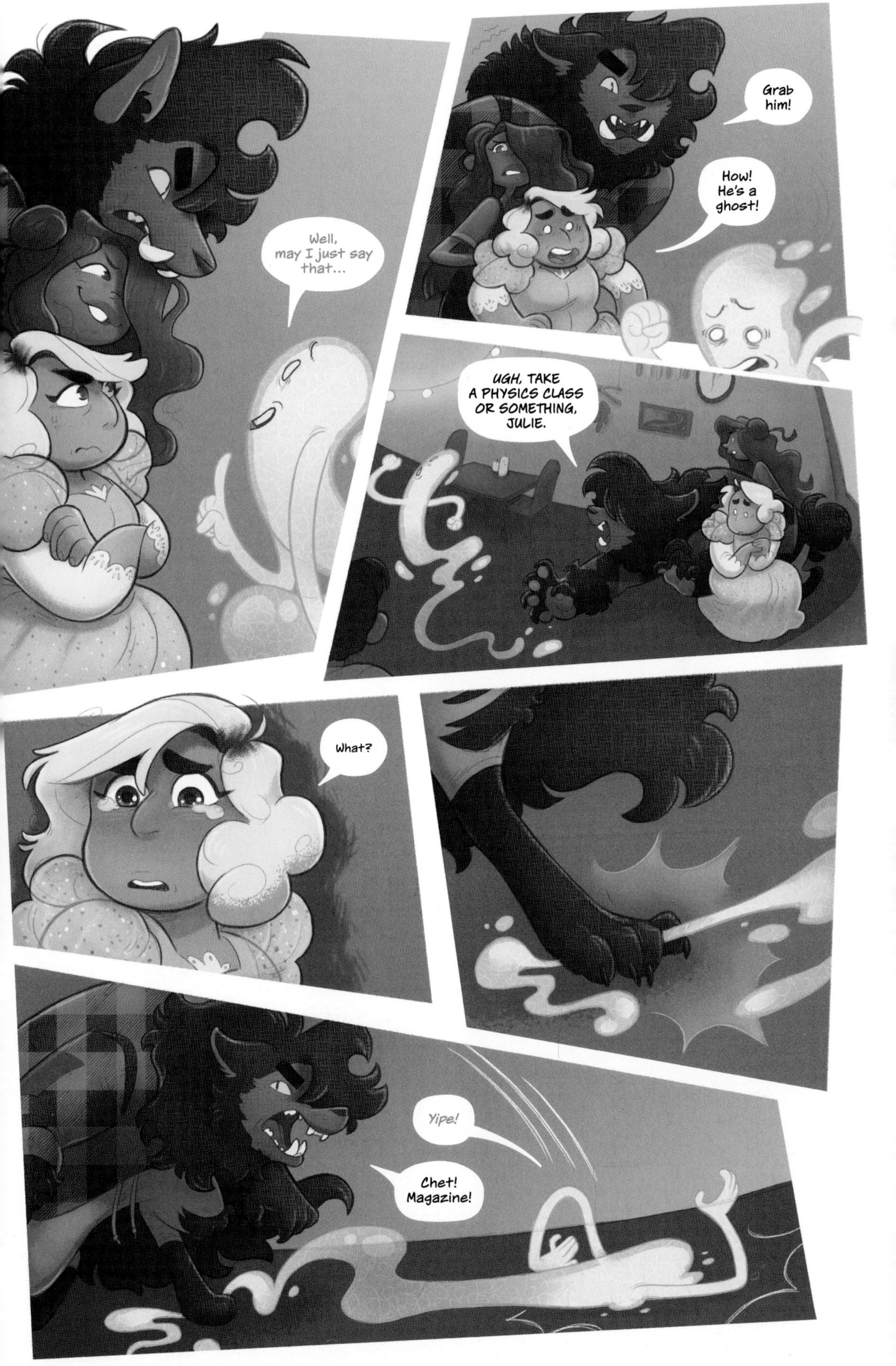
Well, may I just say that...
Grab him!
How! He's a ghost!
UGH, TAKE A PHYSICS CLASS OR SOMETHING, JULIE.
What?
Yipe!
Chet! Magazine!

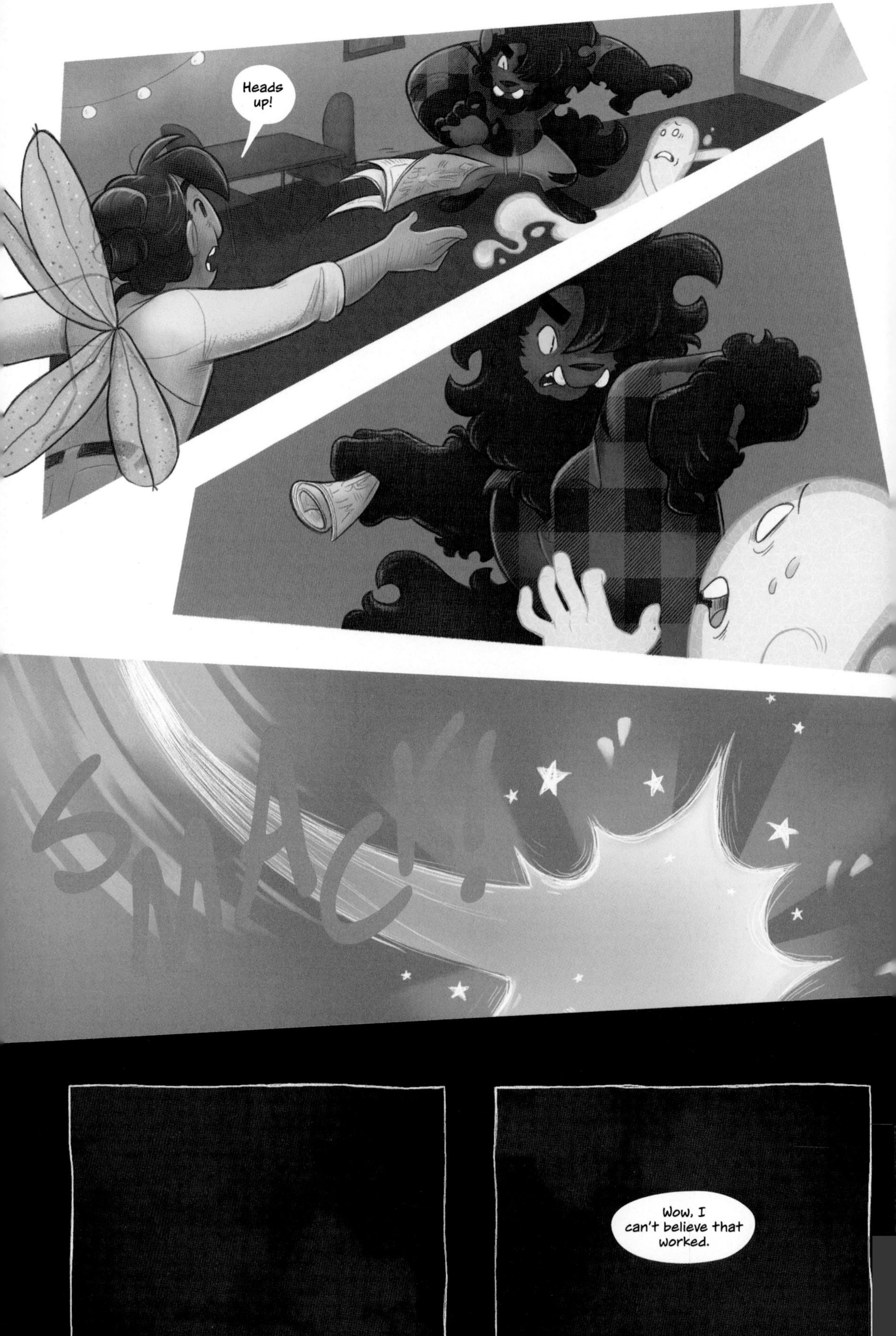
Heads up!
Wow, I can't believe that worked.

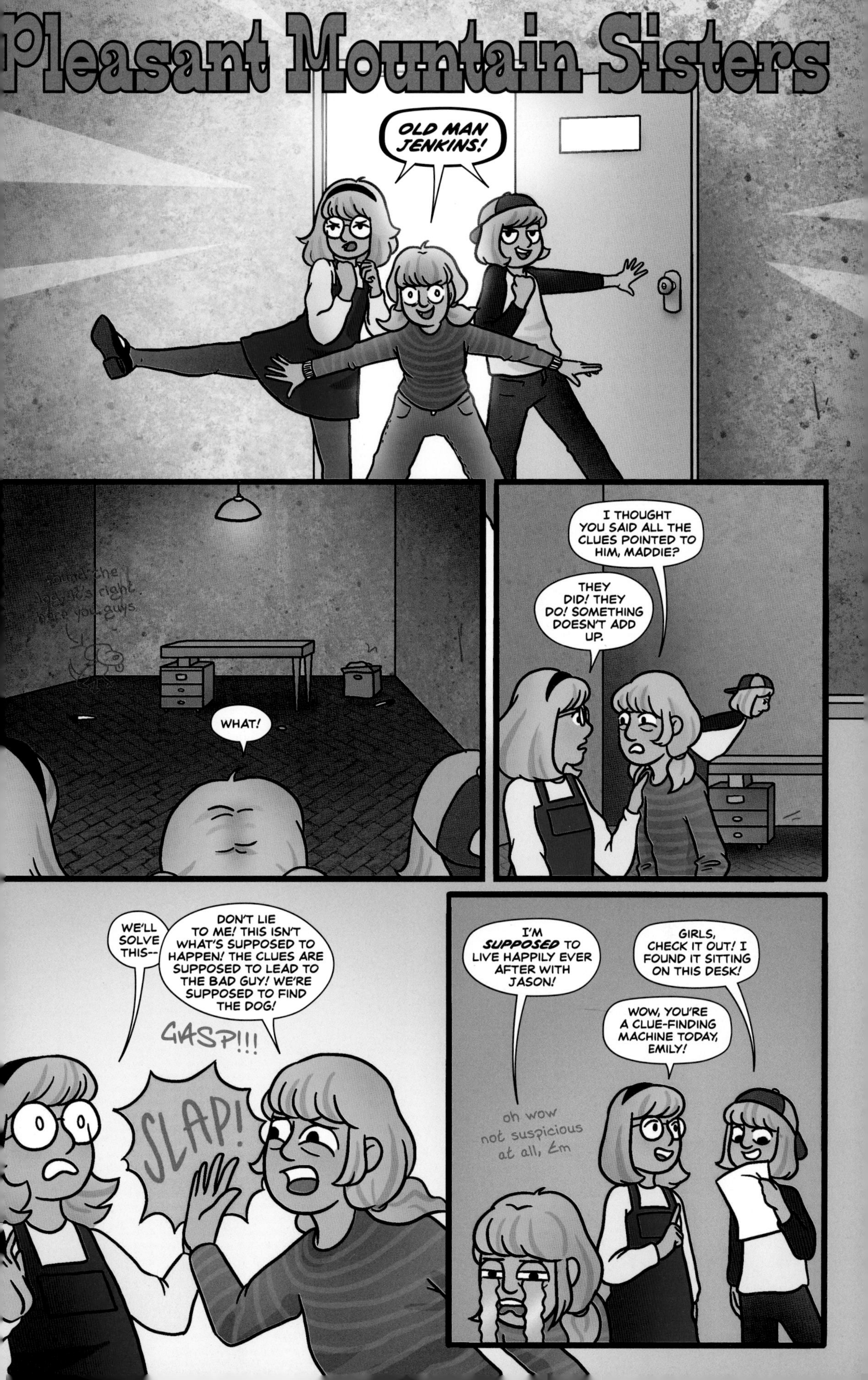

Pleasant Mountain Sisters
OLD MAN JENKINS!
found the dog it's right here you guys.
WHAT!
I THOUGHT YOU SAID ALL THE CLUES POINTED TO HIM, MADDIE?
THEY DID! THEY DO! SOMETHING DOESN'T ADD UP.
WE'LL SOLVE THIS--
DON'T LIE TO ME! THIS ISN'T WHAT'S SUPPOSED TO HAPPEN! THE CLUES ARE SUPPOSED TO LEAD TO THE BAD GUY! WE'RE SUPPOSED TO FIND THE DOG!
GASP!!!
SLAP!
I'M *SUPPOSED* TO LIVE HAPPILY EVER AFTER WITH JASON!
GIRLS, CHECK IT OUT! I FOUND IT SITTING ON THIS DESK!
WOW, YOU'RE A CLUE-FINDING MACHINE TODAY, EMILY!
oh wow not suspicious at all, Em

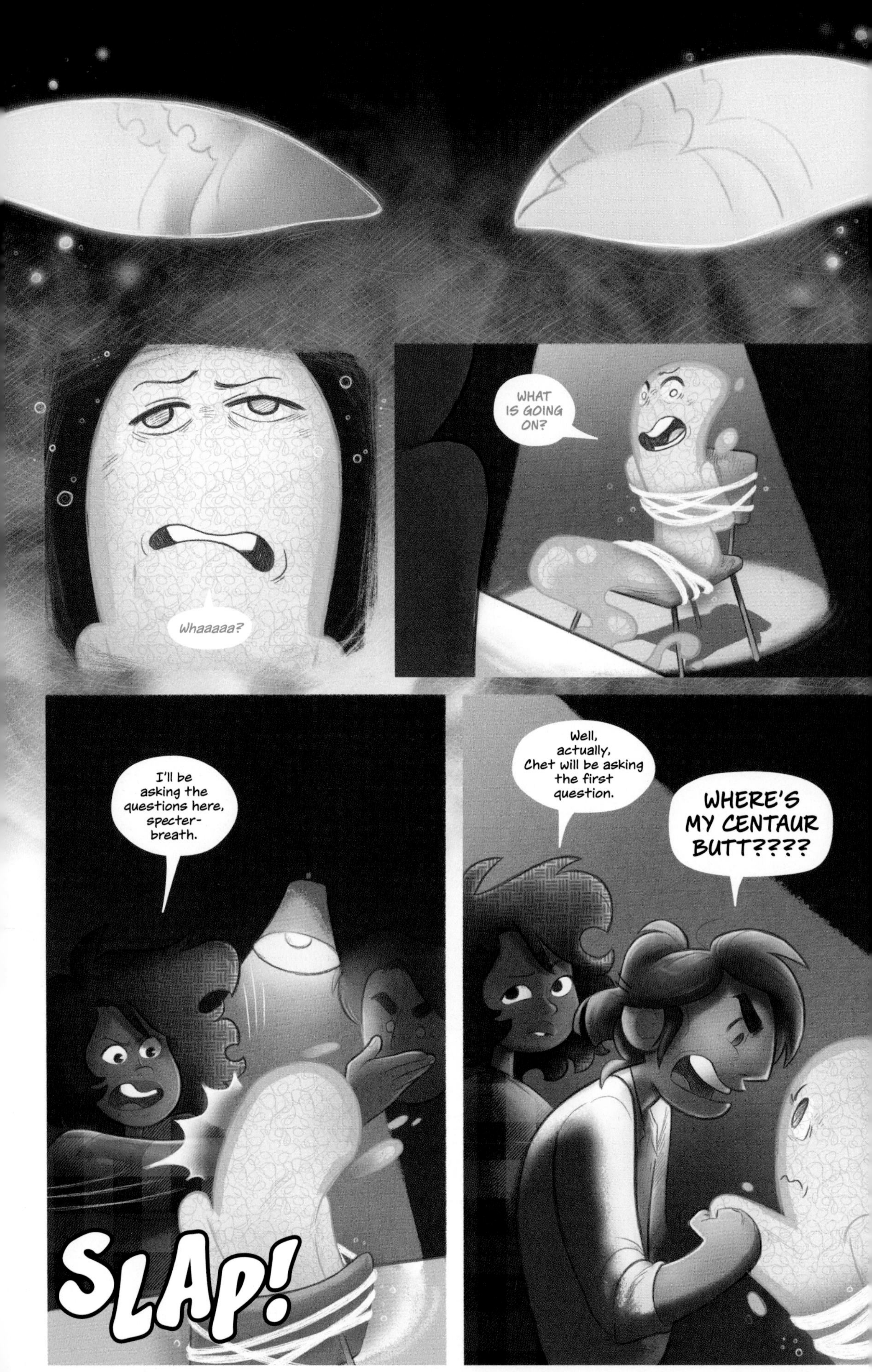
Whaaaaa?
WHAT IS GOING ON?
I'll be asking the questions here, specter-breath.
SLAP!
Well, actually, Chet will be asking the first question.
WHERE'S MY CENTAUR BUTT????

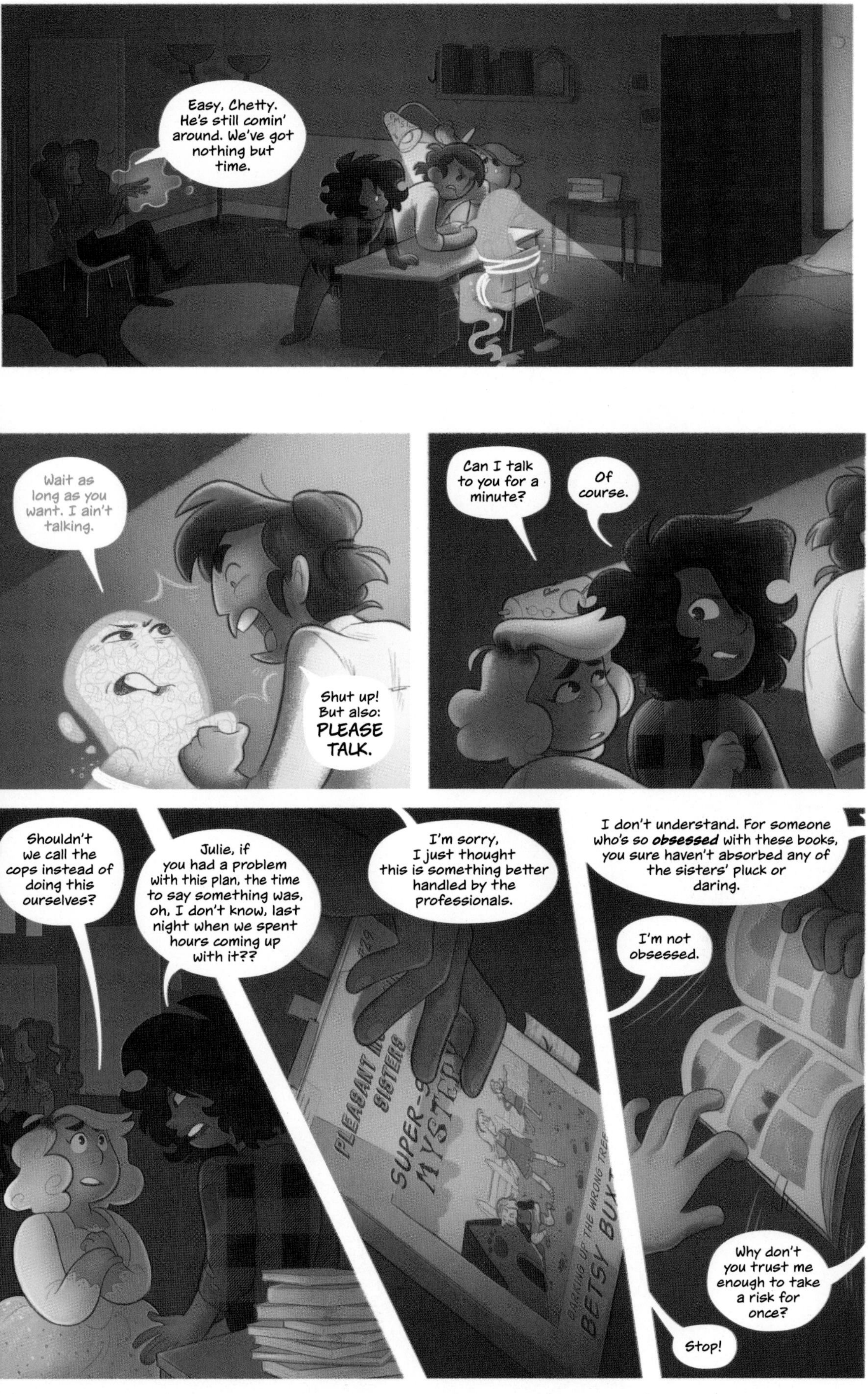
Easy, Chetty. He's still comin' around. We've got nothing but time.
Wait as long as you want. I ain't talking.
Shut up! But also: PLEASE TALK.
Can I talk to you for a minute?
Of course.
Shouldn't we call the cops instead of doing this ourselves?
Julie, if you had a problem with this plan, the time to say something was, oh, I don't know, last night when we spent hours coming up with it??
I'm sorry, I just thought this is something better handled by the professionals.
I don't understand. For someone who's so ***obsessed*** with these books, you sure haven't absorbed any of the sisters' pluck or daring.
I'm not obsessed.
Why don't you trust me enough to take a risk for once?
Stop!

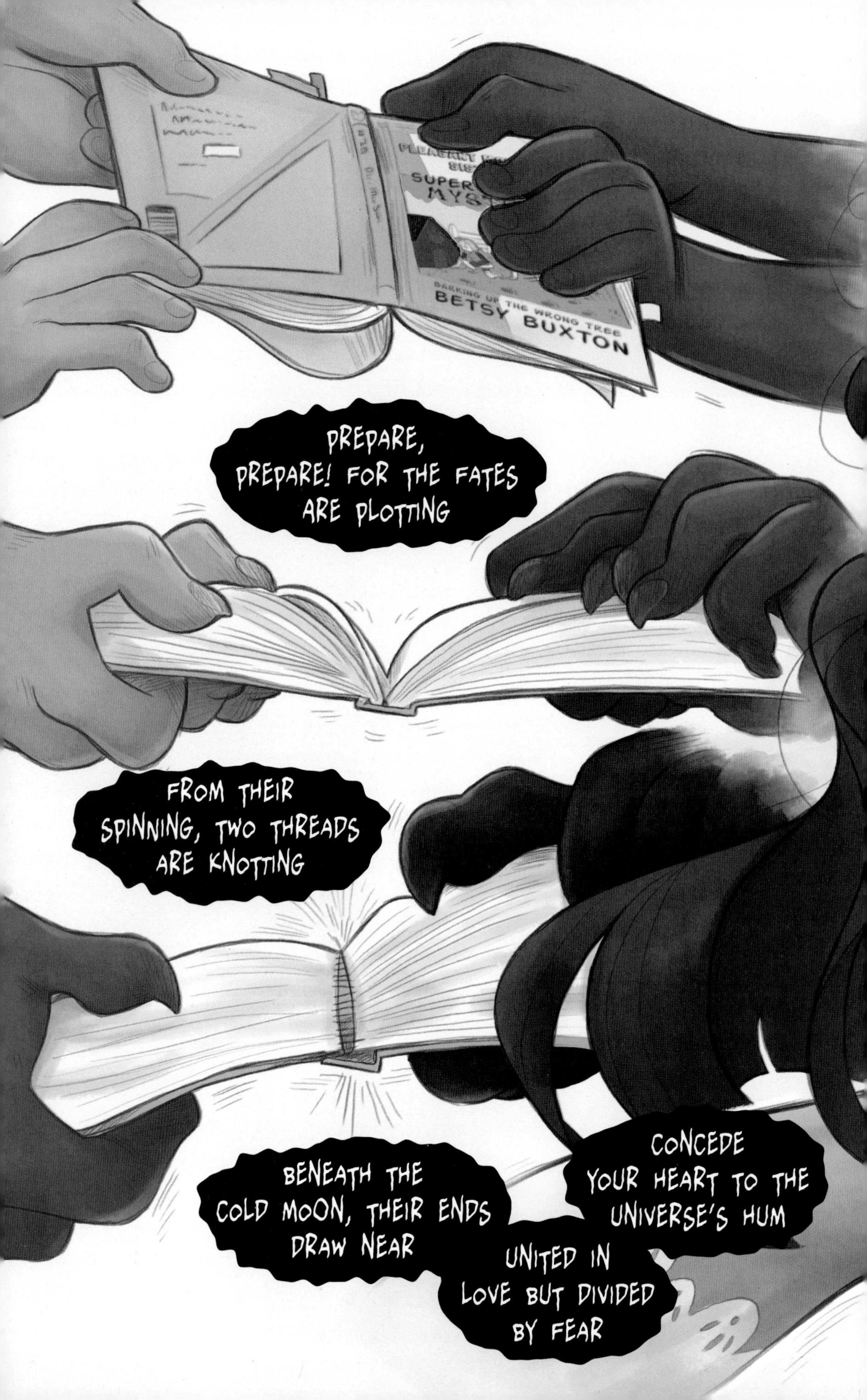
BARKING UP THE WRONG TREE
BETSY BUXTON
PREPARE, PREPARE! FOR THE FATES ARE PLOTTING
FROM THEIR SPINNING, TWO THREADS ARE KNOTTING
BENEATH THE COLD MOON, THEIR ENDS DRAW NEAR
UNITED IN LOVE BUT DIVIDED BY FEAR
CONCEDE YOUR HEART TO THE UNIVERSE'S HUM

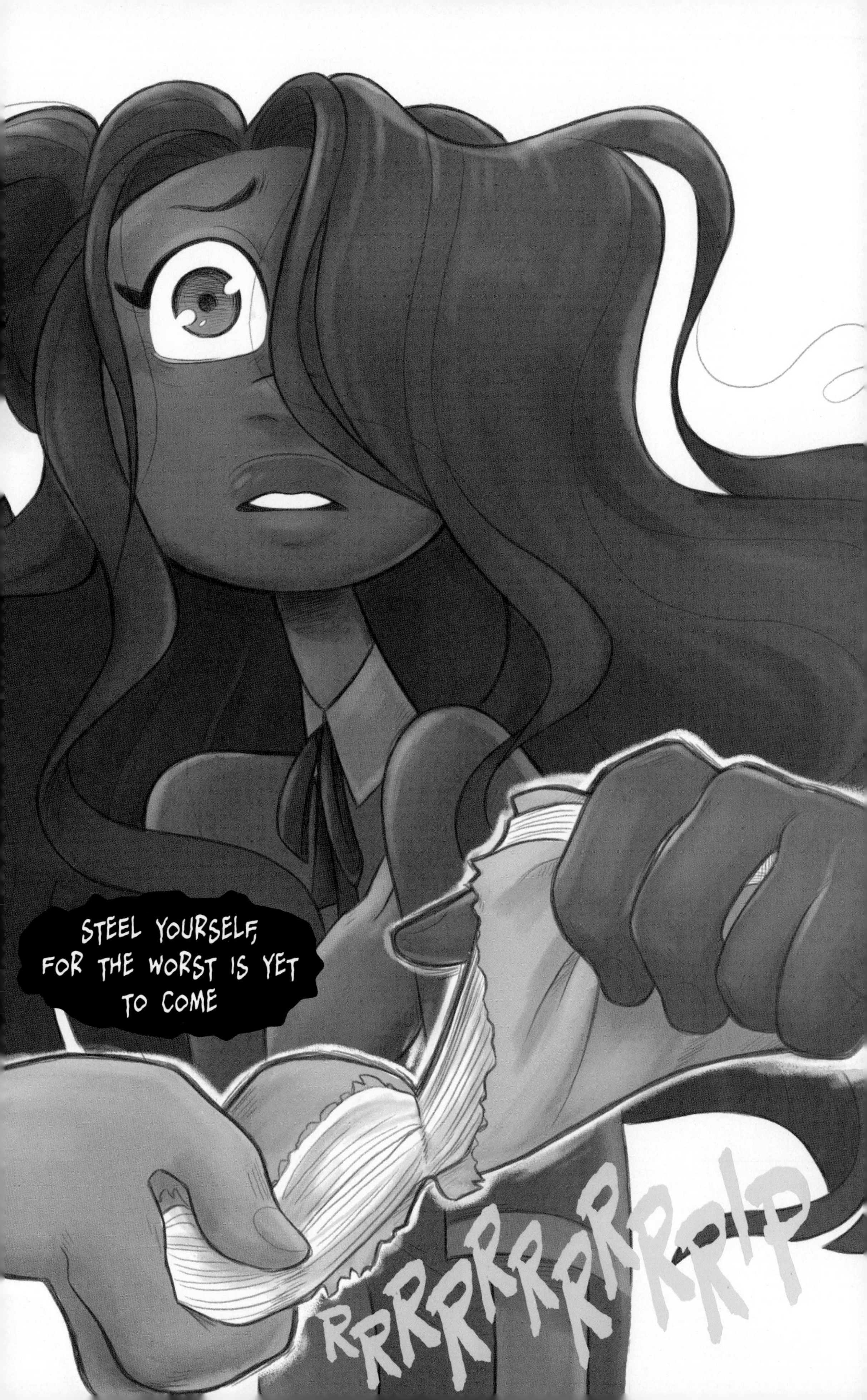
STEEL YOURSELF, FOR THE WORST IS YET TO COME
RRRRRRRRRIP

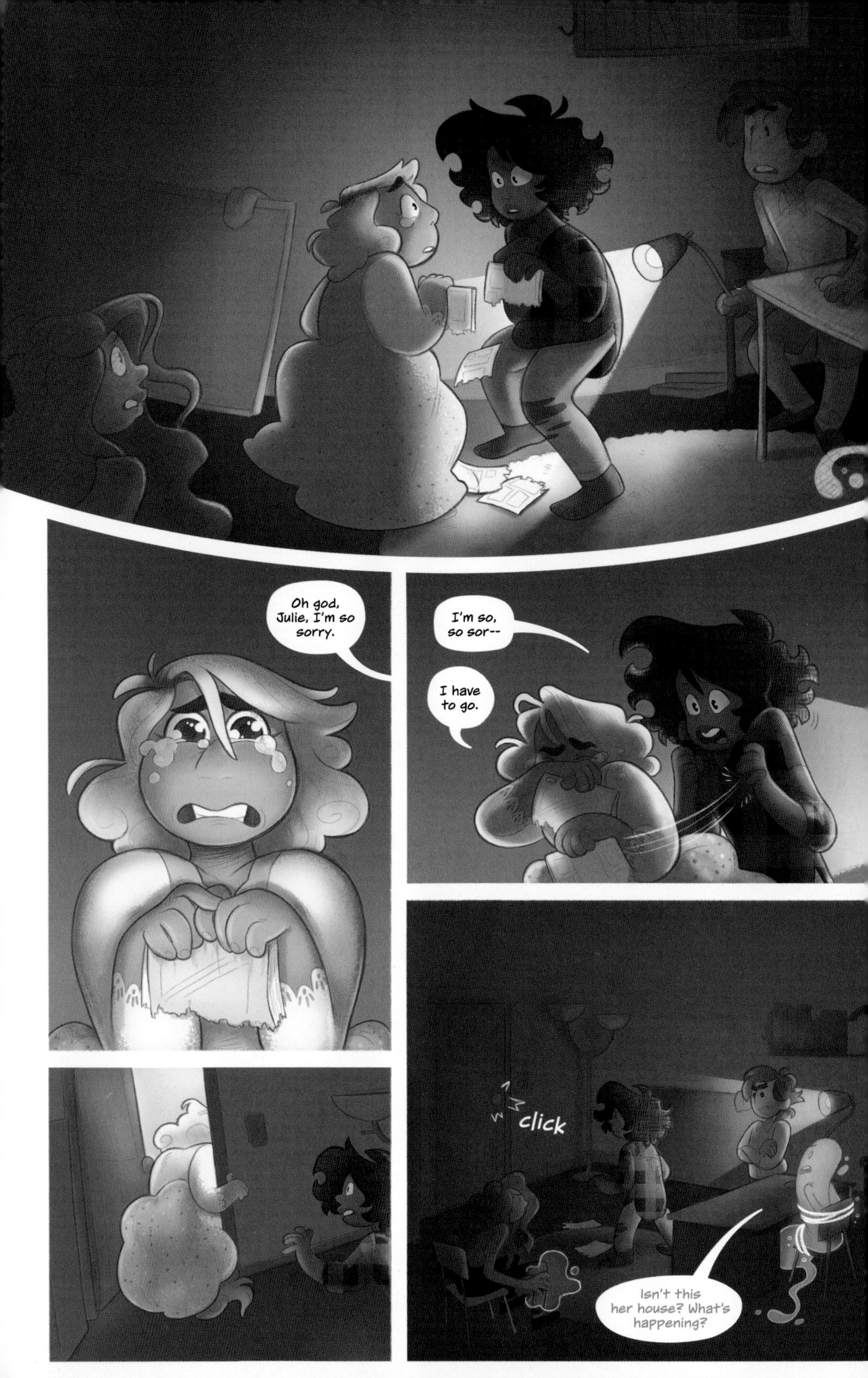
Oh god, Julie, I'm so sorry.
I'm so, so sor--
I have to go.
click
Isn't this her house? What's happening?

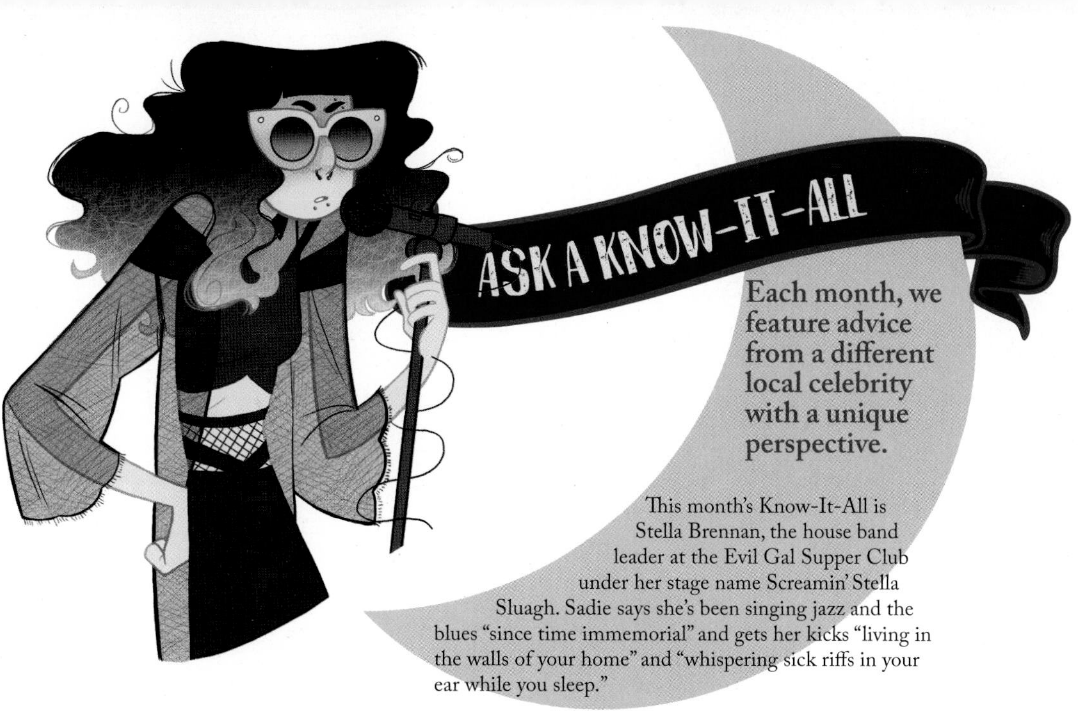
ASK A KNOW-IT-ALL

Each month, we feature advice from a different local celebrity with a unique perspective.

This month's Know-It-All is Stella Brennan, the house band leader at the Evil Gal Supper Club under her stage name Screamin' Stella Sluagh. Sadie says she's been singing jazz and the blues "since time immemorial" and gets her kicks "living in the walls of your home" and "whispering sick riffs in your ear while you sleep."

Dear Know-It-All,
My upstairs neighbor is an early riser. He tries to be, anyway. His alarm starts going off at 6 a.m. and then beeps for a full minute, every five minutes until he gets out of bed, usually an hour later! I'm losing my mind! How can I approach him about his snooze button addiction?

- Rising With The Sun (Unfortunately)

Rising,
Zibby do wah zibby do wah zib zib zib zib zoooo wah how can you be sure there's an alarm clock at all when all you can hear is the beep, the beep, the beep, the beep, the beep, the beep, the beep blasting through your walls?
[Writer's note: At this point, she began snapping.]
Open your mind and consider all the possibilities, like that you don't have an upstairs neighbor. You never had an upstairs neighbor, baby, because you've got something better: a true-ah, a blue-ah, it's a sluagh. It's nothing personal. You may have left your west-facing window open at night, and now you've got yourself a new friend who only wants to party, and by "party" I do mean "drive you crazy." Now-ow-ow-ow of course I personally have no knowledge of your apartment in particular, unless it's the one on the corner of Dennison and 5th, in which case I am going to have to take the fifth myself.

Dear Know-It-All,
Any advice on dealing with someone putting their feet on the back of your seat in a movie theater?

-Vexed in Vancouver

Vexed,
Dah doo ya, dah doo bow, do-doo dah do-doo dah wooo weeeeeee ohh the seats and the feets and the feets on the seats and repeat-eat-eat-eat yeah you eat a bunch of popcorn and you sit down in your seat and before the movie's over yeah you stretch out all your feets and your seats and your popcorn and your Cracker Jack and your candy cane and your marzipan and your zip zip zip zip zop-a-doo day and before
[Editor's note: Grace, what is this? You told me this would be an advice column. How did it devolve into, what is this, whisper scatting?? This is not useful at all. I'm cutting all the scatting from here on out.]

Dear Know-It-All,
My stepdad is impossible to buy gifts for. He's just too picky. I can't keep buying him coffee-related gifts, and a person only needs so many plain white t-shirts. I'm out of ideas. Help?

-Presents of Mind in Pennsylvania

Presents,
In the dead of night, tear into his house and conceal yourself inside his walls and slither into his dreams to witness what he truly desires.
[Editor's note: ...Nevermind, it's way worse without the scatting.]

Dear Know-It-All,
My coworkers are great people whom I love and respect, but they are constantly dealing with so. much. drama. It's to the point where it's tough to want to go to work because I know I'll spend my whole shift talking about their interpersonal issues. How can I stay out of whatever extracurricular problems they're working through?

-In The Land of Increasingly Unsteady Habits

Land,
Diga dat, diga dat, diga ratatata dat, riga ree ree rah rah rah dramatics in the hall and comedy in the workplace. Aww tell me, tell me, tell me could that girl be a sluagh too ah, aye aye fleep a doo bah dah dooway, yeah just a jackknife has MacHeath, dear
[Editor's note: Answer has been edited to remove 1) copyrighted lyrics, 2) an additional 20 minutes of scatting, and 3) bad advice in general.]

Dear Know-It-All,

I didn't treat my man right, and now I'm crying all the time. I said, I didn't treat my man right, and now I'm crying all the time. Yeah, and since my baby left me, that fella's all that's on my mind.

-Lady Singin' The Blues

Lady,

I don't understand the question.
[Editor's note: Grace, come see me in my office.]

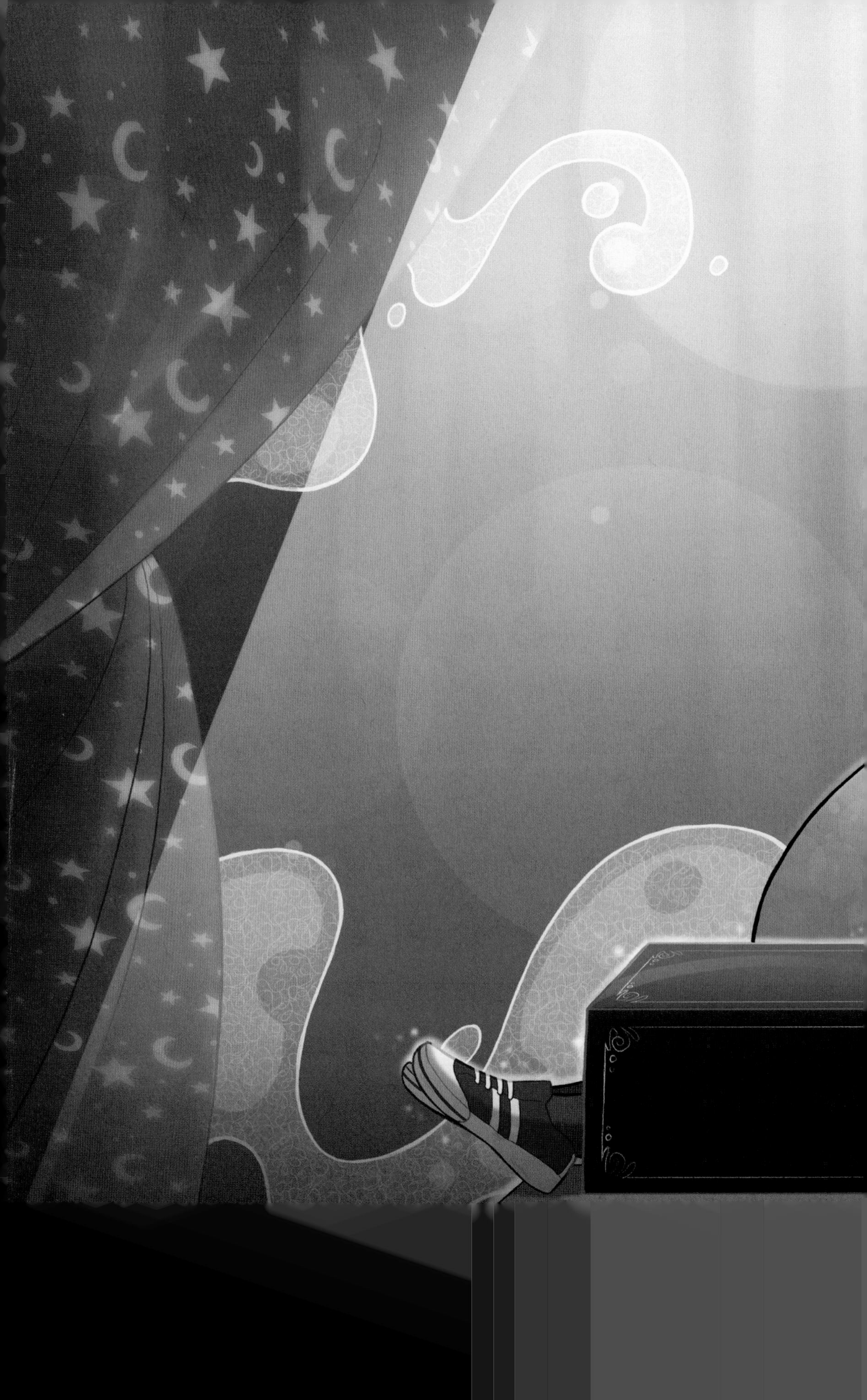

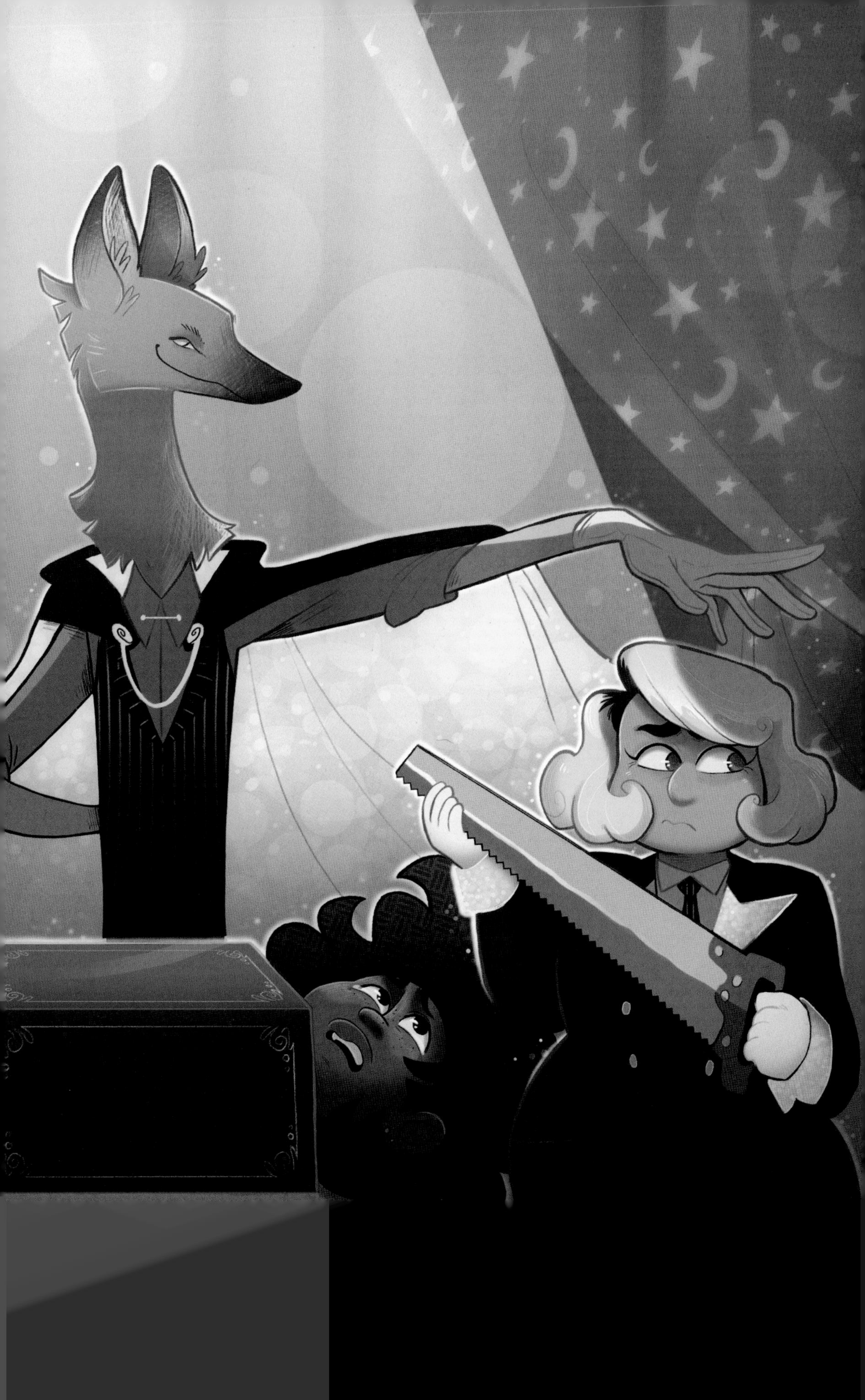

CHAPTER FIVE

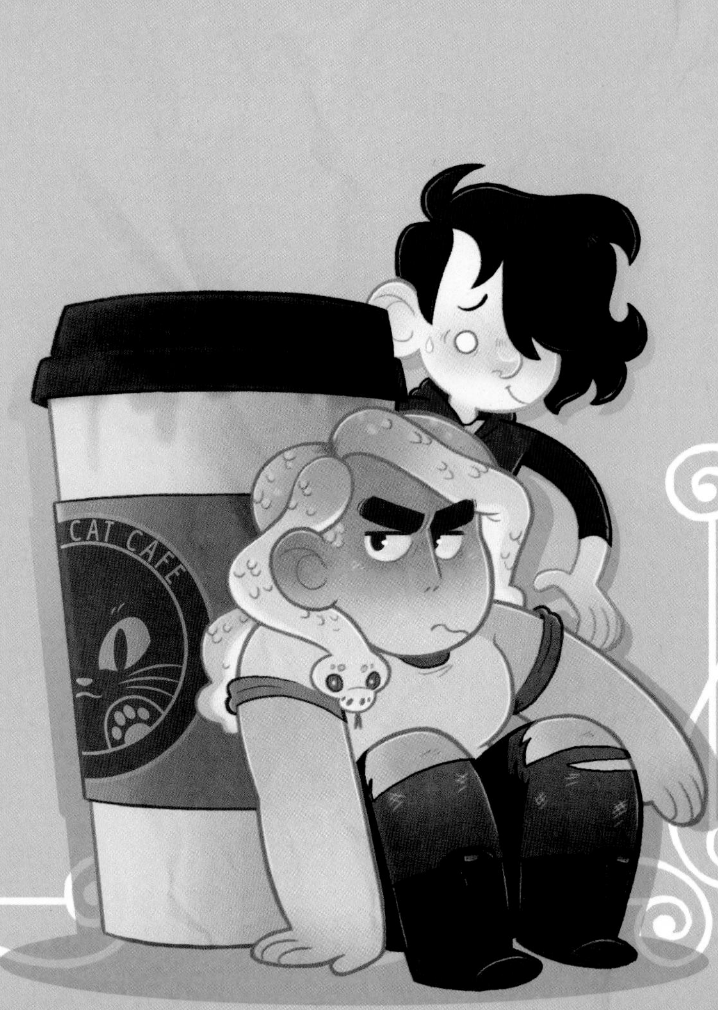
CAT CAFE

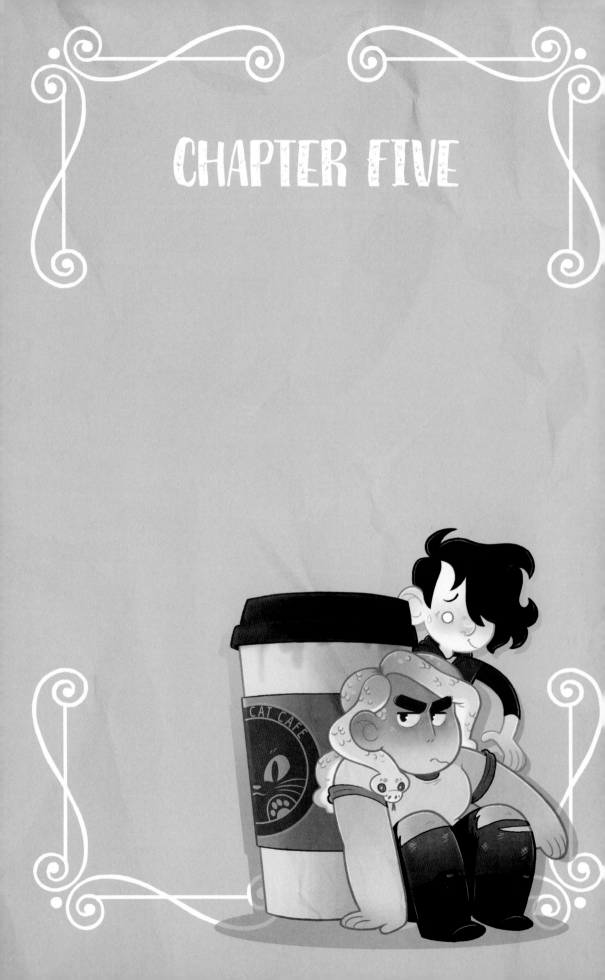

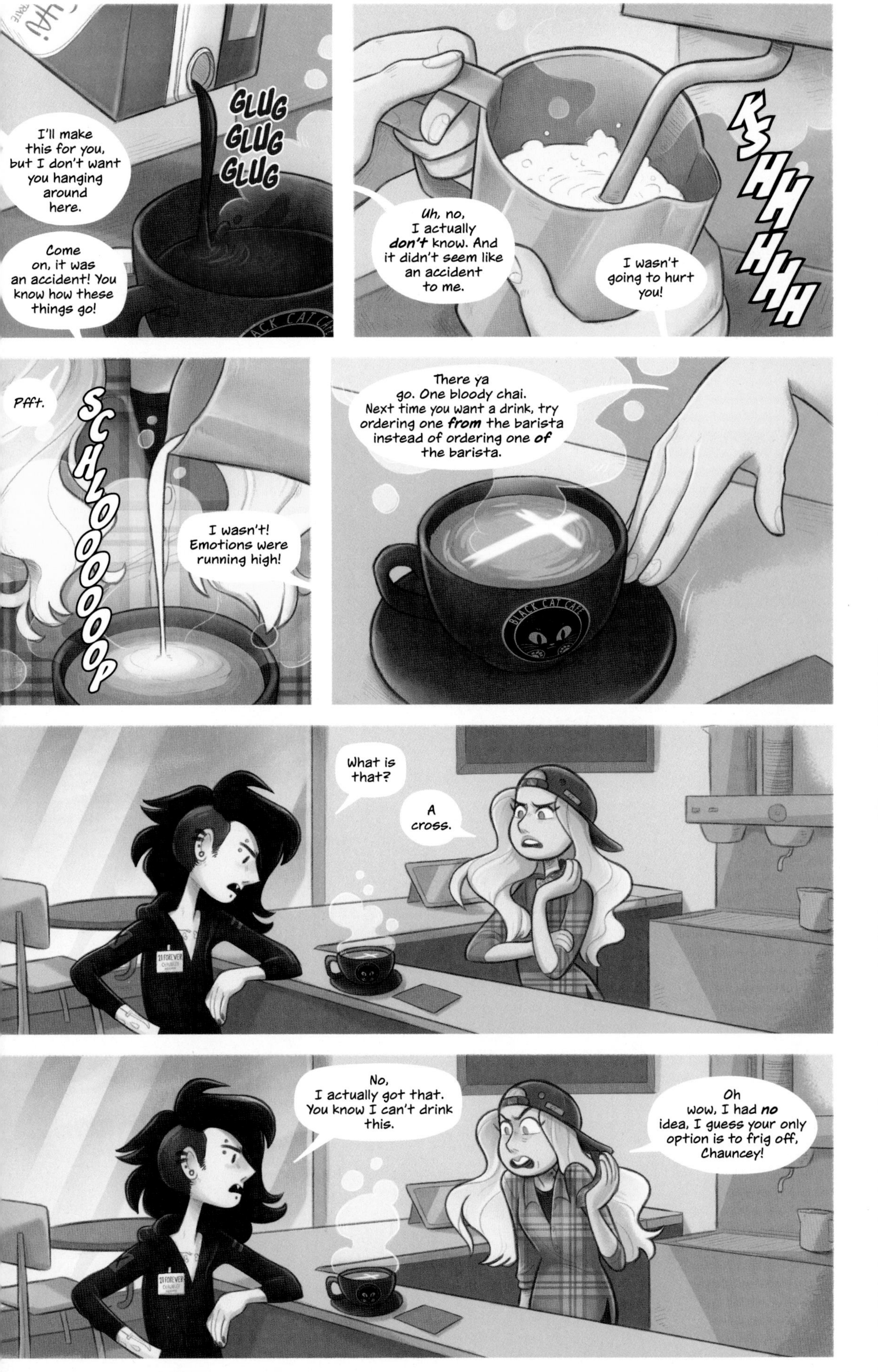
GLUG
GLUG
GLUG
I'll make this for you, but I don't want you hanging around here.
Come on, it was an accident! You know how these things go!
Uh, no, I actually **don't** know. And it didn't seem like an accident to me.
I wasn't going to hurt you!
KSHHHHHH
Pfft.
SCHLOOOOOOP
I wasn't! Emotions were running high!
There ya go. One bloody chai. Next time you want a drink, try ordering one **from** the barista instead of ordering one **of** the barista.
BLACK CAT CAFE
What is that?
A cross.
No, I actually got that. You know I can't drink this.
Oh wow, I had **no** idea, I guess your only option is to frig off, Chauncey!

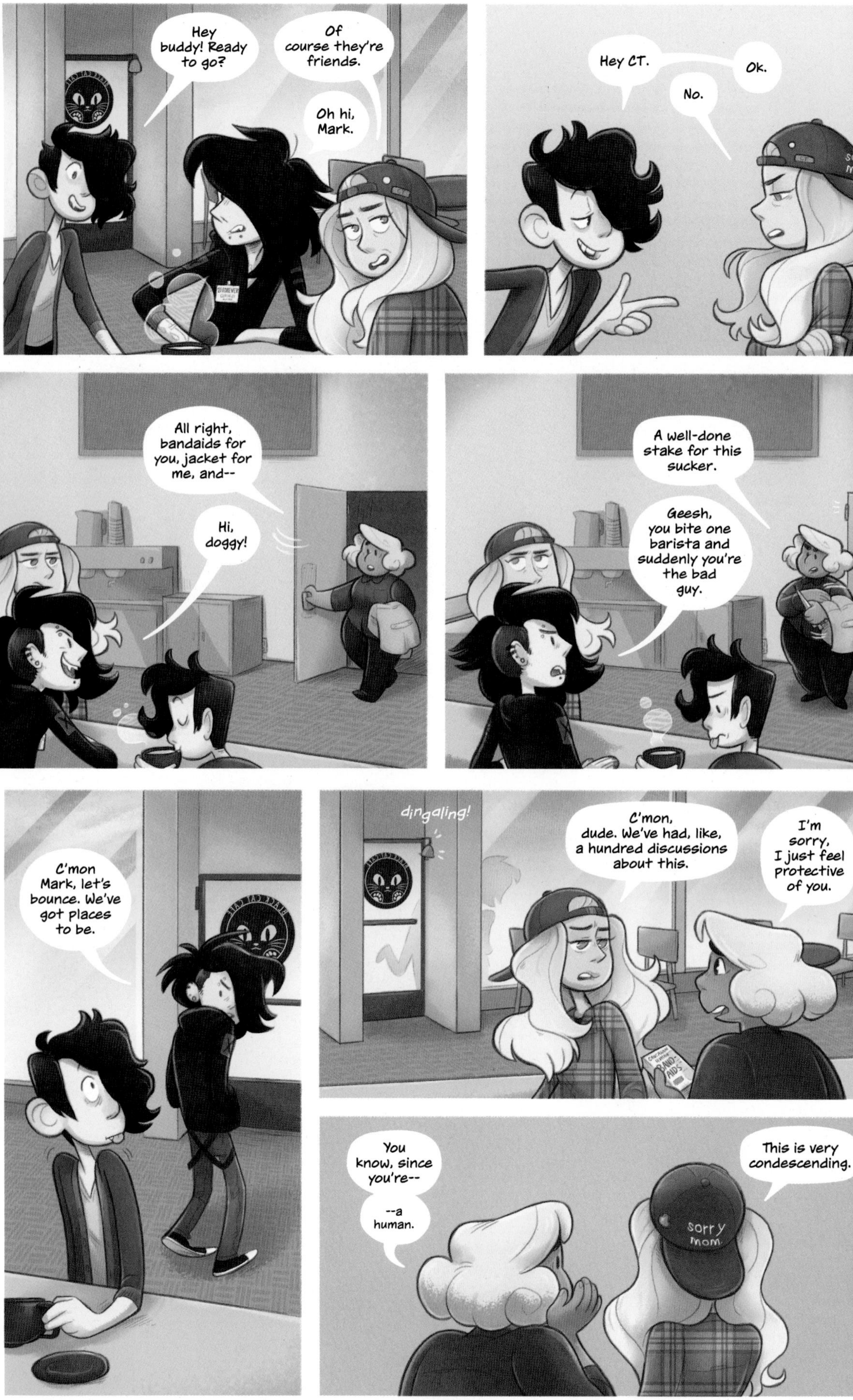
Hey buddy! Ready to go?
Of course they're friends.
Oh hi, Mark.
Hey CT.
Ok.
No.
All right, bandaids for you, jacket for me, and--
Hi, doggy!
A well-done stake for this sucker.
Geesh, you bite one barista and suddenly you're the bad guy.
C'mon Mark, let's bounce. We've got places to be.
dingaling!
C'mon, dude. We've had, like, a hundred discussions about this.
I'm sorry, I just feel protective of you.
You know, since you're--
--a human.
This is very condescending.
sorry mom

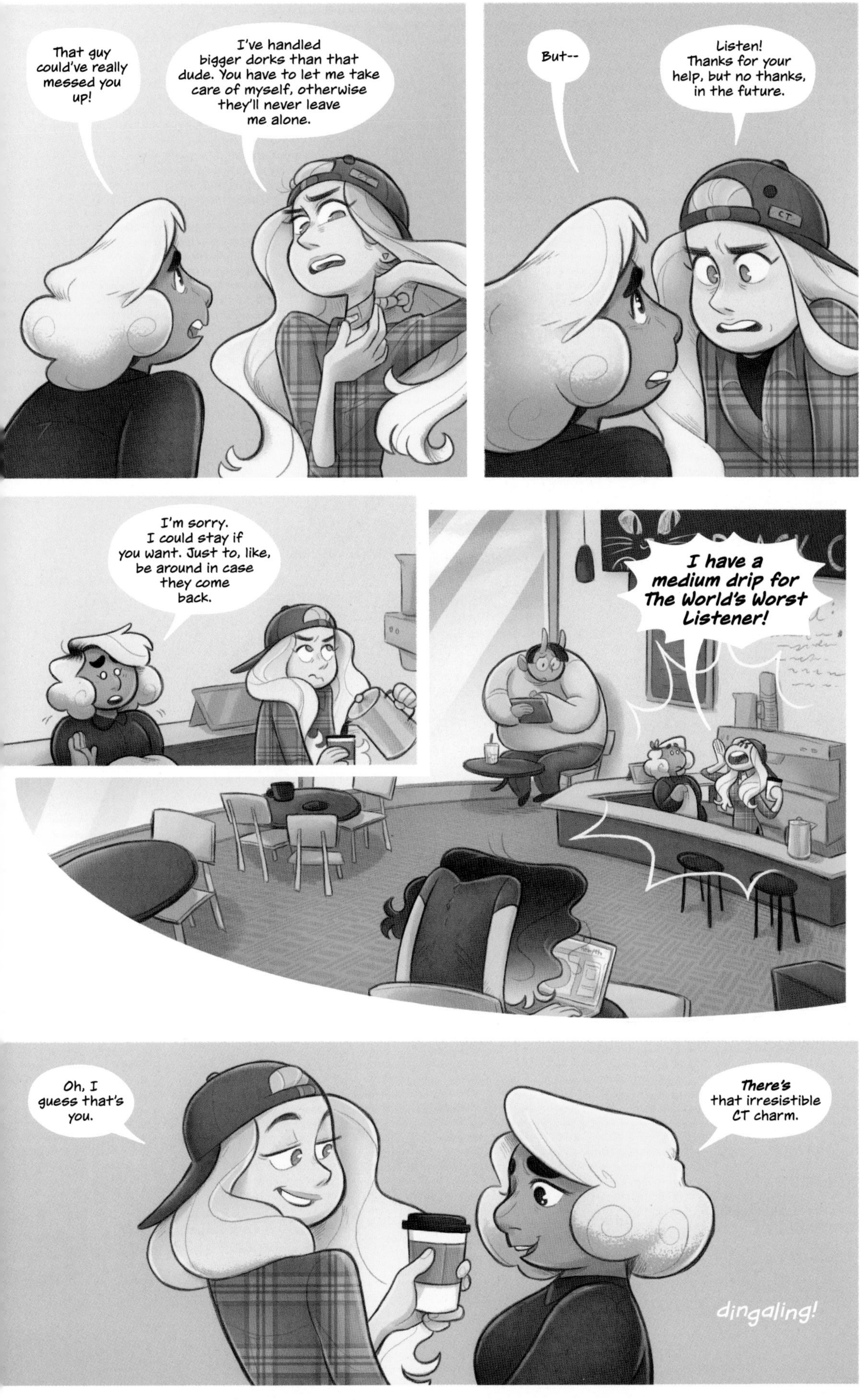
That guy could've really messed you up!
I've handled bigger dorks than that dude. You have to let me take care of myself, otherwise they'll never leave me alone.
But--
Listen! Thanks for your help, but no thanks, in the future.
I'm sorry. I could stay if you want. Just to, like, be around in case they come back.
I have a medium drip for The World's Worst Listener!
Oh, I guess that's you.
There's that irresistible CT charm.
dingaling!

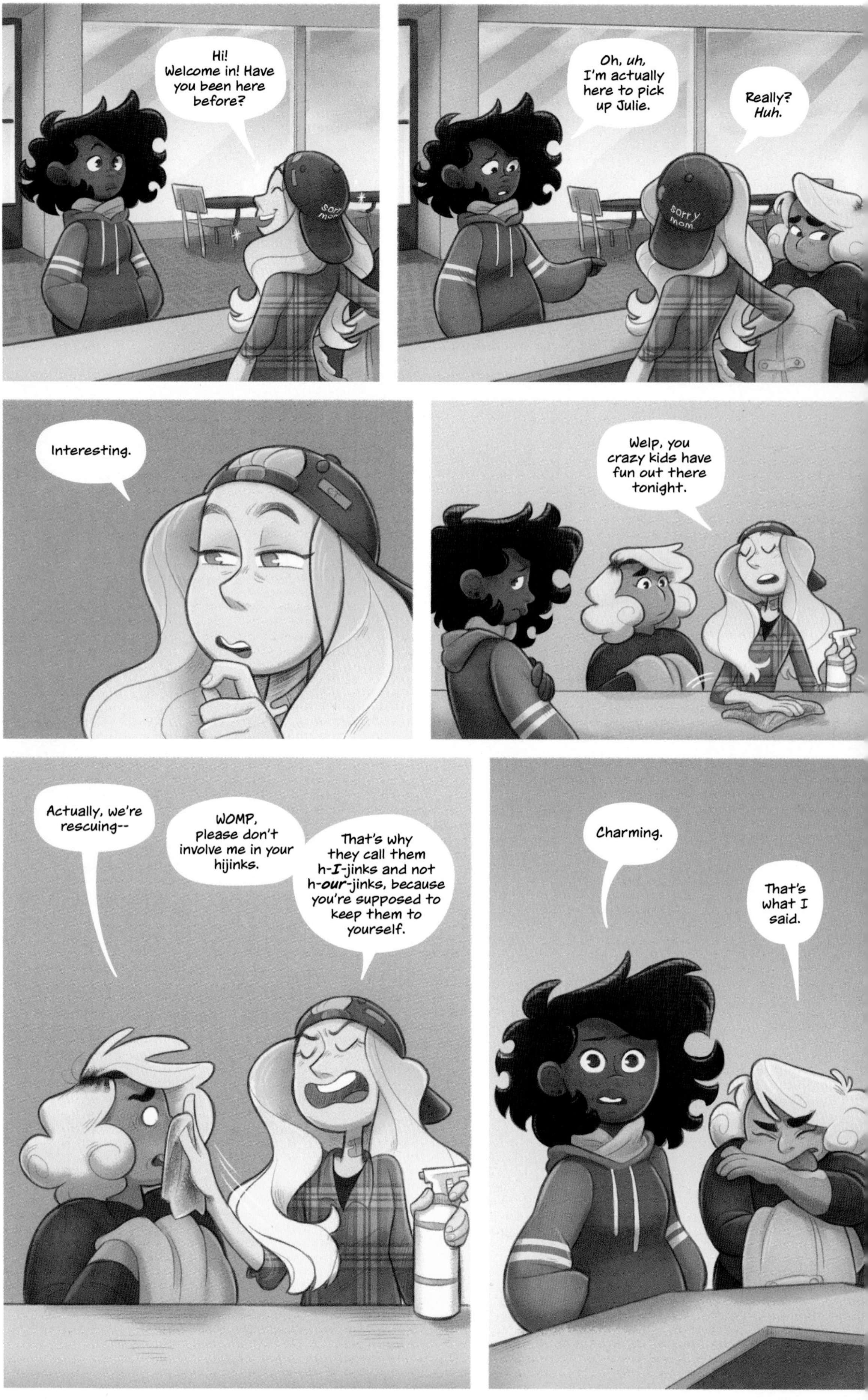
Hi! Welcome in! Have you been here before?
sorry mom
Oh, uh, I'm actually here to pick up Julie.
sorry mom.
Really? Huh.
Interesting.
Welp, you crazy kids have fun out there tonight.
Actually, we're rescuing--
WOMP, please don't involve me in your hijinks.
That's why they call them h-*I*-jinks and not h-*our*-jinks, because you're supposed to keep them to yourself.
Charming.
That's what I said.

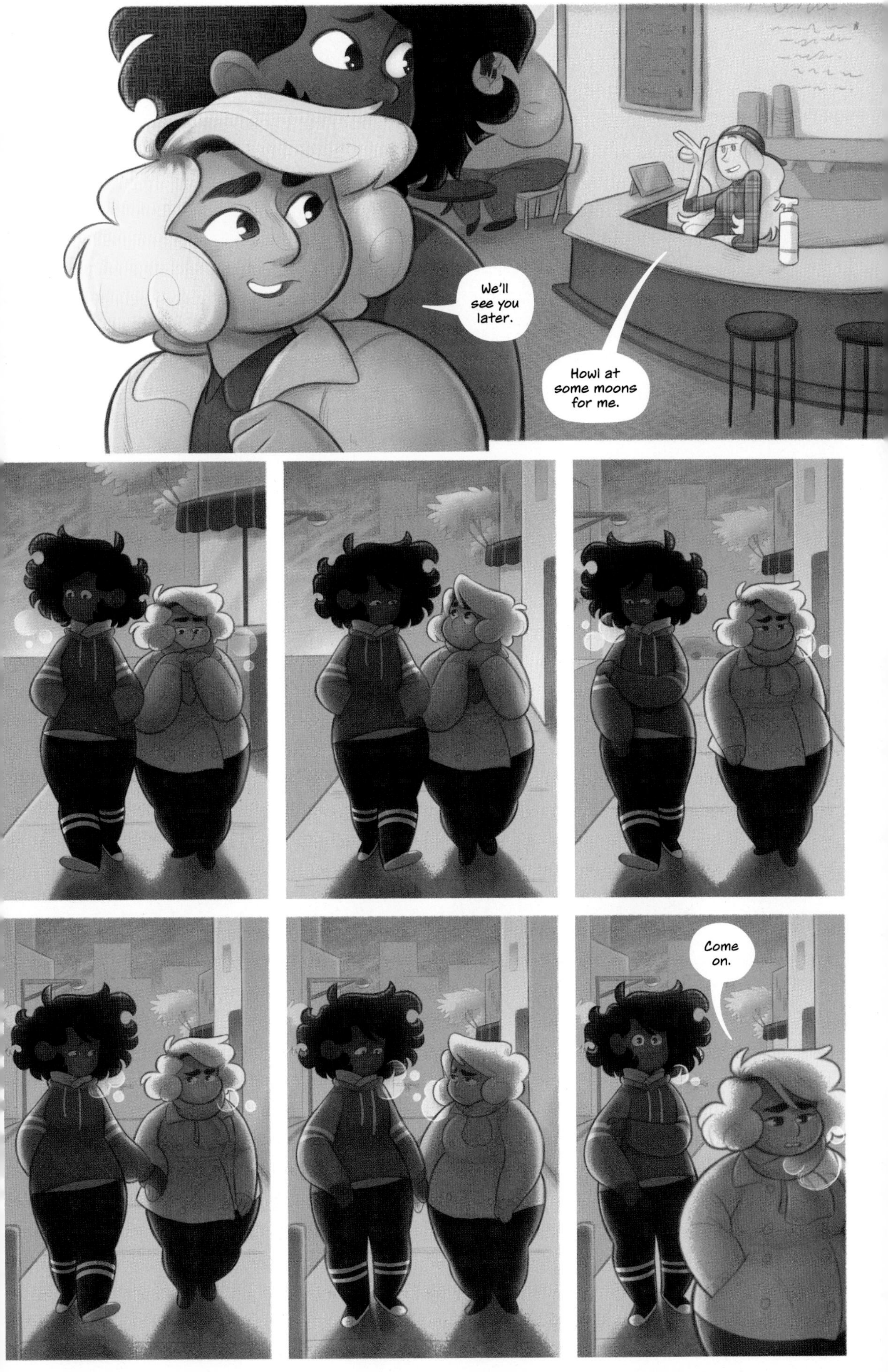
We'll see you later.
Howl at some moons for me.
Come on.

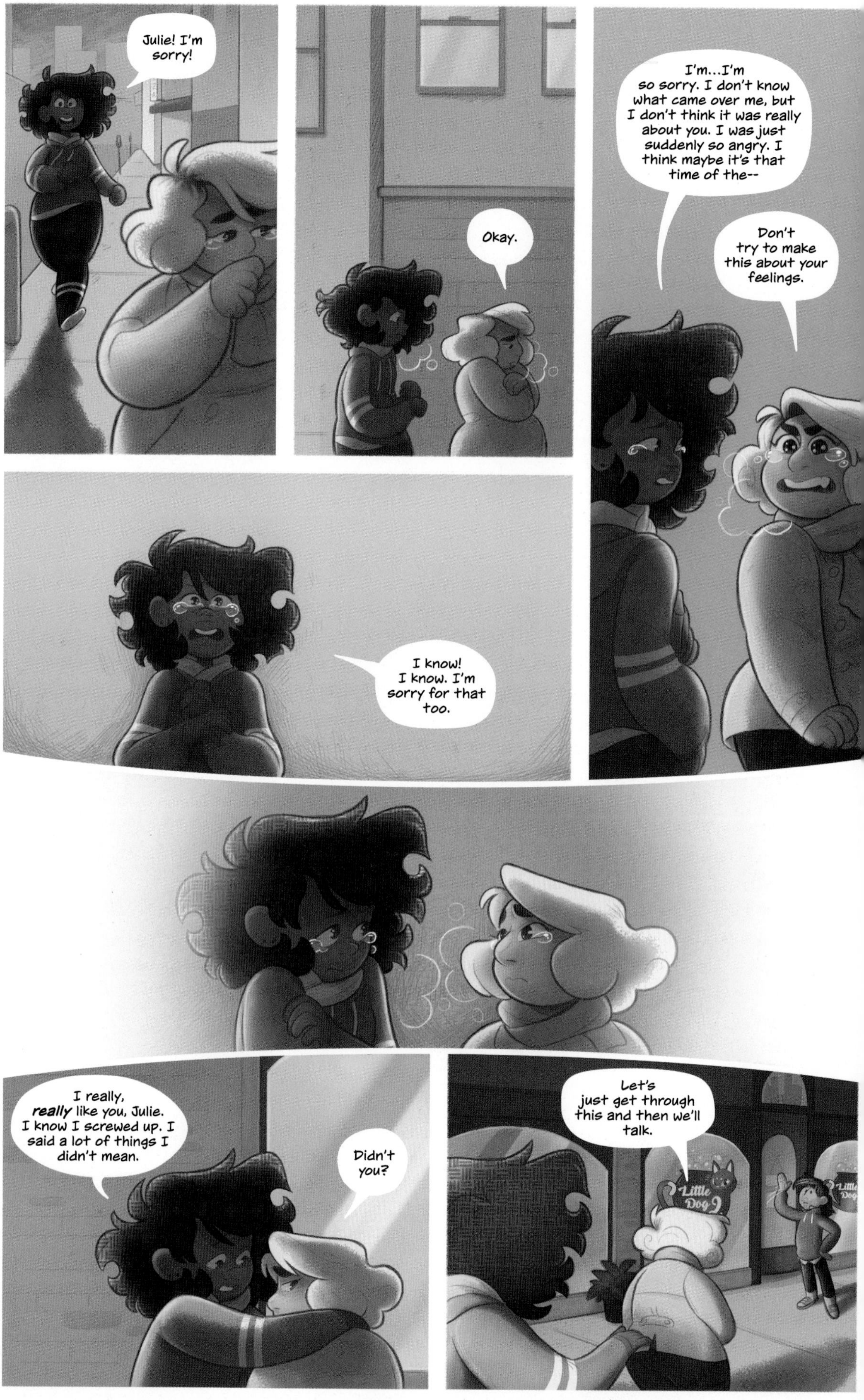
Julie! I'm sorry!
Okay.
I'm...I'm so sorry. I don't know what came over me, but I don't think it was really about you. I was just suddenly so angry. I think maybe it's that time of the--
Don't try to make this about your feelings.
I know! I know. I'm sorry for that too.
I really, ***really*** like you, Julie. I know I screwed up. I said a lot of things I didn't mean.
Didn't you?
Let's just get through this and then we'll talk.
Little Dog

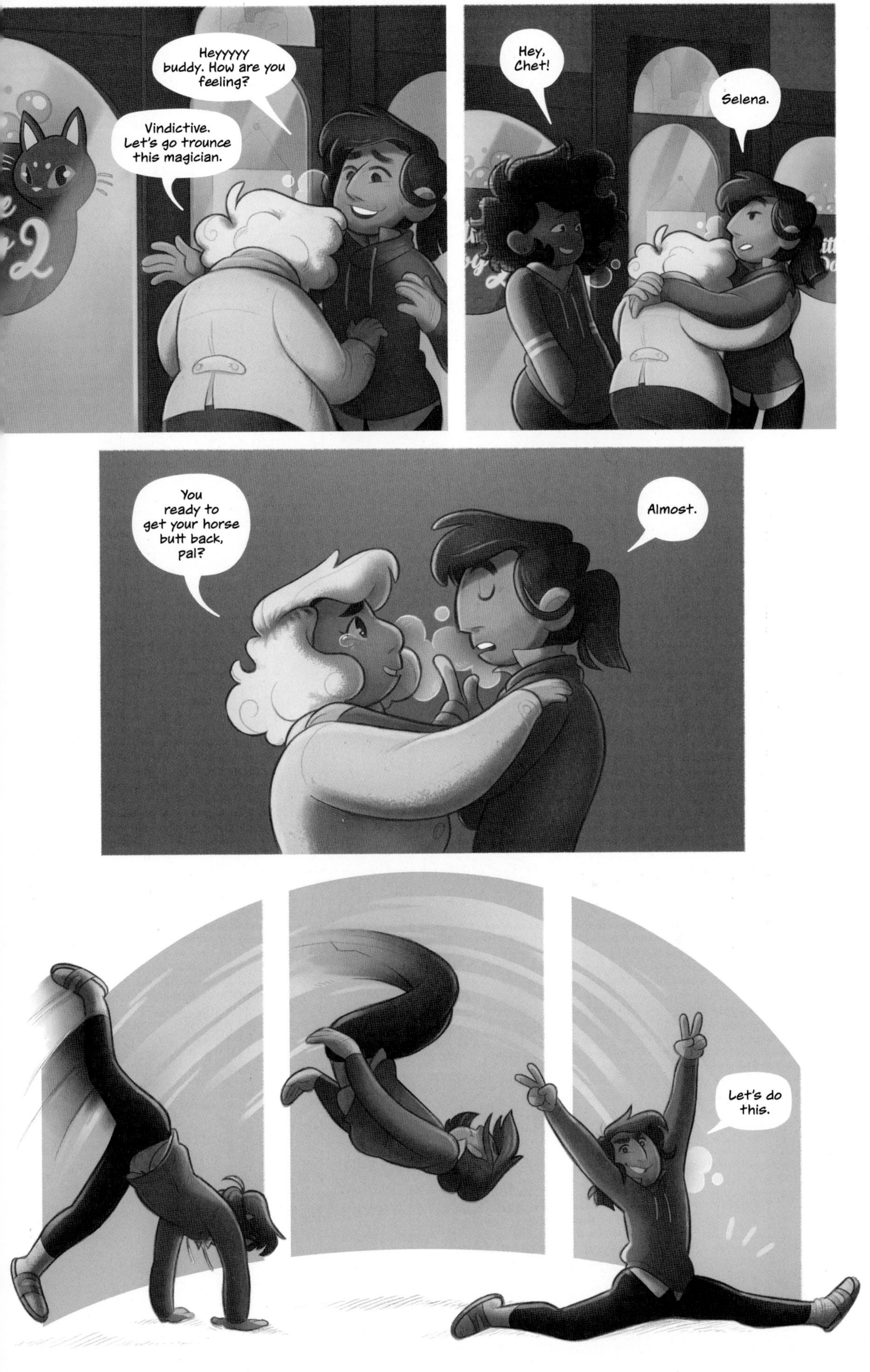

Heyyyyy buddy. How are you feeling?
Vindictive. Let's go trounce this magician.
Hey, Chet!
Selena.
You ready to get your horse butt back, pal?
Almost.
Let's do this.

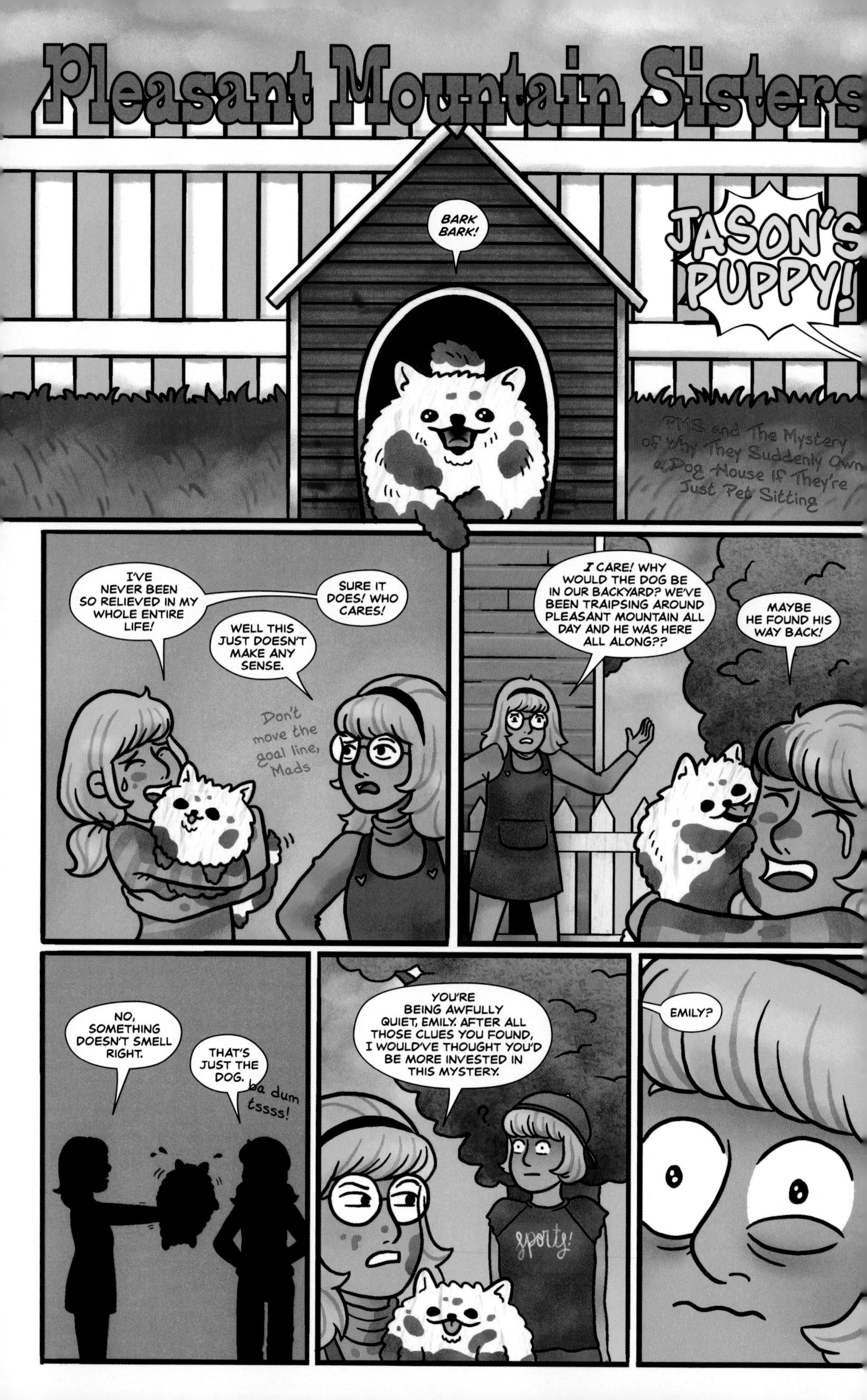
Pleasant Mountain Sisters
BARK BARK!
JASON'S PUPPY!
PMS and The Mystery of Why They Suddenly Own a Dog House If They're Just Pet Sitting
I'VE NEVER BEEN SO RELIEVED IN MY WHOLE ENTIRE LIFE!
WELL THIS JUST DOESN'T MAKE ANY SENSE.
SURE IT DOES! WHO CARES!
Don't move the goal line, Mads
I CARE! WHY WOULD THE DOG BE IN OUR BACKYARD? WE'VE BEEN TRAIPSING AROUND PLEASANT MOUNTAIN ALL DAY AND HE WAS HERE ALL ALONG??
MAYBE HE FOUND HIS WAY BACK!
NO, SOMETHING DOESN'T SMELL RIGHT.
THAT'S JUST THE DOG.
ba dum tssss!
YOU'RE BEING AWFULLY QUIET, EMILY. AFTER ALL THOSE CLUES YOU FOUND, I WOULD'VE THOUGHT YOU'D BE MORE INVESTED IN THIS MYSTERY.
sporty!
EMILY?

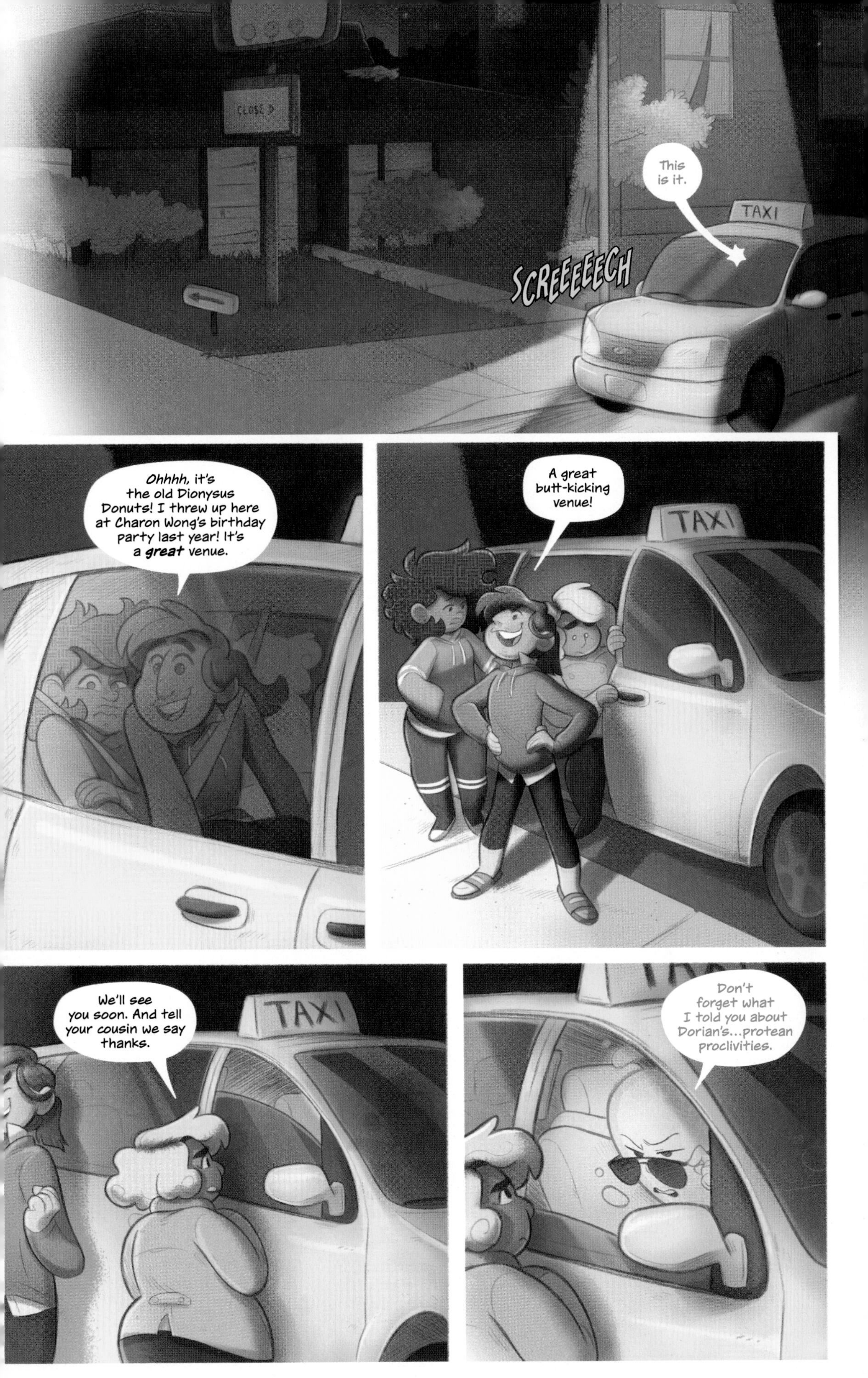
CLOSED
This is it.
TAXI
SCREEEEECH
Ohhhh, it's the old Dionysus Donuts! I threw up here at Charon Wong's birthday party last year! It's a great venue.
A great butt-kicking venue!
TAXI
We'll see you soon. And tell your cousin we say thanks.
TAXI
Don't forget what I told you about Dorian's…protean proclivities.

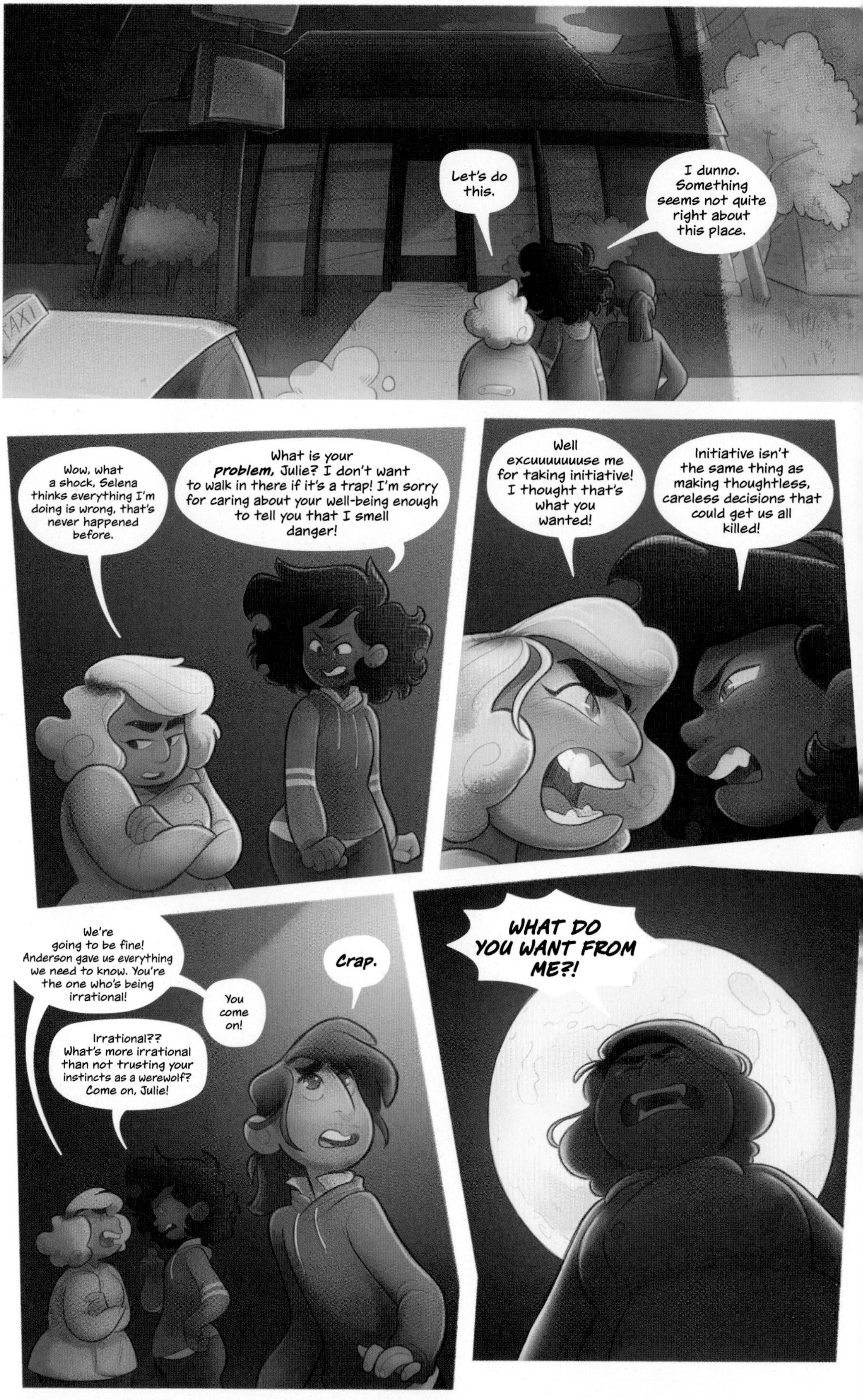
Let's do this.
I dunno. Something seems not quite right about this place.
Wow, what a shock, Selena thinks everything I'm doing is wrong, that's never happened before.
What is your *problem,* Julie? I don't want to walk in there if it's a trap! I'm sorry for caring about your well-being enough to tell you that I smell danger!
Well excuuuuuuuse me for taking initiative! I thought that's what you wanted!
Initiative isn't the same thing as making thoughtless, careless decisions that could get us all killed!
We're going to be fine! Anderson gave us everything we need to know. You're the one who's being irrational!
Irrational?? What's more irrational than not trusting your instincts as a werewolf? Come on, Julie!
You come on!
Crap.
WHAT DO YOU WANT FROM ME?!

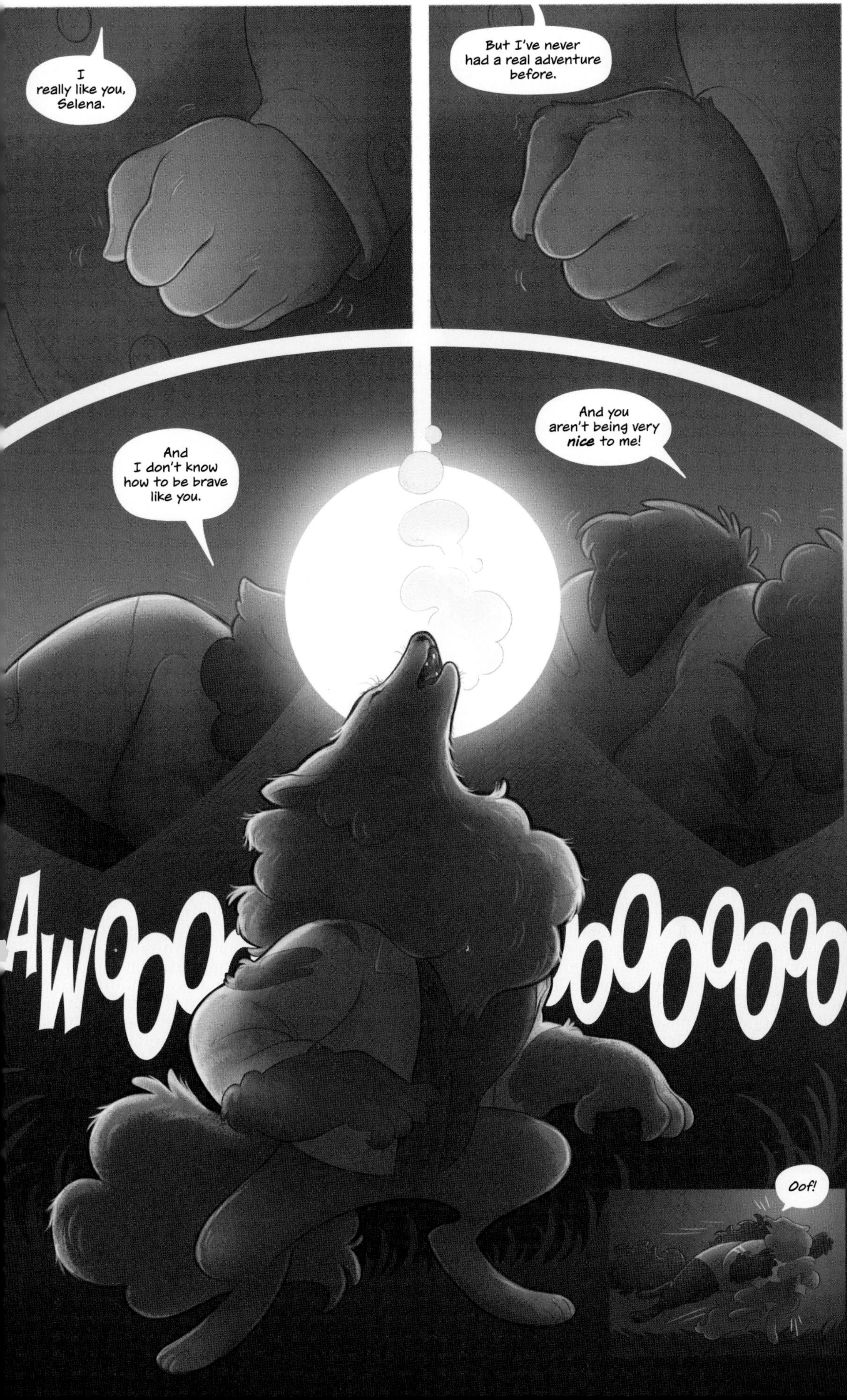
I really like you, Selena.
But I've never had a real adventure before.
And I don't know how to be brave like you.
And you aren't being very *nice* to me!
AWOOOOOOOOOOOO
Oof!

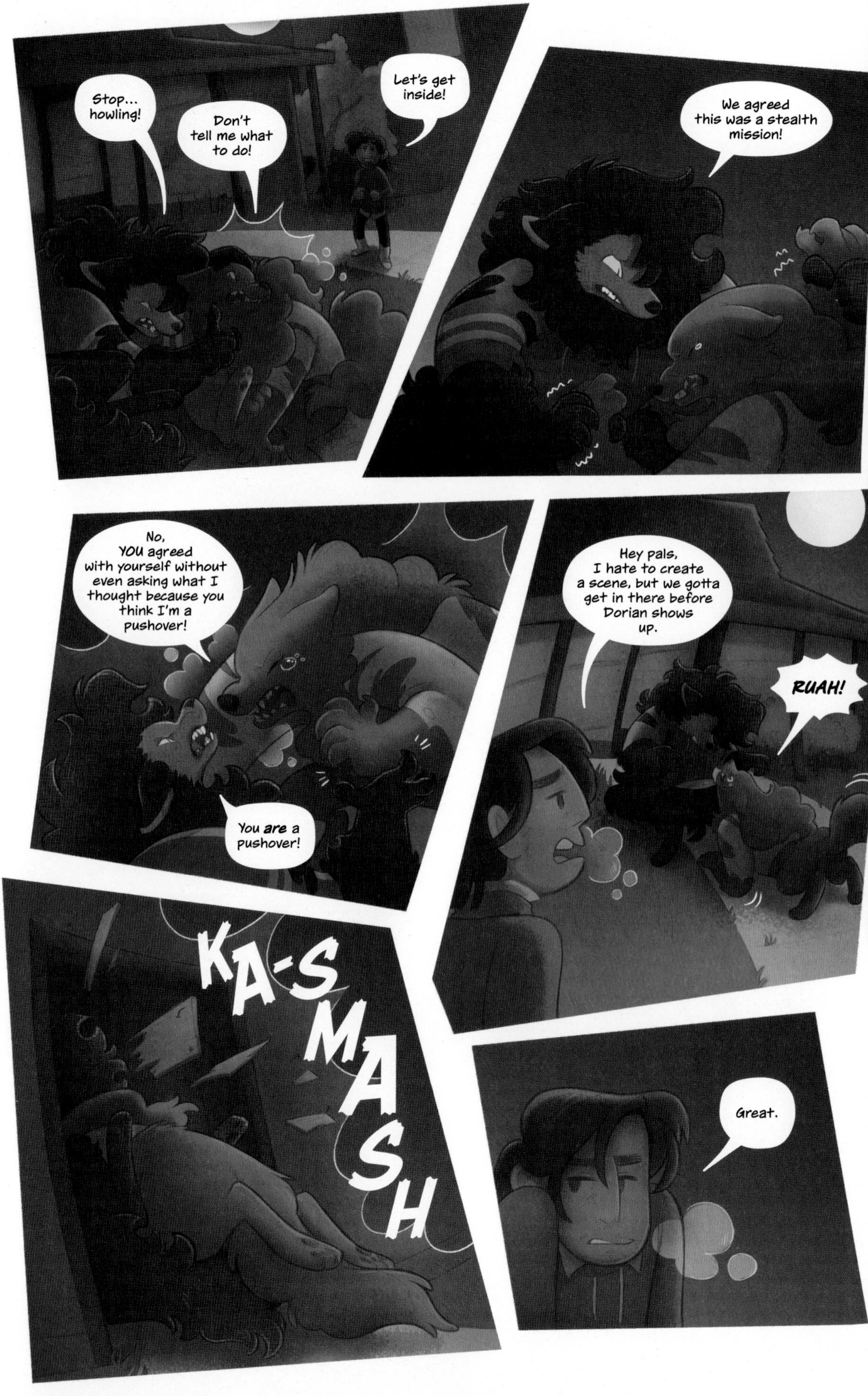
Stop... howling!
Don't tell me what to do!
Let's get inside!
We agreed this was a stealth mission!
No, YOU agreed with yourself without even asking what I thought because you think I'm a pushover!
You *are* a pushover!
Hey pals, I hate to create a scene, but we gotta get in there before Dorian shows up.
RUAH!
KA-SMASH
Great.

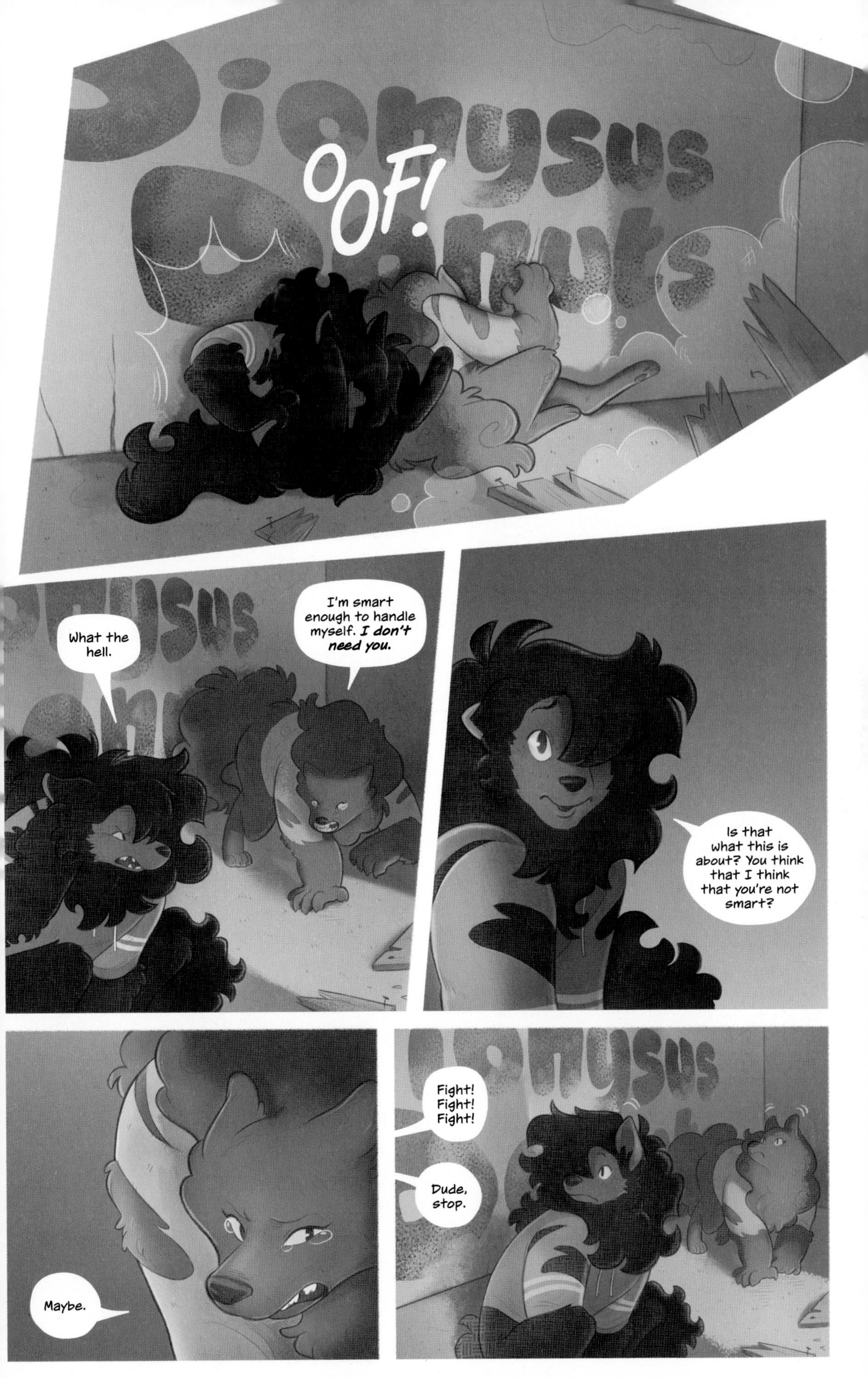
Dionysus
OOF!
What the hell.
I'm smart enough to handle myself. ***I don't need you.***
Is that what this is about? You think that I think that you're not smart?
Maybe.
Fight! Fight! Fight!
Dude, stop.

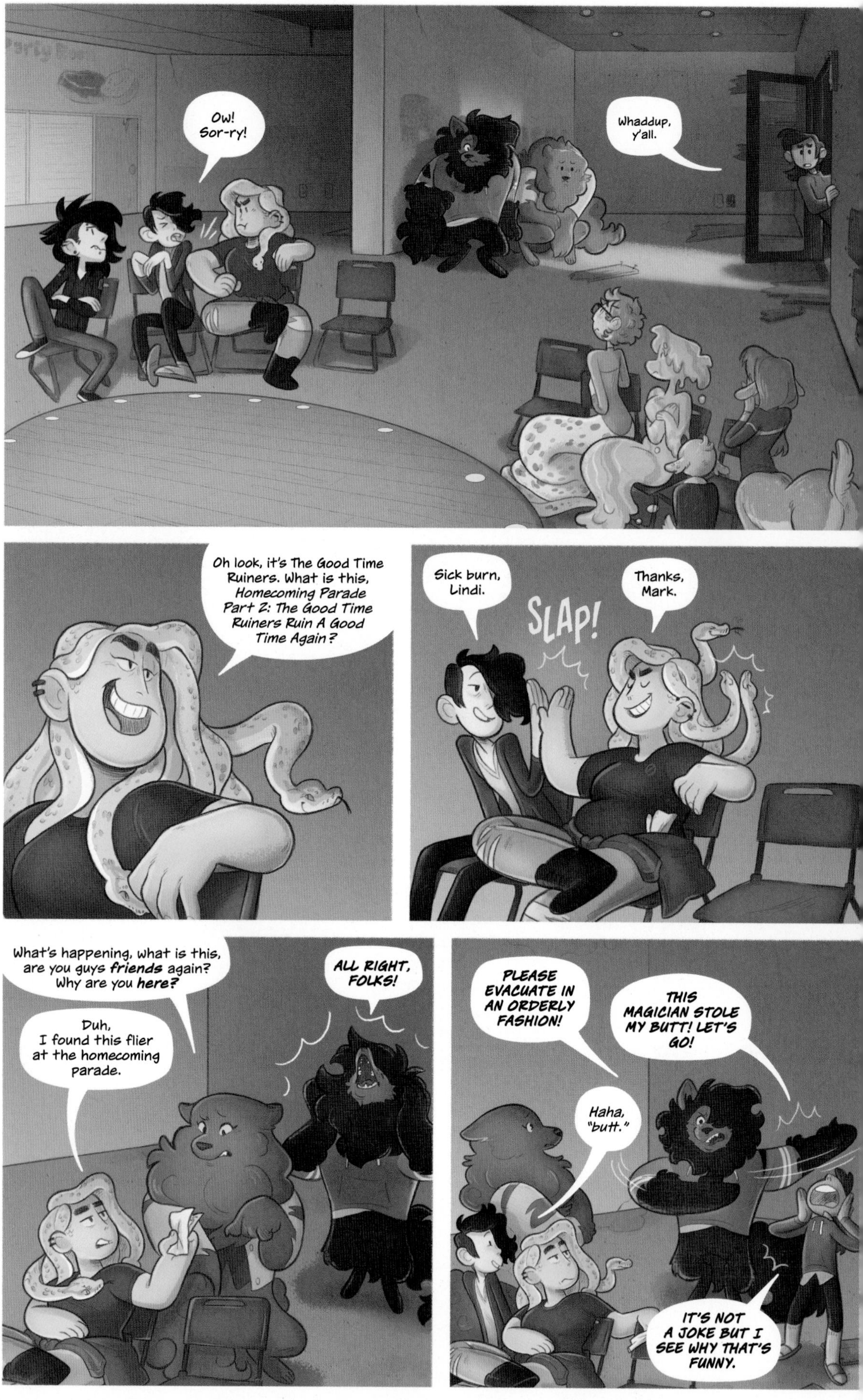
Ow! Sor-ry!
Whaddup, y'all.
Oh look, it's The Good Time Ruiners. What is this, *Homecoming Parade Part 2: The Good Time Ruiners Ruin A Good Time Again?*
Sick burn, Lindi.
SLAP!
Thanks, Mark.
What's happening, what is this, are you guys **friends** again? Why are you **here?**
Duh, I found this flier at the homecoming parade.
ALL RIGHT, FOLKS!
PLEASE EVACUATE IN AN ORDERLY FASHION!
THIS MAGICIAN STOLE MY BUTT! LET'S GO!
Haha, "butt."
IT'S NOT A JOKE BUT I SEE WHY THAT'S FUNNY.

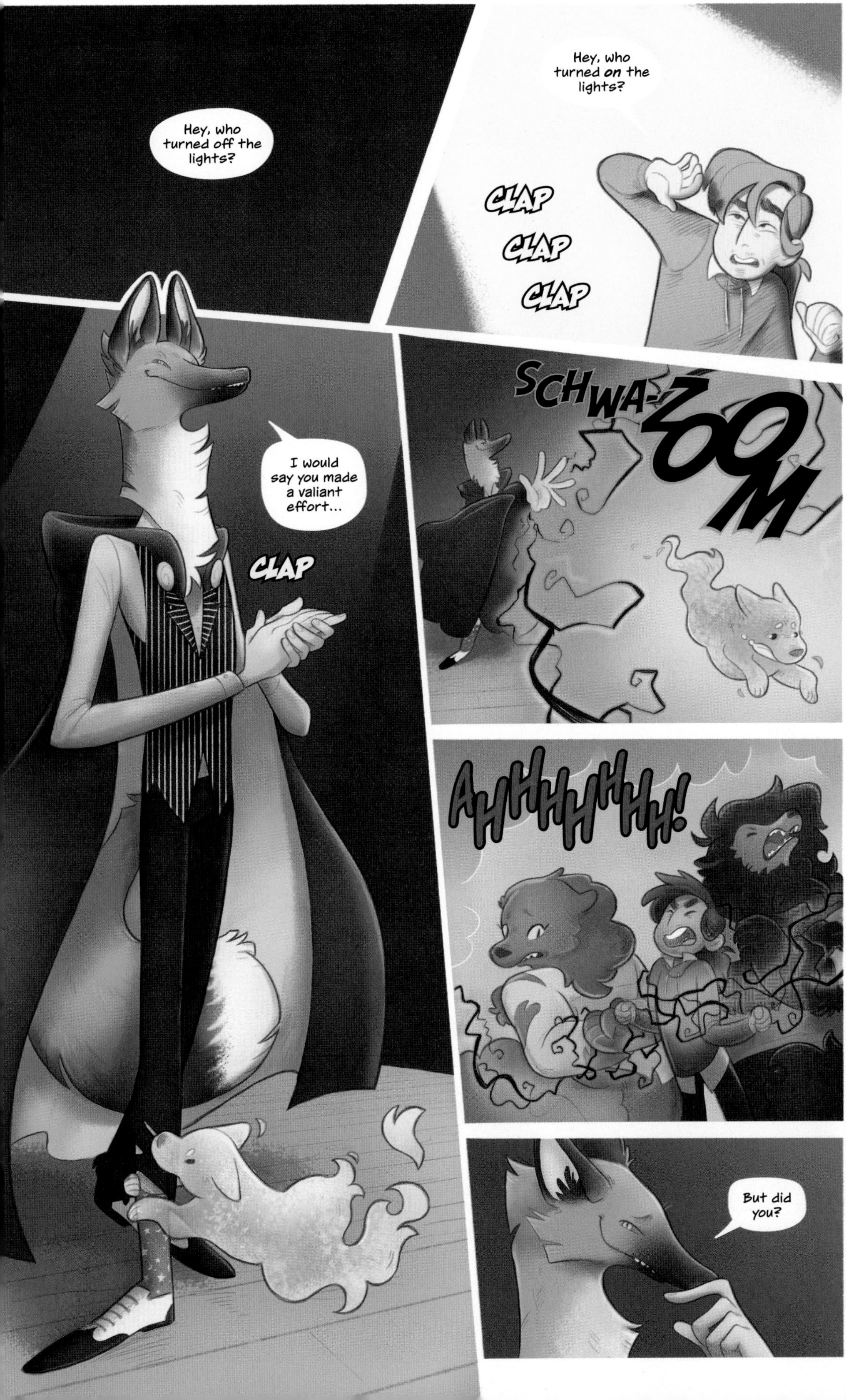
Hey, who turned off the lights?
Hey, who turned on the lights?
CLAP
CLAP
CLAP
I would say you made a valiant effort...
CLAP
SCHWA-ZOOM
AHHHHHHHH!
But did you?

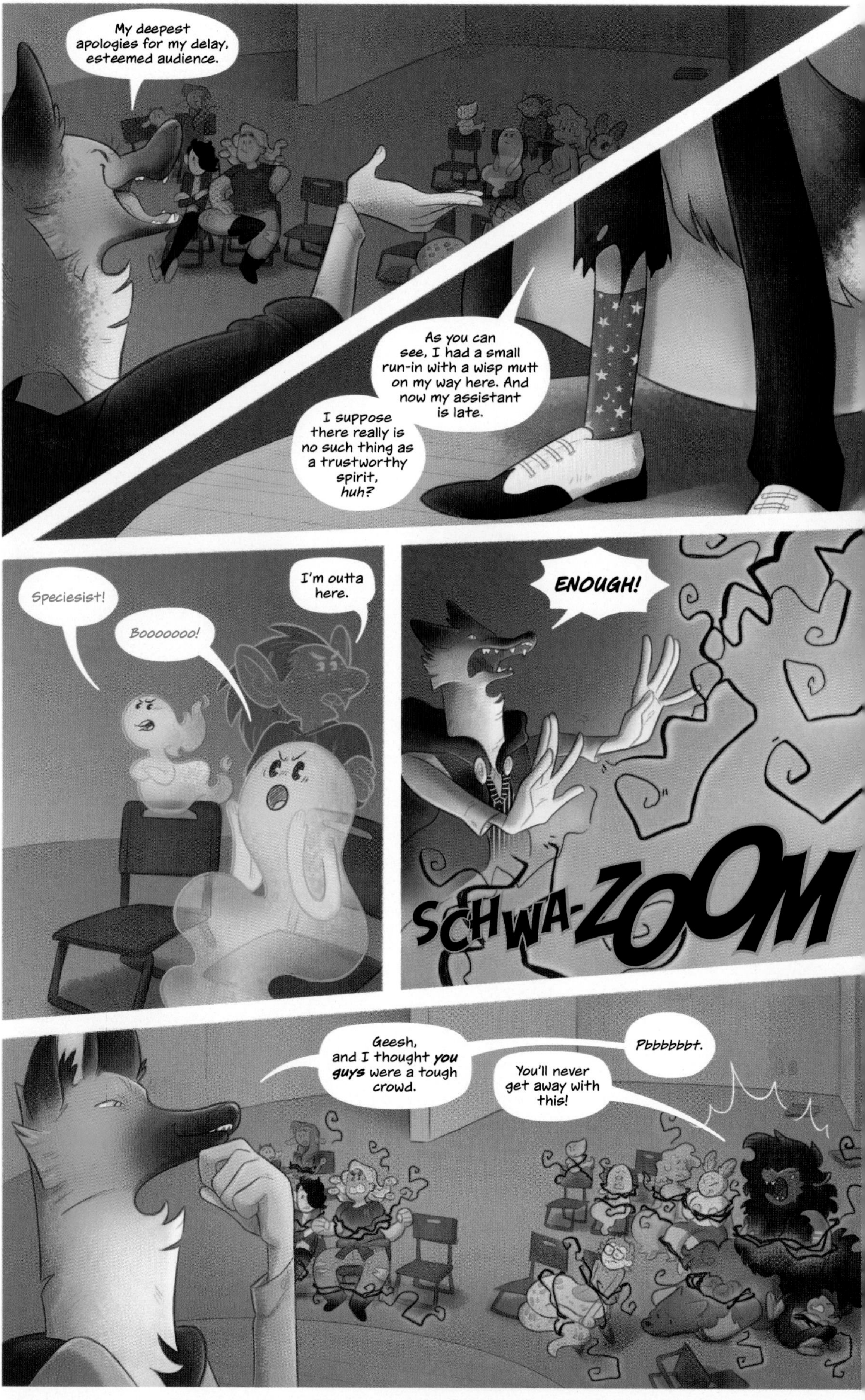
My deepest apologies for my delay, esteemed audience.
As you can see, I had a small run-in with a wisp mutt on my way here. And now my assistant is late.
I suppose there really is no such thing as a trustworthy spirit, huh?
Speciesist!
Boooooooo!
I'm outta here.
ENOUGH!
SCHWA-ZOOM
Geesh, and I thought you guys were a tough crowd.
Pbbbbbbt.
You'll never get away with this!

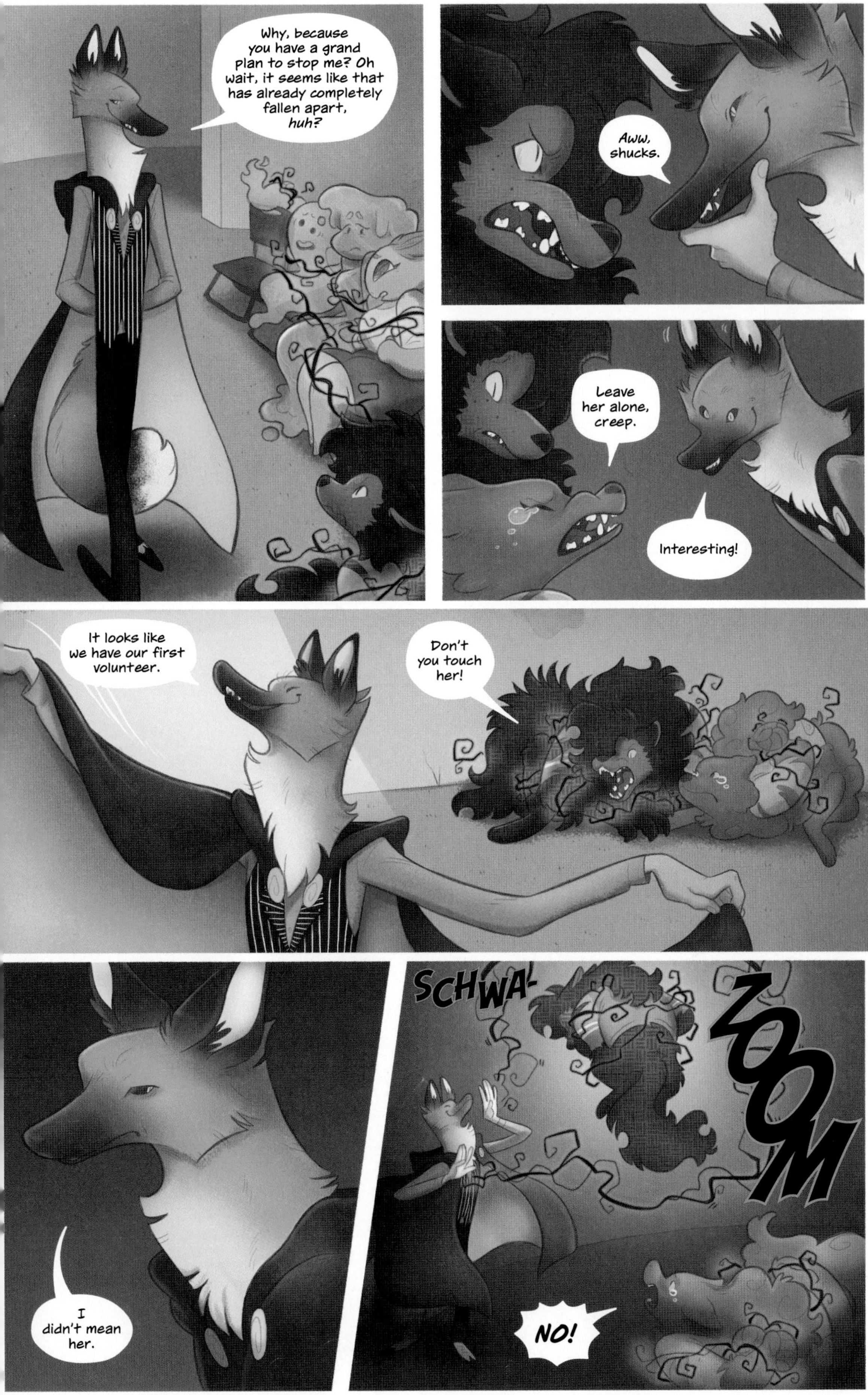

Why, because you have a grand plan to stop me? Oh wait, it seems like that has already completely fallen apart, huh?
Aww, shucks.
Leave her alone, creep.
Interesting!
It looks like we have our first volunteer.
Don't you touch her!
I didn't mean her.
SCHWA-
ZOOM
NO!

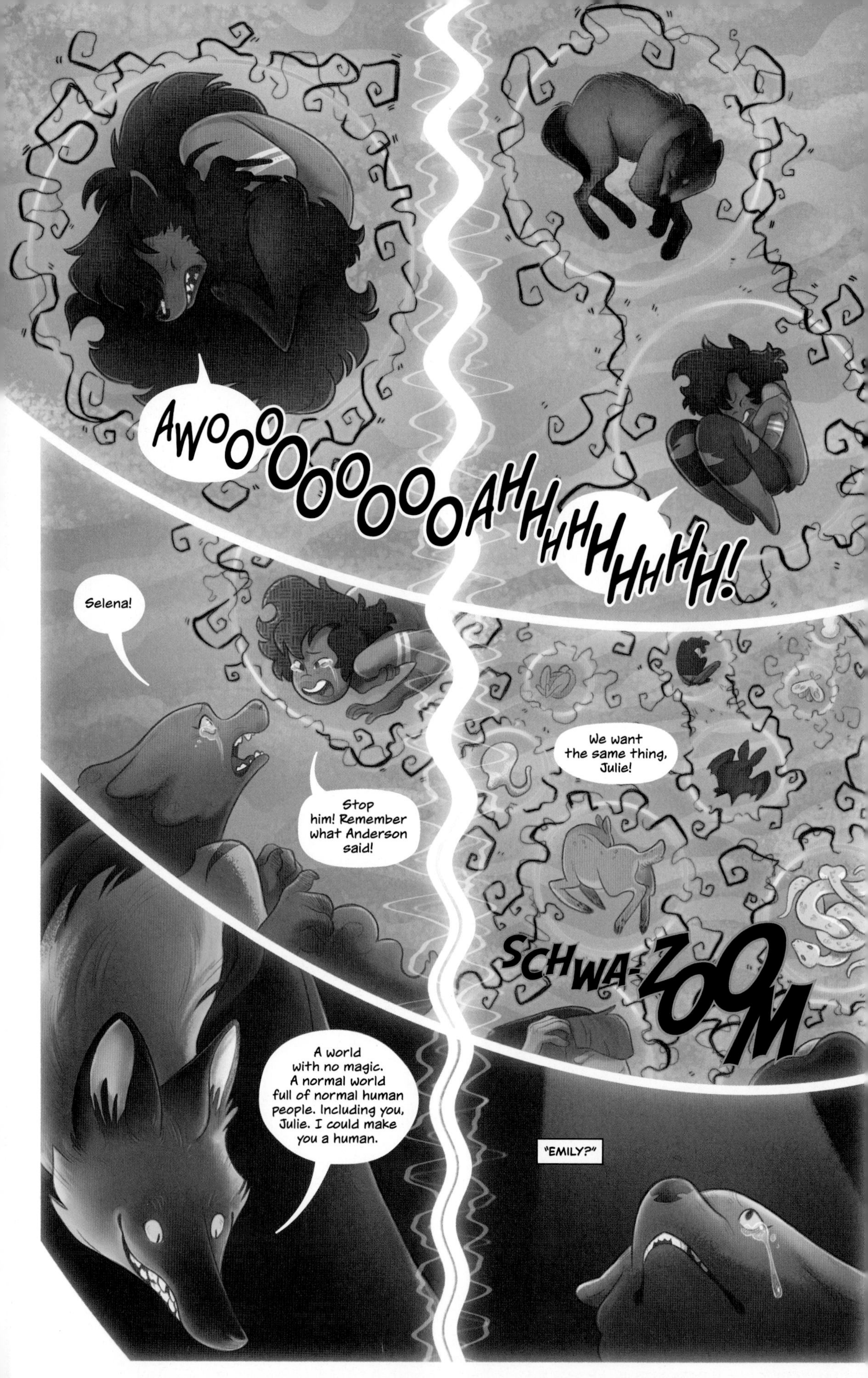
AWOOOOOOOOOAHHHHHHHHHH!
Selena!
Stop him! Remember what Anderson said!
We want the same thing, Julie!
SCHWA-ZOOM
A world with no magic. A normal world full of normal human people. Including you, Julie. I could make you a human.
"EMILY?"

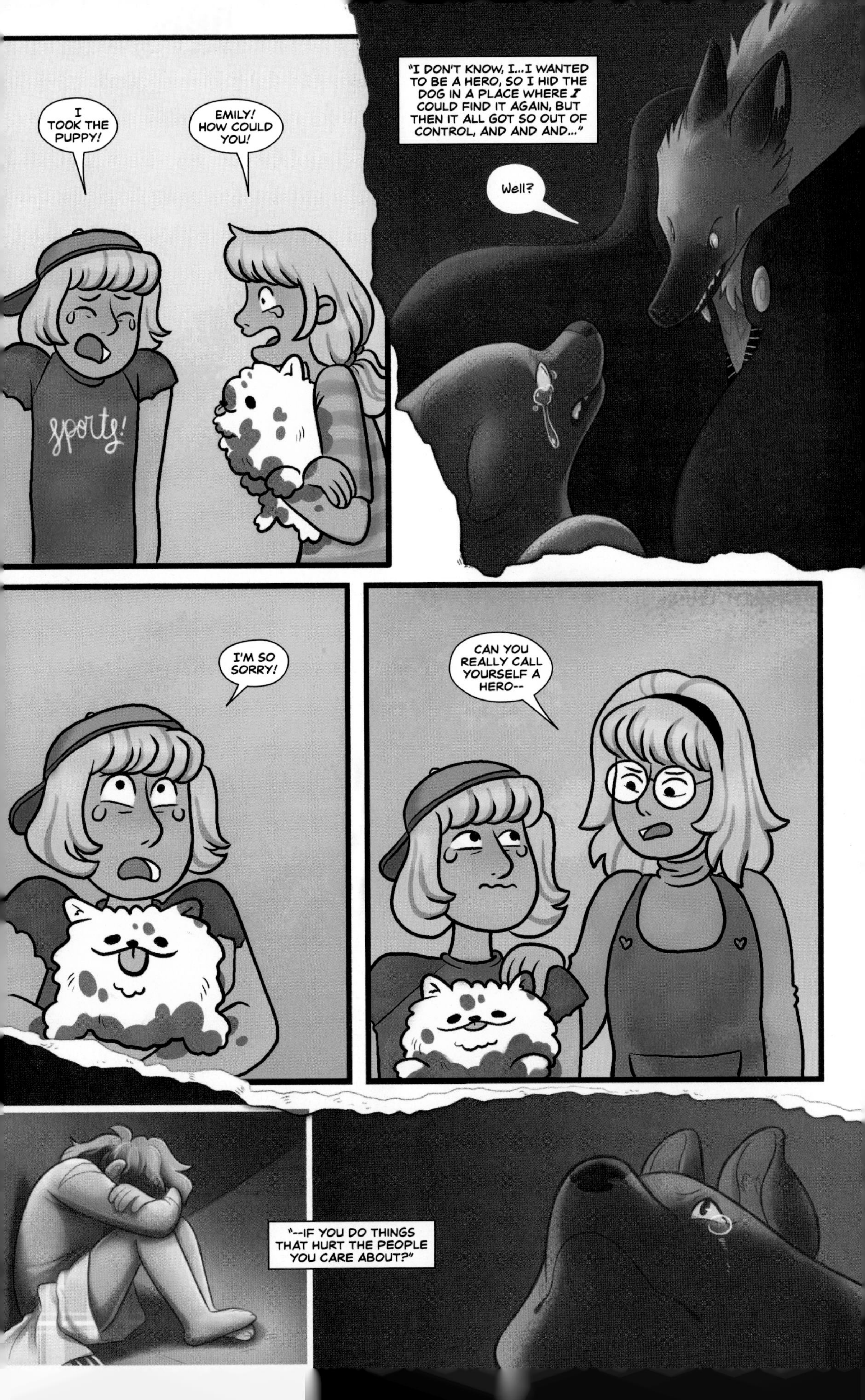
I TOOK THE PUPPY!
EMILY! HOW COULD YOU!
"I DON'T KNOW, I...I WANTED TO BE A HERO, SO I HID THE DOG IN A PLACE WHERE I COULD FIND IT AGAIN, BUT THEN IT ALL GOT SO OUT OF CONTROL, AND AND AND..."
Well?
sporty!
I'M SO SORRY!
CAN YOU REALLY CALL YOURSELF A HERO--
"--IF YOU DO THINGS THAT HURT THE PEOPLE YOU CARE ABOUT?"

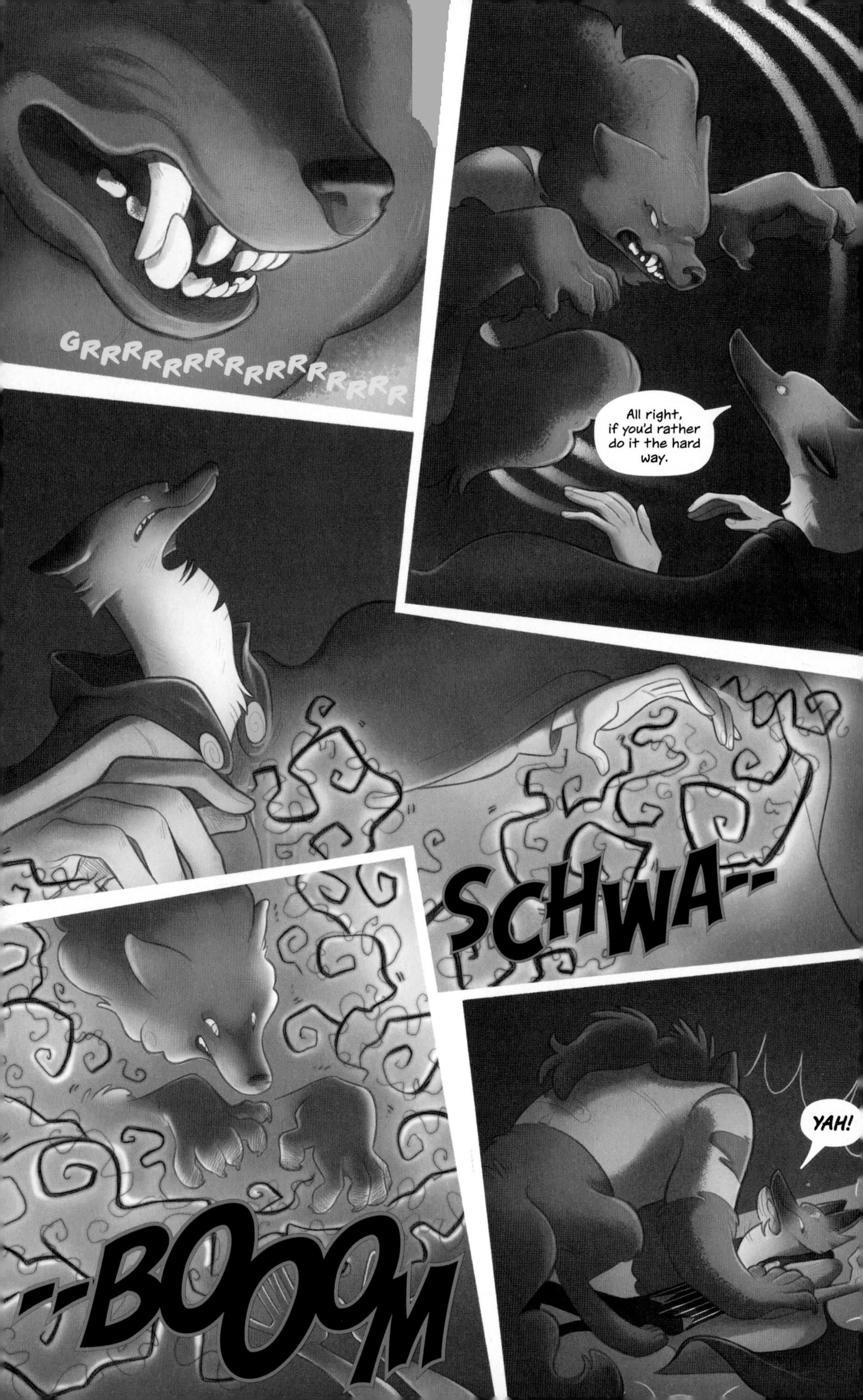
GRRRRRRRRRRRRRRRR
All right, if you'd rather do it the hard way.
SCHWA--
--BOOOM
YAH!

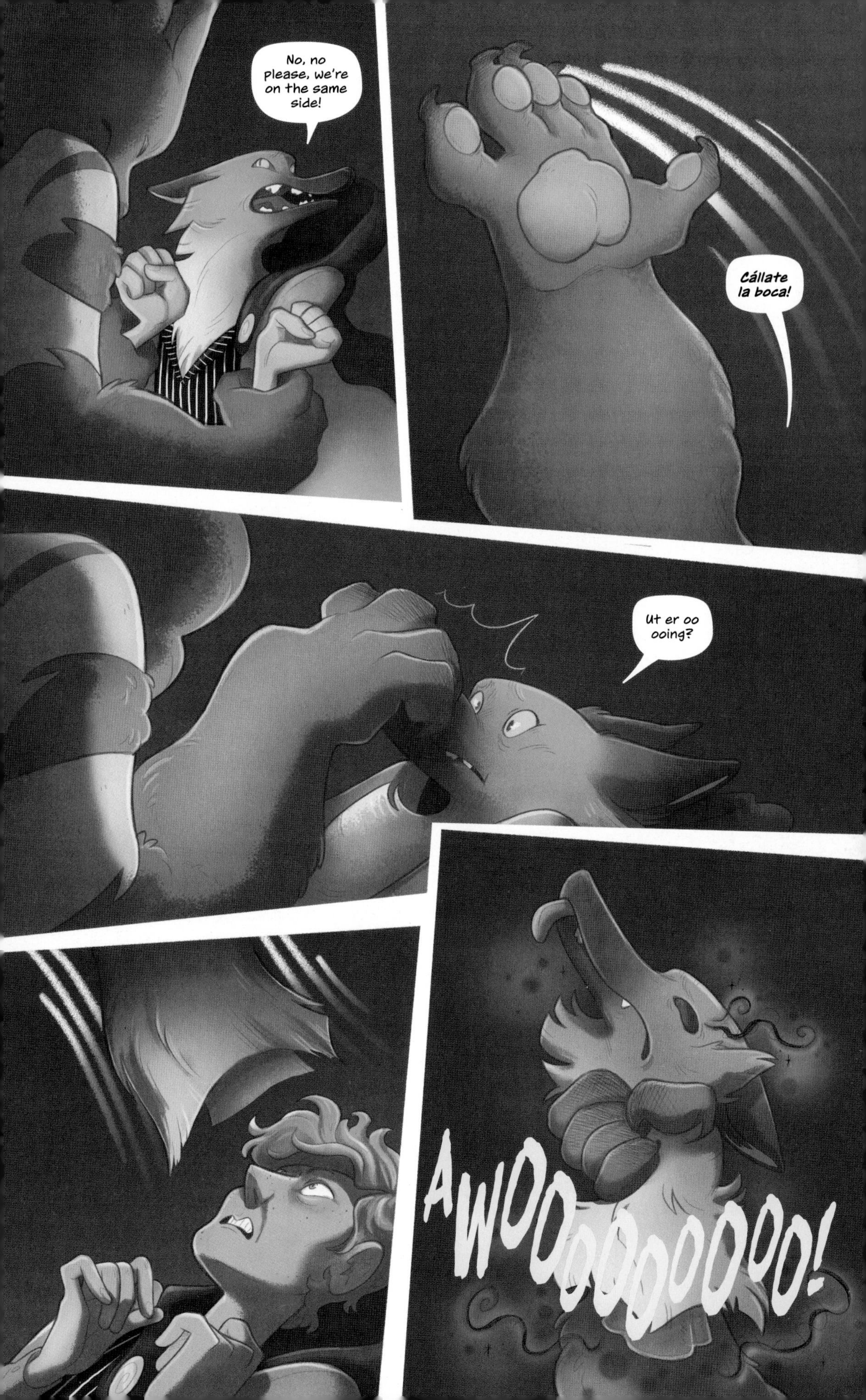
No, no please, we're on the same side!
Cállate la boca!
Ut er oo ooing?
AWOOOOOOOOOO!

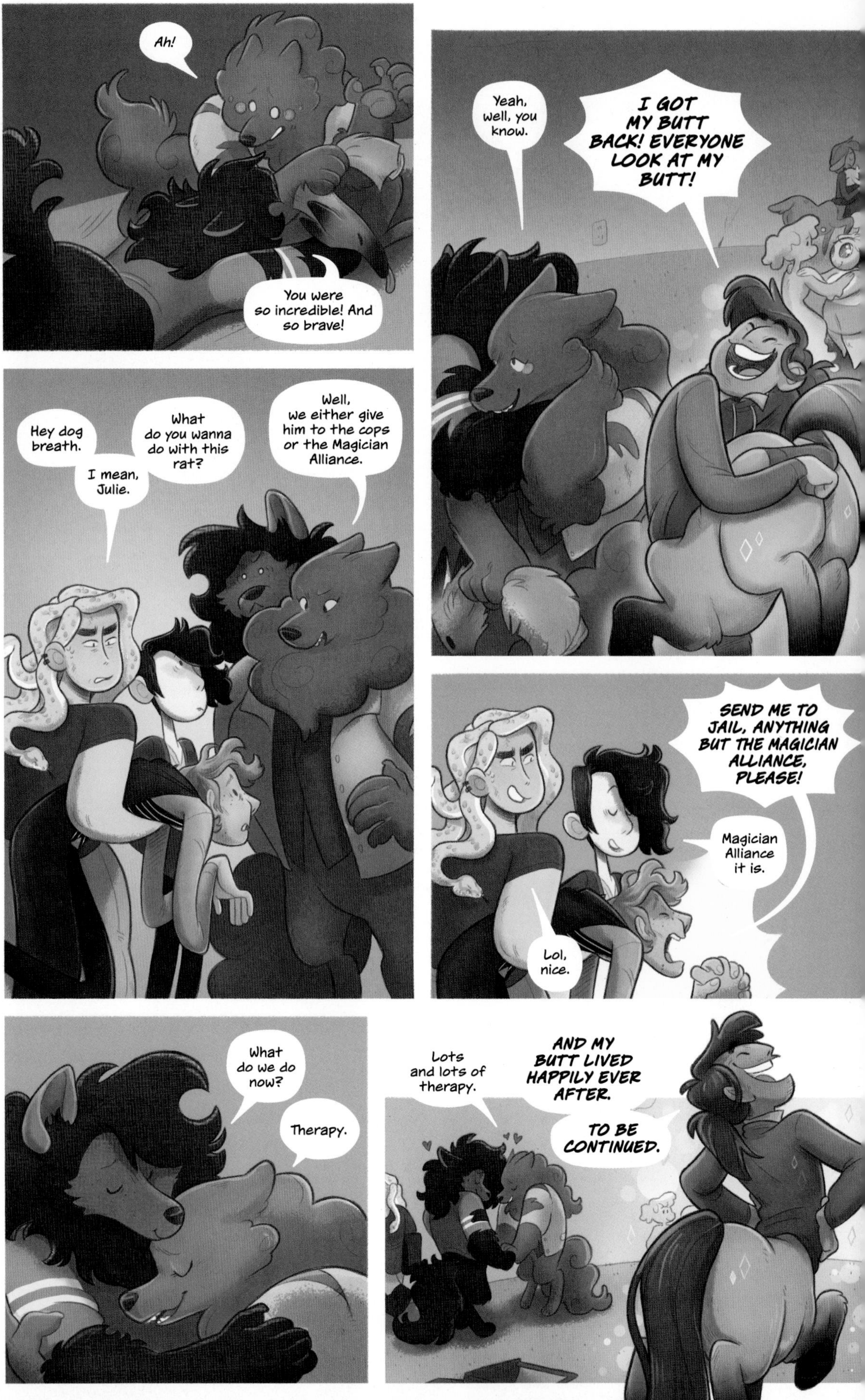
Ah!
You were so incredible! And so brave!
Yeah, well, you know.
I GOT MY BUTT BACK! EVERYONE LOOK AT MY BUTT!
Hey dog breath.
I mean, Julie.
What do you wanna do with this rat?
Well, we either give him to the cops or the Magician Alliance.
SEND ME TO JAIL, ANYTHING BUT THE MAGICIAN ALLIANCE, PLEASE!
Magician Alliance it is.
Lol, nice.
What do we do now?
Therapy.
Lots and lots of therapy.
AND MY BUTT LIVED HAPPILY EVER AFTER.
TO BE CONTINUED.

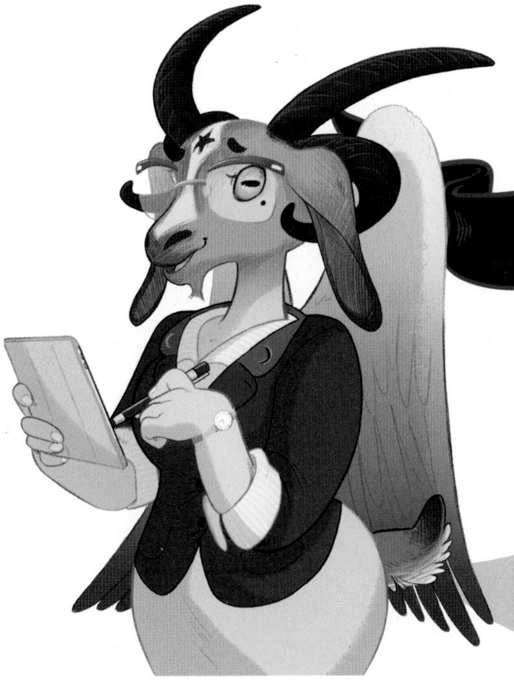

ASK A KNOW-IT-ALL

Each month, we feature advice from a different local celebrity with a unique perspective.

This month's Know-It-All is Sophia Atbash, assistant dean at Blitheton State University. A BSU alumna herself, Sophia "prefers to be called Ms. Atbash" and can often be found "getting roped into interviews that the dean herself doesn't want to do." Oh. But she's "always happy to help whenever she can!"

Dear Know-It-All,

What's the *hiccup* best remedy to get *hiccup* rid of hiccups? *hiccup*

- On A Highway To Hiccup Hell

Dear Highway,

What a wonderful question! I happen to have a fool-proof solution to hiccups! It's been passed down from generation to generation in my family, and it never fails. First... wait, just so we're clear, am I supposed to be answering as myself or offering advice that the dean herself would give? Whatever I'm comfortable with? Hmm. Well, one time, I heard the dean tell a student to get out of her office until they got their caustic slime under control, so... maybe consider that?

Dear Know-It-All,

My downstairs neighbor is playing mind games with me. She recently left a note on my door saying she could hear my alarm going off in the morning and could I please turn it off sooner? And it's like, guess what, my alarm doesn't even go off in the morning. Like, what's her deal, even?

- Nocturnal Nathanial in 4C

Dear Nathanial,

That's a real toughie, pal. I'm just gonna shoot the dean a little text and we'll see what she has to say about it. ***(Editor's note: A long pause.)*** I don't want to put any words in her mouth. ***(Editor's note: Another long pause.)*** Maybe she's in a meeting. I'm sure she'll text back soon. ***(Editor's note: The longest pause of all.)*** Maybe we should just move on for now and come back to this one later? ***(Editor's note: Reader, we did not come back to this one later.)***

Dear Know-It-All,

So uh, we're trying to throw a raging party in a couple weeks, but uh, my bro Kevin, oh wait, I should change his name... his name is actually uh, Buttface. Haha. So Kevin, I mean Buttface, invited these total nerds to our party! Like, my dude, it's our senior year! I just want to enjoy our house without any nerds!

- Josh, Beta Psi Epsilon. Wait no, what's a good fake name? Anyway it's not Josh.

Dear Josh,

Josh Josh Josh Josh Josh! No! We've talked about this a hundred times! You can't discriminate against students on the basis on whether or not they're cool! Honestly, Josh, I'm surprised at you. When you were in my office last week, I thought for sure we'd settled this, and now I'm not sure what to think. I'm sure your mom will be thrilled to hear that you went behind my back. Yeah, that's right, I'm going over BOTH our heads now. For gosh sake, Josh, do better.

Dear Know-It-All,

I like to troll people online, but my friends say I'm being mean. It's not my fault that they don't get my style of humor, but I don't want them to think I'm a bad guy.

- Grendel the Good-Humored

Dear Grendel,

I think I speak not only for the dean (although I of course welcome her correction) but for everyone when I say: Stop being horrible to people on the internet.

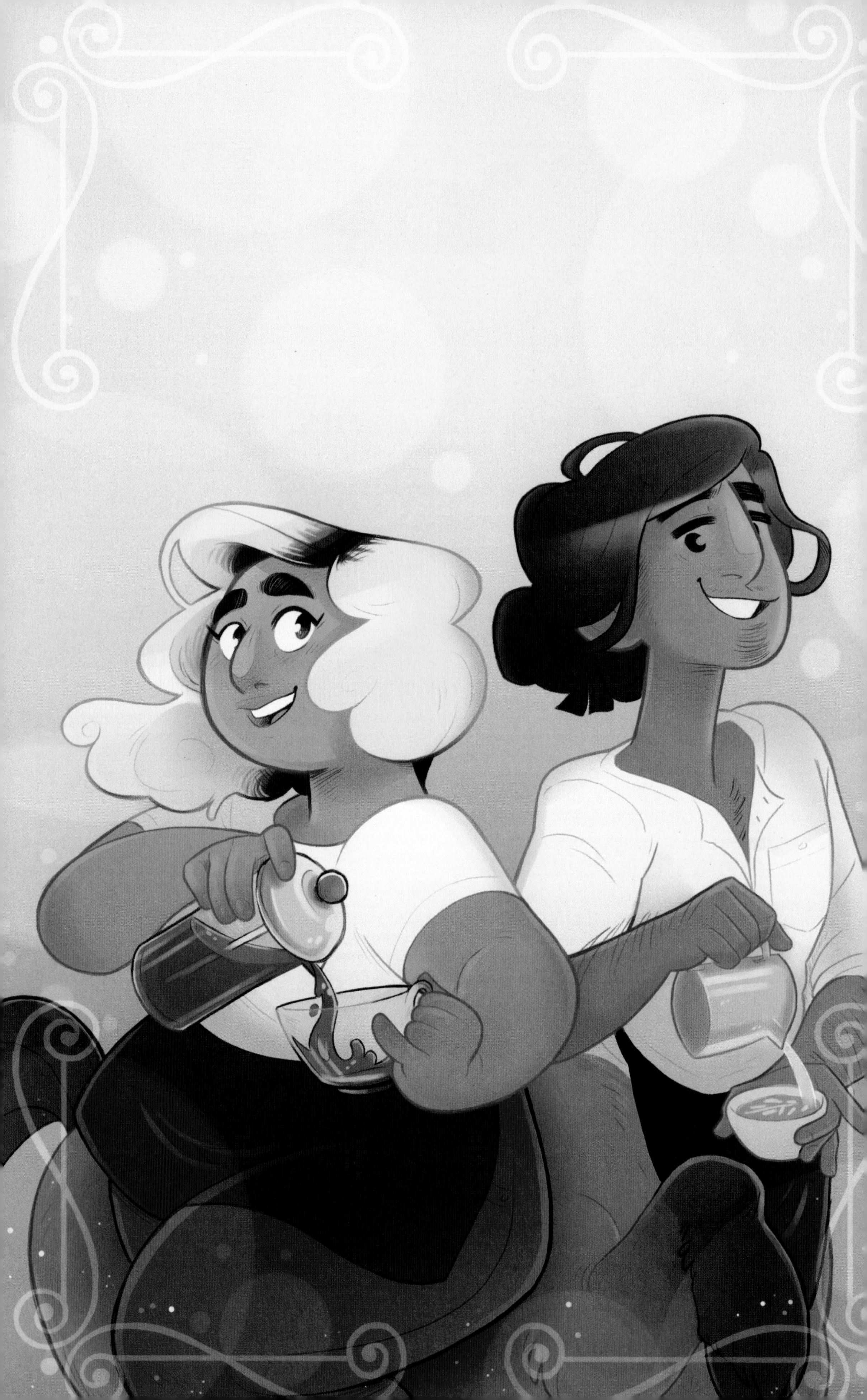

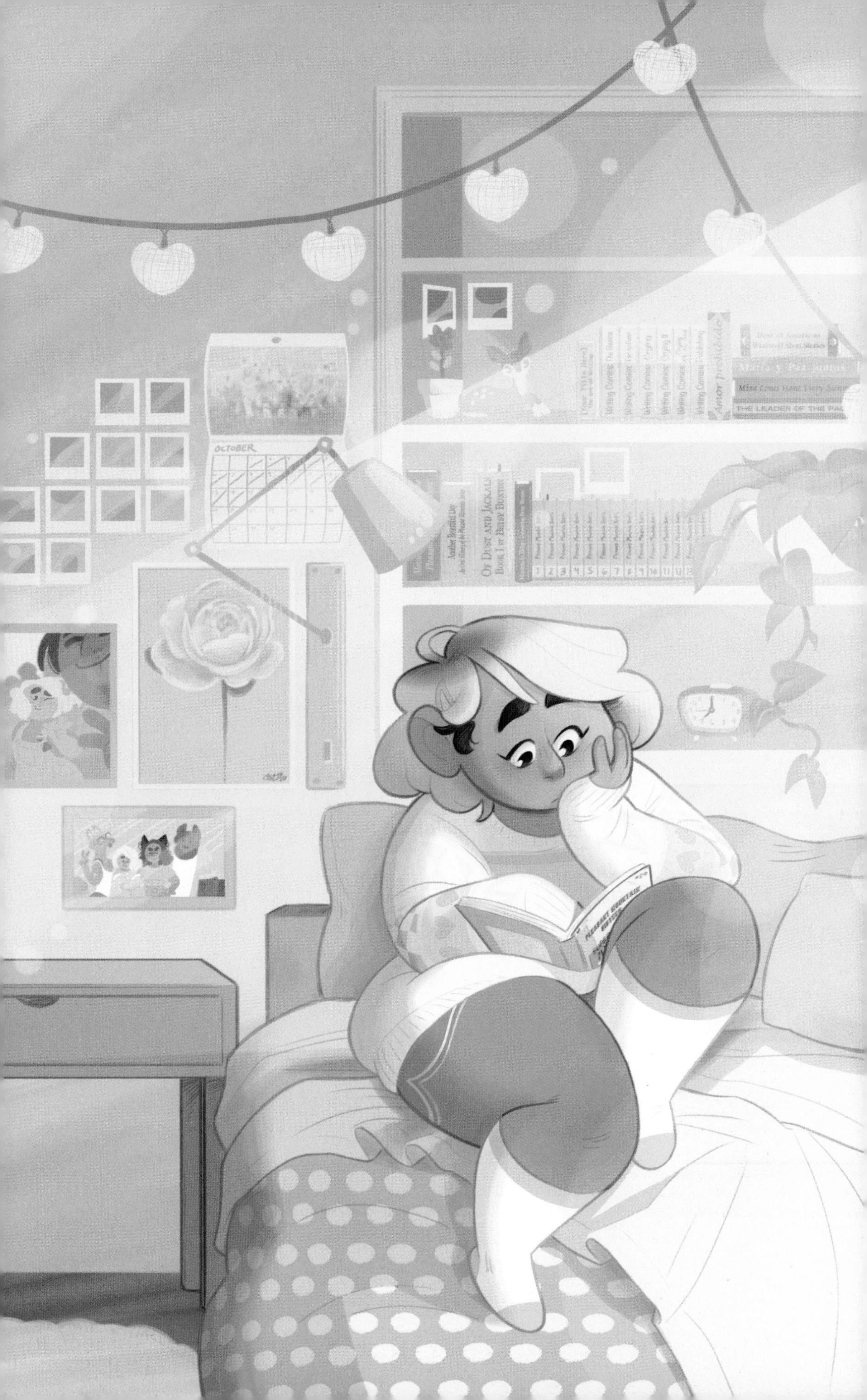

OCTOBER
Amor prohibido
Best of American Werewolf Short Stories
THE LEADER OF THE PA
Another Beautiful Day
Of Dust and Jackals Book I by Betsy Buston
1 2 3 4 5 6 7 8 9 10 11 12

GRACE ELLIS SHAE BEAGLE

MOONSTRUCK

MCCUBBIN COWLES

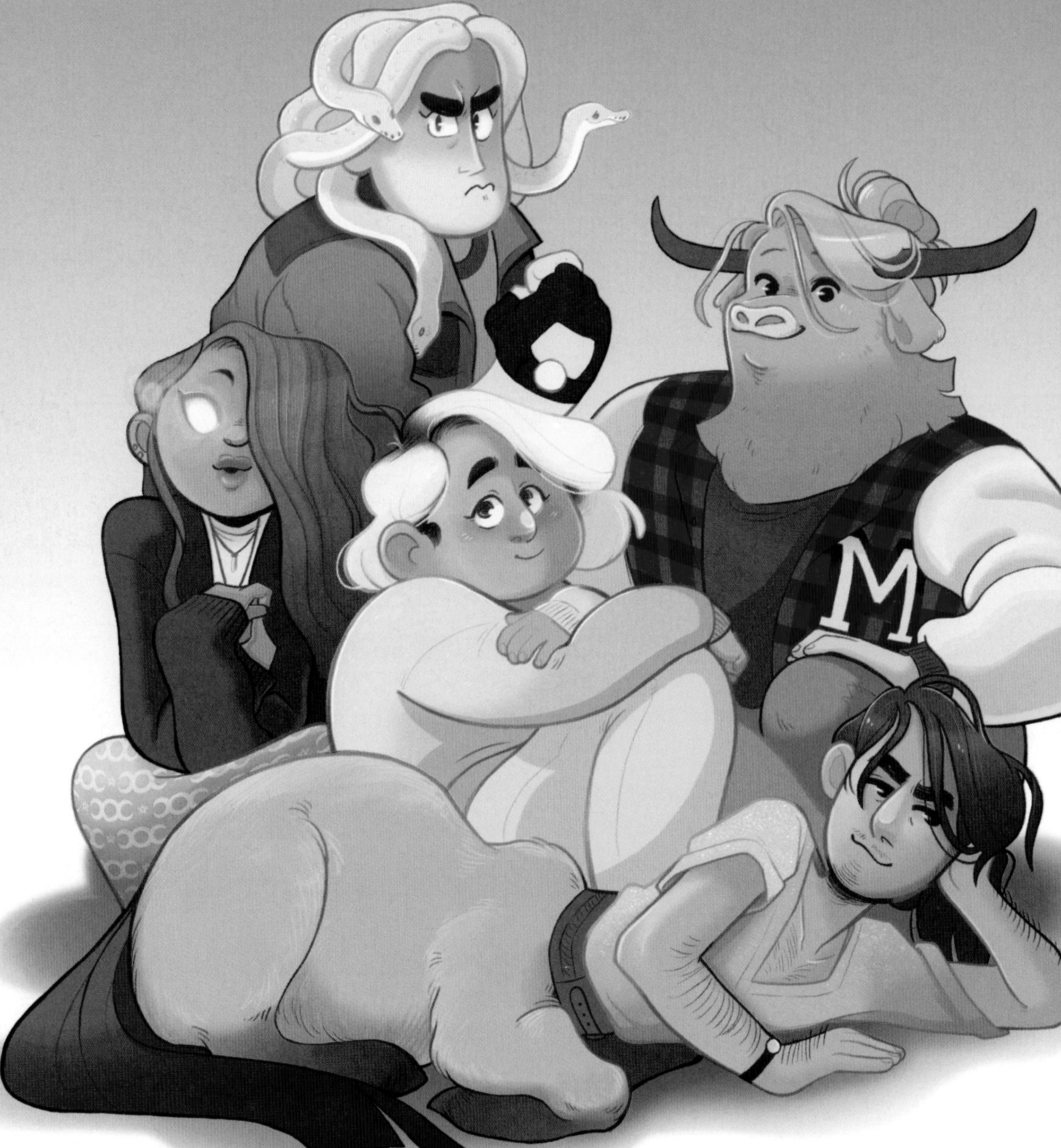

M

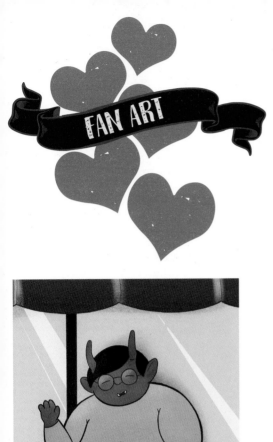

FAN ART

We've been SUPER lucky to get some amazing fan art for this arc, and we're sharing some of our favorites with you here. Do you have a favorite MOONSTRUCK character that you'd like to draw for us? We'd love to see it! Email us! teammoonstruck@gmail.com

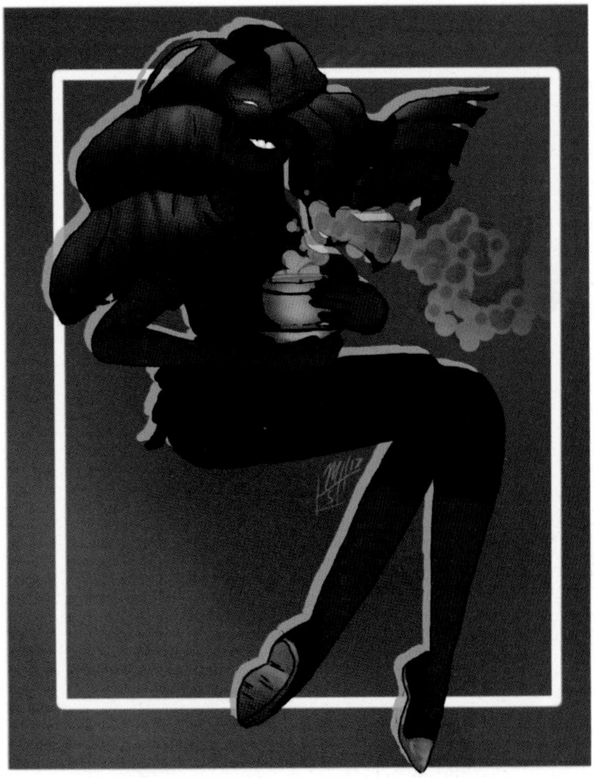

Cass by Chelle Hall
Instagram: @swell.chelle.arts

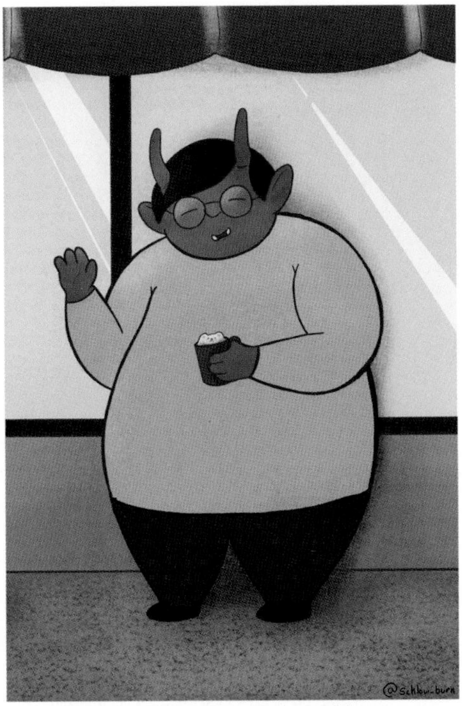

"Cutie Background Character" by Chloe Carpenter
Twitter: @schlow_burn

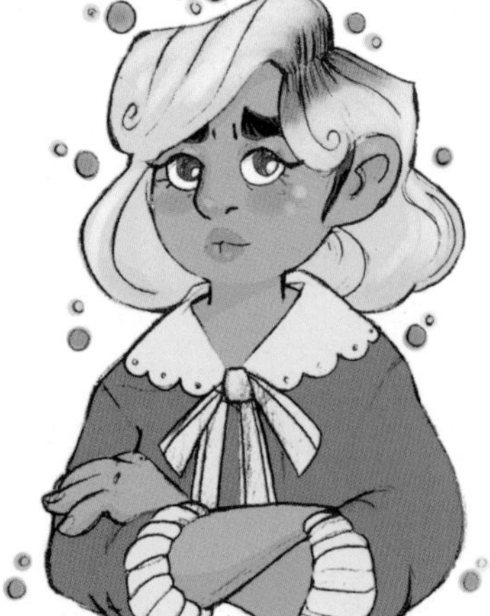

Julie by Seven Bury
Instagram: @sevenkbb

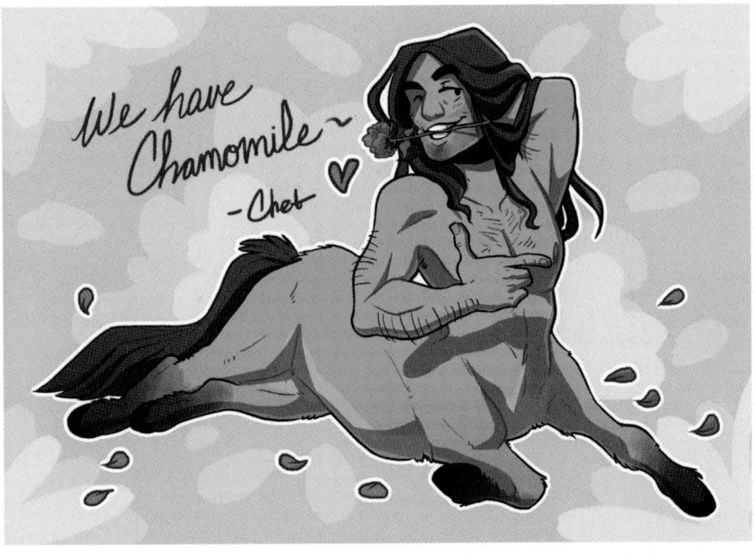
We have Chamomile~
-Chet

Chet by Lauren Myers
Instagram: @nukeillustration

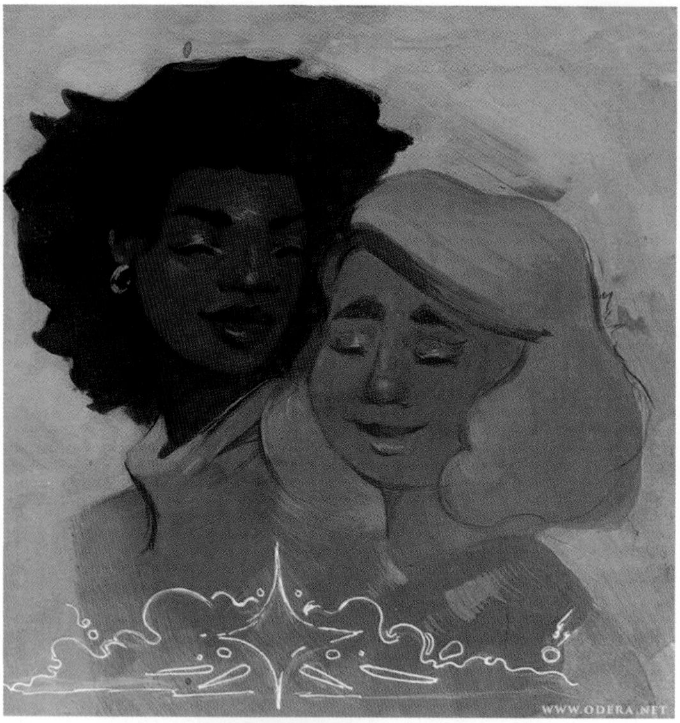
WWW.ODERA.NET

Selena & Julie by Odera Igbokwe:
www.odera.net
Twitter & Instagram: @odyism

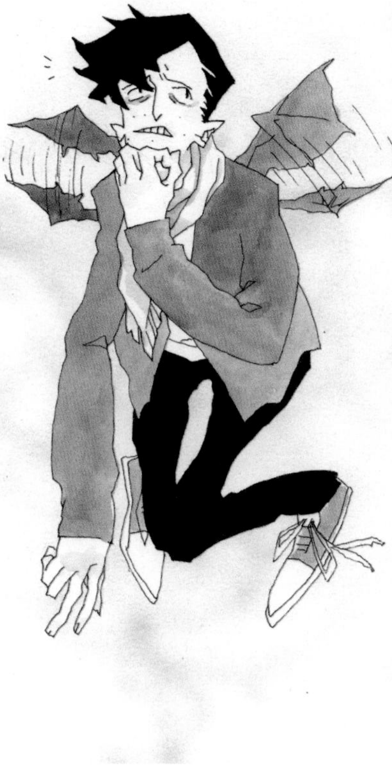

Cass by Caitlin Quirk
Instagram: @cquirkart

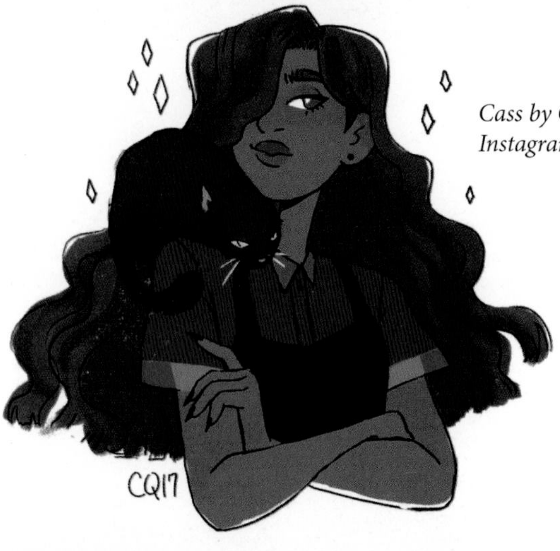
CQ17

Mark by Alissa Sallah
Instagram: @sallataire

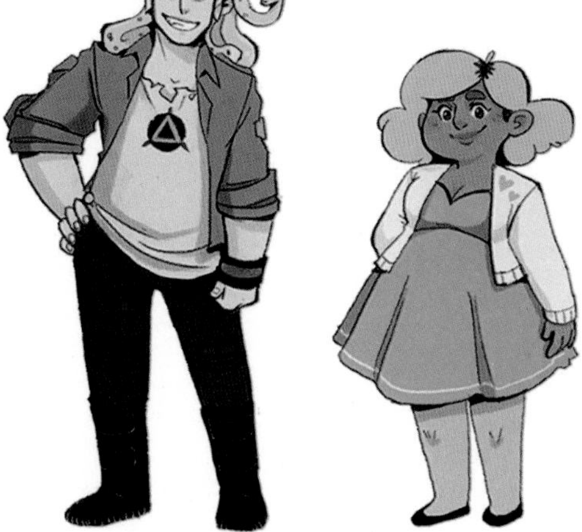

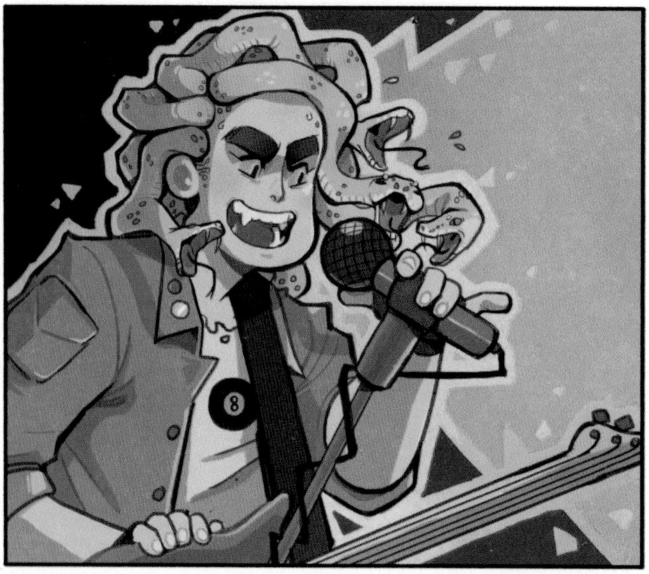
8

Lindi & Julie and Lindi and her snakes
by Amasugiru